Parenting Culture Studies

Parenting Culture Studies

Ellie Lee, Jennie Bristow, Charlotte Faircloth and
Jan Macvarish
School of Social Policy, Sociology and Social Research, University of Kent, UK

First published 2014 by
PALGRAVE MACMILLAN

Palgrave Macmillan in the UK is an imprint of Macmillan Publishers Limited,
registered in England, company number 785998, of Houndmills, Basingstoke,
Hampshire RG21 6XS.

Palgrave Macmillan in the US is a division of St Martin's Press LLC,
175 Fifth Avenue, New York, NY 10010.

Palgrave Macmillan is the global academic imprint of the above companies
and has companies and representatives throughout the world.

Palgrave® and Macmillan® are registered trademarks in the United States,
the United Kingdom, Europe and other countries.

ISBN 978–1–137–30460–5   hardback
ISBN 978–1–137–30463–6   paperback

This book is printed on paper suitable for recycling and made from fully
managed and sustained forest sources. Logging, pulping and manufacturing
processes are expected to conform to the environmental regulations of the
country of origin.

A catalogue record for this book is available from the British Library.

A catalog record for this book is available from the Library of Congress.

Typeset by MPS Limited, Chennai, India.

Contents

List of Figures and Tables

Figures

Table

Foreword

Parenting has emerged as one of the most hotly debated issues of the twenty-first century. Western culture attaches such significance to parenting because it is represented as the source of virtually every social problem that afflicts our communities. Poor parenting, or the absence of so-called parenting skills, is held responsible for the cultivation of dysfunctional children who in turn become maladjusted grown-ups. From this fatalistic perspective, the 'parenting deficit' is blamed for children's mental health problems, educational difficulties, anti-social behaviour, and poor coping skills, and the destructive consequences of bad parenting lasts throughout a person's life. According to the wisdom that prevails amongst policymakers and experts, everything from crime and drug addiction to teenage pregnancy and self-harm can be traced back to the way that mothers and fathers brought up their children.

Parenting as such is rarely depicted explicitly as one of the major problems of our times. Indeed, politicians and commentators often take care to state that most parents are doing a fine job of raising their children: before proposing another new policy or initiative that implicates inadequate parenting as the source of many of society's ills. Back in September 2006, the then prime minister, Tony Blair, made a remarkable statement about the necessity for policing parents who were likely to produce children and who had the potential to become a 'menace to society'. His demand to spot potential problem parents before birth was coupled to an argument for intervening in potential problem families before the children were even born. That only a handful of public figures challenged this statement is testimony to the prevalence of the belief in parental determinism.

The belief that the child will be punished for the sins of the parents has its origins in biblical times. Exodus 20:5 warns people that the Lord is a 'jealous God, visiting the iniquity of the fathers upon the children'. However, in today's secular world the term 'sin' has been demoralized and transformed into a deficit. Divine intervention is not necessary where children are seen to be punished by the mere act of bad parenting.

The pathologization of parenting should not be construed as merely the secular variant of a very old religious theme. God's warning was addressed to those fathers and mothers who actually committed a sin.

In present times, it is not just a small group of irresponsible mothers and fathers who are seen to constitute a problem but *all* parents. In its pure form, the condemnation of the parent as a problem was first crystallized in the writing of eighteenth-century French philosopher Jean Jacques Rousseau. Rousseau's belief that people had to be saved from the detrimental effects of customs and traditions underlay his hostility to the authority of the father and the mother, for 'parents are the agents who transmit false traditions and habits from one generation to the next' (Shklar, 1987, p. 170).

The theme of curbing the influence that mothers and fathers exercise over their children has recurred periodically throughout modern times. However, it is only since the 1970s that parenting has come to be seen as one of the central issues facing policymakers and their experts. The remarkable expansion of public interest in childrearing is underpinned by the assumption that there is a direct causal link between the quality of parenting and social outcomes. This proposition has been particularly welcomed by policymakers, who find intervention in the sphere of parenting far more straightforward than engaging with wider social issues.

Over recent decades, the tendency to link social problems to childrearing practices has led to its elaboration as a causal relationship. The idea of a one-dimensional, causal relationship between parenting and socioeconomic outcomes tends to be conveyed through discrete and specific claims, such as the allegation that a lack of proper nurturing has a significant influence on the development of children's brains.

The transformation of parenting into a self-contained cause of childhood dysfunction has led to its politicization. However, parenting is not simply politicized; it is also transformed into a cultural accomplishment that can be cultivated to produce positive outcomes. So parents supposedly have the power either to damage their child, or to improve their life chances, through the exercise of such everyday practices as how one reads to one's child, or the form of discipline that is used. With so much at stake, it is not surprising that parenting is more and more regarded as a subject that requires the constant attention of policymakers and experts.

As the contributors to this book indicate, parenting is no longer an issue that confines itself to the relationship between mothers and fathers and their children. Parental determinism has its focus not only on the child but also on the society as a whole. Like the economic determinism or the biological determinism of the past, parental determinism is alleged to explain a bewildering variety of behaviours. When leading politicians on both sides of the Atlantic can argue that bad parenting harms more children than poverty, then it becomes evident that parental determinism has become the mirror image of economic determinism.

The essays in this book provide an innovative approach towards the conceptualization of what is distinctive about contemporary parenting culture. Their arguments suggest that this issue is too important to be monopolized by one academic discipline. This book provides a compelling case for a new orientation towards what I very much hope will become a new field of scholarship.

Frank Furedi
Professor Emeritus
University of Kent

Acknowledgements

This book is the product of research, discussions, and debates that have been organized through the Centre for Parenting Culture Studies (CPCS) over the past six years. During this time hundreds of people have come along to our events, discussed ideas, and shared their own research with us, and we want to thank all those who have taken an interest in what CPCS has been doing. We would like to offer particular thanks to the following, many of whom are Associates of the Centre, whose work and support has been invaluable: Geraldine Brady, Sue Davis, Esther Dermott, Stuart Derbyshire, Ros Edwards, Sarah Evans, Frank Furedi, Val Gillies, Janet Golden, Helene Guldberg, Emma Head, Jennifer Howze, Gary Hughes, Tracey Jensen, Mary-Ann Kanieski, Stephanie Knaak, Rebecca Kukla, Pam Lowe, Nancy McDermott, Sally Millard, Elizabeth Murphy, Heather Piper, Stefan Ramaekers, Helen Reece, Jane Sandeman, Sally Sheldon, Stuart Waiton, Glenda Wall, Zoe Williams, and Joan Wolf. We would also like to thank those who have funded our work in recent years, especially the Economic and Social Research Council, the Foundation for the Sociology of Health and Illness, the Leverhulme Trust, the Wenner-Gren Foundation, and the Faraday Institute, and thanks also to the School of Social Policy, Sociology and Social Research at the University of Kent for providing a home for CPCS.

Finally, inevitably our 'other halves' (Amol, Ben, Mark, and Tony) and our own children (Annia, Emma, Reuben, Louis, Paul, and Lauren) have played their part in helping us understand better the problems of today's parenting culture, and we thank them, most of all, for their love.

About the Authors

Ellie Lee is Reader in Social Policy at the University of Kent, and Director of the Centre for Parenting Culture Studies (CPCS). She established CPCS as a Research Centre based at the University of Kent with the other authors of this book in 2010. Her research to date has been about abortion, teenage pregnancy, feeding babies, 'welfare of the child' assessments in infertility clinics, drinking and pregnancy, and neuroscience and family policy. She has published books and papers about this research, and also frequently discusses her views in the print and broadcast media.

Jennie Bristow is a PhD candidate and Allcorn Box Memorial Fund Scholar at the University of Kent. Her research is in the sociology of generations and specifically in the construction of the Baby Boomer as a social problem in Britain. Jennie is the author of *Standing Up to Supernanny* (2009) and the co-author, with Frank Furedi, of *Licensed to Hug* (2008) and *The Social Cost of Litigation* (2012). She is also the Editor of the online journal *Reproductive Review*.

Charlotte Faircloth is a Leverhulme Trust Early Career Fellow in the Centre for Parenting Culture Studies at the University of Kent, where her research explores gender, intimacy and equality. She is author of *Militant Lactivism? Attachment Parenting and Intensive Motherhood in the UK and France* as well as co-editor (with Diane Hoffman and Linda Layne) of *Parenting in Global Perspective: Negotiating ideologies of kinship, self and politics*, both of which were published in 2013.

Jan Macvarish is Research Fellow at the Centre for Health Services Studies at the University of Kent. Her research interests are the culture and politics of family and intimacy, in particular, contemporary singles culture, teenage pregnancy and parenthood, issues in fertility services, and the influence of neuroscience. She is currently working in a study titled, 'Biologising parenting: Neuroscience discourse and English social and public health policy', as part of the Faraday Institute's Uses and Abuses of Biology research programme.

Introduction

Ellie Lee

The origin of this book lies back in the mid-2000s, when Charlotte Faircloth and I became involved in separate research projects about a very necessary, but ostensibly mundane, aspect of being a parent: feeding babies. We both spent time interviewing and talking with mothers, reading and reviewing existing research about this topic from disciplines including sociology, political science, anthropology, philosophy, and history, and carried out desk research about the history of infant feeding policy. As we wrote up and published our work (for example, Faircloth, 2010, 2013; Lee, 2007a, 2007b, 2008, 2011; Lee and Bristow, 2009), we also developed an active dialogue with colleagues doing similar research to our own (Blum, 1999; Knaak, 2005, 2010; Kukla, 2005, 2006, 2008; Murphy, 1999, 2000, 2003, 2004; Wall, 2001; Wolf, 2007, 2011) and discussed our research in many non-academic forums (with healthcare providers, advocacy groups, in newspapers, and in TV and radio debates).

These are typical comments sent to us, in response to observations we have made in such public forums:

> Let me get it out there – I am a non-breastfeeding mum. I breastfed my daughter for six long weeks. Long for me and long for her. It's simple. Breast milk did not agree with her. But, here I am, yet again, finding myself explaining why I did not breastfeed for the recommended six months. It's like I have to give an excuse, a plausible one at that, as to why I failed my daughter. And failure it is considered. (Emily)

> I am a mother of a seven-month-old and I have chosen to formula feed. I have been amazed at the amount of pressure placed on women to breastfeed. In the early days following my daughter's birth, I felt

under a huge amount of pressure to attempt breastfeeding at a time when I was too tired and emotionally vulnerable to protest. (Sabina)

The conclusions we drew from this research experience inform the central propositions of this book. These can be summarized as follows:

- We live at a time when mothers will inevitably be informed, more or less explicitly, that they are mistaken if they think that the work of raising a child involves making straightforward decisions. So Emily, for example, soon discovered that what she thought was a 'simple' decision was certainly not viewed that way by others.
- Mothers will encounter the idea that they need to understand that what they do is far more complicated and much more important than they might imagine. Furthermore, they will receive the message that a great deal is at stake that they may not recognize when they make what seem to them to be practical, simple decisions.
- In sum, the message to mothers (and also fathers) is that the health, welfare, and success (or lack of it) of their children can be directly attributed to the decisions they make about matters like feeding their children; 'parenting', parents are told, is both the hardest and most important job in the world. Tomorrow depends on it.

Parental action, in most areas of everyday life, is now considered to have a determining impact on a child's future happiness, healthiness, and success. It is because of this that Sabina found there was manifest 'pressure to breastfeed'; others communicated to her there was a great deal at stake if she opted against breastfeeding and so she should do all she could to feed her baby from the breast. This was also why Emily found herself needing to 'account' repeatedly for what she ended up doing, when she found breastfeeding did not work out. Both these women indicate they experienced not breastfeeding as a measure of failure; indeed Emily states she had to 'give an excuse ... as to why I *failed my daughter*'. The relation between success, failure, and how a baby is fed is, this suggests, deemed to be a direct one, and so Emily's decision about this is not viewed by others as a practical or pragmatic matter. Rather, it is deemed powerfully and casually linked to the future well-being of her child.

As historical studies indicate, how babies are fed has long been construed as a matter of public debate and public interest (Kukla, 2005; Murphy, 2003). Yet as the accounts from Sabina and Emily show, public surveillance and monitoring of maternal decisions has certainly not receded, regardless of drastic declines in infant mortality and morbidity associated with very early childhood in the past. This monitoring is stronger than ever, and as we indicate in other parts of this book, has become connected to an ever-widening set of claims about children's 'success' or 'failure'. For example, the biological core of a person – their brain – has come to be viewed as profoundly and directly impacted by the way that person was fed as a baby (O'Connor and Joffe, 2013).

Research also shows how even ostensibly 'doing the right thing' does not offer protection from monitoring and surveillance. The accounts above bring to light something of the way the mantra that characterizes official views – that 'breast is best' – works itself out. However *breastfeeding* (especially if a mother decides to carry on giving her baby milk this way for a lengthy time) can *also* be viewed as a matter of concern for others (Faircloth, 2013). Far from being an 'expert-free cultural space', this way of feeding a baby is medicalized and professionalized (Avishai, 2011, p. 27). Indeed a whole new professional sector, that of the 'lactation specialist', has emerged over the past 40 years, with its own publications, 'academic' journals, and claims to be heard by both policymakers and parents, on the grounds that there is such a thing as breastfeeding expertise.

This book has four authors, each of whom has researched different, but related, aspects of parenting culture over the past few years. Our aim in writing the book is to explain why the everyday and routine matters of being a parent, typified by the example of feeding babies, have become the 'big issues' they now appear to be. Centrally, we highlight the main development in parenting culture, which is the growth and influence of what Furedi (2002/2008a) has termed 'parental determinism', a form of deterministic thinking that construes the everyday activities of parents as directly and causally associated with 'failing' or harming children, and so the wider society. The project of Parenting Culture Studies[1] is grounded in an attempt to understand better the roots and trajectory of parental determinism, and overall, this project is informed by two central propositions.

First, in common with the tradition of Family Studies (Ribbens-McCarthy and Edwards, 2011), a genuinely interdisciplinary approach is of most value, starting less with discipline-based concerns than with an interest in bringing together insights from any scholarship that can help shed light on the development and contours of this form of determinism. As such, Parenting Culture Studies seeks to draw upon scholarship that is attentive to the need to try and answer the question of how and why the task that should properly be shared by *all* adults – that of shaping and developing the next generation – has come to be thought of and fetishized as 'parenting'. While the approach taken by this book's authors is primarily sociological, we have pursued the development of Parenting Culture Studies by engaging with and debating academics from other disciplines, such as the philosophy of education, anthropology, psychology, law, and history, and from many countries other than England. We hope that is reflected in what you read here.

Second, a key challenge is to develop the best understanding we can of the relationship between continuity and change. The proposition that the sociocultural context in which parents raise their children has changed in recent years seems, to us, to be strongly supported by the evidence. For example, as we discuss below, a distinct and specific terminology is now used to discuss (and make problematic) what parents do, and this is most clear in the way that raising children is now called 'parenting'. The verb 'to parent' is itself relatively new, and Figure I.1 below shows how interest in this new practice of 'parenting' has escalated in recent decades.

A useful starting point is to ask questions about the new language for describing the task of raising children and explore what appears to be new. However, as Frank Furedi suggests in his Foreword, and the chapters that follow make clear, important continuities with the past also emerge. For example, for many centuries there have been 'child experts' or self-proclaimed 'authorities' who set out their views on the mistakes they think parents make. The relation between past and present is thus posed as a key question for the study of parenting culture, leading to the matter of the future, that is, how might our parenting culture develop and change for the better? How might the concept of parental determinism best be interrogated and challenged? We return to these questions at the end of the book.

Here, we make a few further preliminary comments about our general approach. Two written works in particular have inspired our efforts to develop the study of parenting culture; these are Sharon Hays' 1996 work, *The Cultural Contradictions of Motherhood* and Frank Furedi's *Paranoid Parenting*. (This was published first in 2001. A revised edition with new introduction appeared in 2008, and an American version was published in 2002. We make it clear in the text to which of these versions we refer.) Both Hays' and Furedi's texts stand as influential works, each having been cited hundreds of times. The terms developed in these books to capture contemporary experience – 'intensive motherhood' in the former and 'paranoid parenting' in the latter – have become reference points within and beyond the world of scholarship. This book, and the wider project of Parenting Culture Studies, aims to take forward

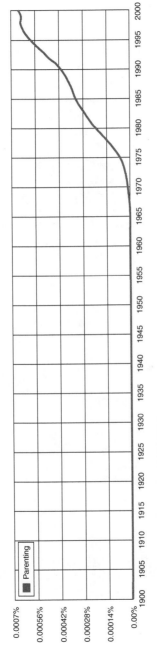

Figure 1.1 Books about parenting, 1900–2000
Note: Graph generated by Google Books Ngram viewer.

an ongoing conversation about these two terms and explore what they capture about the emphasis now placed on 'parenting'.

There are three related ideas that, in the view of the authors of this book, emerge from *The Cultural Contradictions of Motherhood* and *Paranoid Parenting* as especially important, and all the chapters that follow engage with them in different ways. One is the **historical specificity** of contemporary parenting culture; 'intensive motherhood' or 'paranoid parenting' are contemporary phenomena. While their history can be traced, and their roots and antecedents identified, they constitute a novel cultural development. The second is the usefulness of the concept **risk consciousness** for understanding the development of parental determinism. The third idea is the emphasis that Hays and Furedi place on viewing 'parenting' (in its 'intensive' or 'paranoid' form) as **socially constructed**. Later chapters further engage and explore these ideas: here, we offer some preliminary comments to highlight the core themes of the book.

'Parenting': what's new?

It will become rapidly apparent to those who start to research the way that any routine aspect of bringing up children is now talked about that a particular language is used to describe these activities. Central to this language is the term 'parenting'. If one looks, for example, at the question of how to discipline children, it will become clear this is rarely discussed as a community task or the responsibility of adult society as a whole. Rather, discipline is discussed as a 'parenting strategy', focused primarily on changing parental behaviour so as to discourage spanking or shouting at children, which is often expressed in the advocacy of 'positive parenting' (Daly, 2013; Reece, 2013). There are 'parenting manuals', 'parenting guides', 'parenting classes', and 'parenting education' that all purport to be able to improve matters in this area of the everyday life of parents (Beck and Beck-Gernsheim, 1995). The same is true for every aspect of raising a child. Feeding children, talking to them, sleeping with (or separate from) them, and even playing with children have become areas of action subsumed under the overall umbrella term 'parenting', and there is 'parenting advice' relating to all of them.

A central source of scholarship for Parenting Cultures Studies is that which has made efforts to understand the development of this terminology and its usage and meaning. In the first instance *Paranoid Parenting* provides us with this account:

> Child-rearing is not the same as parenting. In most human societies there is no distinct activity that today we associate with the term

parenting. In agricultural societies, children are expected to participate in the work and routine of the community and are not regarded as requiring special parenting attention or care ... The belief that children require special care and attention evolved alongside the conviction that what adults did mattered to their development. These sentiments gained strength and began to influence public opinion in the nineteenth century. The work of mothering and fathering was now endowed with profound importance. It became defined as a distinct skill that could assure the development of character traits necessary for a successful life ... Once children are seen as the responsibility of a mother and father rather than of a larger community the modern view of parenting acquires salience. (Furedi, 2002, p. 106)

From this point of view, a trajectory towards placing particular significance on the role and contribution of *the parent*, using their 'skills' to ensure a child's 'successful life', has a long history. It is at least as old as industrialization and, as Hays (1996) details, it may be considered that the basis for contemporary parenting culture lies in the working through of the separation out of 'the family' from the wider economy and society. However, despite its long history, it is also recognized that 'parenting' has acquired specific connotations more recently. 'Whoever invented the term *parenting* was not primarily interested in the lives of children', notes Furedi. 'Until recently, the term *to parent* referred exclusively to the act of begetting a child. Today it is deployed to describe the behaviour of mothers and fathers' (Furedi, 2002, p. 197). It is this more recent turn towards an *explicit focus on the parent and their behaviour* that emerges as the general, distinctive attribute of the contemporary term 'parenting' and the determinism it brings with it.

The decade since the publication of *Paranoid Parenting* has seen an expansion of research efforts looking into the meaning of the words that are now used so commonly to refer to (and make problematic) what parents do (for example, Ramaekers and Suissa, 2012). The history of the term has been explored usefully by some; Faircloth *et al.* (2013) suggest that 'parenting' as a term became widely used first in specific fields – for example, by psychologists and self-help practitioners – from the 1950s. It would seem, however, as we indicated above, that its popularization into more everyday language (for example, in titles of mass-market books) took place a little later. An interesting contribution from Smith, whose research focus is explicitly on 'changes in language', comments that '[t]o "parent" as a verb and the idea of parenting are relatively recent arrivals', with 'an explosion' in use from the 'early and mid-1970s' (Smith, 2010, p. 360).

Smith also comments on the changing *meaning* of the term. Much older uses of the term 'parenting', he contends, came to give way by the last quarter of the twentieth century to a view that 'parenting' is a 'technical' matter which can therefore be generalized about (rather than a personal relationship, by definition not appropriately subjected to technical criteria). Additionally, notes Smith, *'parenting* does not tend to depict the relationship with one's child as an easy or comfortable one' (2010, p. 360, emphasis in original). This suggests that from the outset, the term 'parenting', when used widely, has been associated with the view that parent–child relationships are problematic or deficient. It is, notes Smith, conceived of, 'as a dour business, and in which experts ... have a proper role' (2010, p. 360).

By looking at the language of 'parenting', a picture emerges of a growing momentum from the 1970s onwards towards the targeting of *parental behaviour* as deficient and also 'parenting' as something of a joy-less task or 'job', to be conducted under the watchful gaze of experts. As well as being inherently bound up with the idea of a *deficit* in parental behaviour that must be addressed if children are to succeed, studies of 'parenting' also thus indicate this term is inherently bound up with the idea that *people other than parents* have special insights that can and should be brought to bear. Indeed, one of the dominant observations from studies is that 'parenting' is now viewed as an activity that cannot be effectively carried out 'naturally'. '(Good) parenting' is, in contrast, considered to be a form of learned interaction, widely discussed as a 'skill set'. In their contribution exploring what it means to view parents as 'educators' of their children, Ramaekers and Suissa thus persuasively identify the way that 'parents are expected ... to do things with their children that are in a very specific sense goal-oriented' (2011, p. 198). In this sense, the parent today is not a person who, in their informal, everyday interaction with their child, teaches and guides the child about the world, on the basis of their own experience. Rather, the idea of 'education' associated with 'parenting' is a far more formal one, coming from the outside; indeed, argue these authors, it has become 'something that parents can (and should) do on the basis of scientific research' (2011, p. 199).

Another area addressed by recent research is the relation between 'parenting' and gender (Shirani *et al.*, 2012). 'Mother-blaming' has been a long-standing theme in literature on the history and sociology of the family, and scholarship has exposed how the perceived inadequa-cies of mothers have been frequently highlighted as the cause of wider social problems (we discuss this further in Chapter 2). Relatively less scholarly attention has been paid to 'fathering' and its history, although it is clear that 'fathering' has certainly been considered problematic by experts and opinion formers from at least the nineteenth century onwards (Lupton and Barclay, 1997). 'Parenting', however, is manifestly a gender-neutral term purporting to include both mothers and fathers (Sunderland, 2006), and as we discuss further in Part II of this book, those concerned about 'parenting' suggest that today's fathers, just like today's mothers, need to 'acquire skills' through 'expert help', in order to play their critical role as a parent adequately. For this reason, it has been observed that policymakers' efforts to 'engage fathers' form an important part of parental determinism (Gillies, 2009).

Scholarship about 'parenting' that analyses developments in the realm of policymaking has developed considerably in recent years, with research exploring various ways that policymakers have organized what they do around the assumption of direct, causal connections between how children are 'parented' and problems of social concern. A recent contribution from one of the authors of this volume (Bristow, 2013) looking at political commentary about the riots that occurred in Britain in 2011 highlights, for example, the uniformity of the view among policymakers that 'parenting' was in some way to blame. Some have drawn attention to just how distinctive is this turn towards a new politics of parenting (Edwards and Gillies, 2011; Gillies, 2008, 2012). As Edwards and Gillies explain:

> There has been a remarkably explicit and sustained focus on the minutiae of everyday parenting practices as linked to the good of society as a whole. (Edwards and Gillies, 2011, p. 141)

A prominent theme in the literature concerned with parental determinism is that of 'targeting', or a preoccupation on the part of policymakers with the 'parenting' practices of those who claim welfare benefits. In Chapter 3 we discuss this very important area of parenting culture in more detail.

The central proposition to emerge from this preliminary assessment is that we can be sure that 'parenting' is not a neutral term to describe what parents do as they raise their children. Rather, the transformation of the noun 'parent' into the verb 'parenting' has taken place through a sociocultural process centring on the belief that 'parenting' is a highly important and problematic sphere of social life; indeed, 'parenting' is almost always discussed as a social problem and in some way blamed for social ills. In turn, 'parenting culture' can be summarized to mean the more or less formalized rules and codes of conduct that have emerged over recent years which reflect this deterministic view of parents and define expectations about how a parent should raise their child.

Risk culture and risk consciousness

The emergence of 'parenting' as described above has thus become a growing focus for scholarship. The chapters in Part I of this book detail further what emerges from the relevant work about central aspects of this process. Questions we have frequently been asked by students when teaching about the insights of this scholarship in recent years are: How did this happen? Why has the work of bringing up and raising children come to be re-defined as 'parenting'? Before moving on, we now offer some general answers to these questions to situate what comes next.

A feature of some of the work that analyses parental determinism is its use of 'risk' as a core concept to understand the rise of this way of thinking. 'Risk' is an underlying concept in *Paranoid Parenting*, a book that forms one of a series of studies by Furedi about the workings of risk culture (see Furedi, 1997, 2005, 2007). The concept of risk is also central to books about specific topics that have been influential for our thinking. These include, for example, Armstrong's study of the regulation of alcohol consumption in pregnancy (2003), Lupton's work on the monitoring of pregnant women (1999a, 2013a, 2013b), and Wolf's critique of the 'breast is best' discourse (2011). Scholarship about 'risk' has noted, however, that this is a concept that is understood and conceptualized in the vast literature that uses the term in different and contradictory ways (Denney, 2005; Lupton, 1999b). The approach that informs the arguments set out in this book draws on a perspective that is concerned primarily with a *consciousness of risk*, and we now summarize briefly what 'risk consciousness' means. We set out four features of this way of understanding 'risk' and then return to them through the book, as we work through our arguments about contemporary parenting culture.

(1) *Risk as untoward possibility not probability*
Analysis of risk consciousness begins with the observation that there is an important difference between what 'risk' has meant at previous points in history and what it comes to mean in the present. Fox outlines the shift as follows:

> Before the era of modernity, *risk* was a neutral term, concerned merely with probabilities, with losses and gains. A gamble and/or endeavour

that was associated with high risk meant simply that there was great potential for significant loss or significant reward. However, in the modern period, *risk* has been co-opted as a term reserved for a negative or undesirable outcome, and as such, is synonymous with the terms *danger* or *hazard*. (Fox, 1999, p. 12, emphasis in original)

The meaning ascribed to the term 'risk' today, then, is different to the past. Where it once meant 'probability' understood via calculation to generate a balanced assessment, it now connotes the possibility of an *unwanted* or *dangerous* outcome.

Risk consciousness, from this perspective, is a way of thinking about the future in which *possibilities that are untoward* are taken into account more than *probabilities*. This outlook, Furedi explains, 'invites speculation about what can possibly go wrong' and 'frequently what can possibility go wrong is equated with what is likely to happen' (2009b, p. 205).

This redefinition of risk as possible danger suggests, in turn, the development of a particular view of *uncertainty* (that is, outcomes about which we cannot be sure at the outset). Rather than uncertainty being perceived as something which can be confronted rationally, or which opens up possibilities as well as pitfalls, the 'unknown' is viewed with anxiety. Indeed, '[o]ne of the defining features of our times is that anxiety about the unknown appears to have a greater significance than the fear of known threats', notes Furedi (2011, p. 97).

This sort of 'possibilistic' risk-thinking has been assessed as having wide influence. Most famously, it was associated by the former US Defence Secretary Donald Rumsfeld with the conduct of war; there are, he explained with reference to 'weapons of mass destruction' in Iraq, 'unknown unknowns – the ones we know we don't know', and it is these that should form the focus for strategic decisions (Furedi, 2009b, p. 199). As Furedi notes, however, although Rumsfeld was ridiculed for his 'unknown unknowns' comment, the possibility that there are speculative threats has become the organizing principle for action and policy-making in many instances.

The focus on speculative threats – the 'what ifs' of everyday life – has had a significant impact on the way that children, and also fetuses, are now perceived. Both children and 'pre children' are, we suggest through this book, more and more defined as *de facto* 'at risk', but what exactly the 'risk' *is* is often admitted to be uncertain or unknown. It is a 'worst case scenario', a possibility rather than a probability. Yet 'risks' of these kinds exert powerful influence over all discussions about childhood and children, from pregnancy behaviour to children's play, to the interaction between adults and children within local communities. This perception of risk as applied to children also forms a key underpinning of the redefinition of the parent as determinant of the future well-being of the child; indeed what arises from it is the construction of the parent as a *manager of risk*, who has in their power the ability to decide the fate of the child according to how well they perform this task (an idea that we dwell upon throughout this text).

(2) *Risk as free-floating anxiety*

The second important observation about risk consciousness is that this way of looking at the world finds as its focus not collective concerns about specified dangers faced by groups, so much as *individualized fears about uncalibrated risks*. The recognition that this sort of anxiety has become the typical way of thinking about children is fairly widely noted.

Stearns, for example, writes that in America 'at some point in the past four decades', a view has taken hold that children, 'operate amid significant dangers about which they need to be warned and from which they need to be protected'. This outlook, he suggests, is distinguishable from longer standing ideas about 'vulnerability' in that in the past, the idea of risk bound up with the notion vulnerability 'did not, initially, assume that *the larger social context itself* had to be viewed in terms of danger' (Stearns, 2009, p. 48, our emphasis). More recently, in contrast, it is precisely this context, society itself, which has come to be viewed as risky (or 'toxic', as we discuss further in Part II). Thus, what the child is 'vulnerable to' becomes far less specific; 'unsanitary conditions' or 'accidents', for example, are replaced by a generalized sense that 'society' places children 'at risk'. This, argues Stearns, means that the child 'must be surrounded by a host of precautions and constraints previously unnecessary ... A culture already installed was greatly intensified towards new levels of monitoring and regulation' (Stearns, 2009, p. 48).

As Furedi has pointed out, this unfocused, generalized sense of anxiety has fundamental importance for the definition of 'parenting':

> Traditionally, good parenting has been associated with nurturing, stimulating and socializing children. Today it is associated with monitoring their activities. An inflated sense of risk prevails, demanding that children should never be left on their own ... Permitting youngsters to be home on their own after school is presented as an act of parental irresponsibility. (Furedi, 2002, p. 5)

As we detail further in Chapter 1, the meaning of parenthood is reworked through the re-redefinition of the child as 'at risk' in this generalized way; 'Parenting', with its deterministic connotations, is the outcome of this inflation of risk.

(3) *Risk consciousness and morality*

Risk consciousness has become more pervasive, but why has this happened? A third feature of the relevant literature is the answer it provides to this question. Understanding the growth of risk consciousness, it has been suggested, lies in grasping the relation between an outlook that elevates fear of the unknown and conditions where 'cultural authority is weak' (Furedi, 2011, p. 92). A powerful preoccupation with the untoward effects of 'not knowing' develops, grows, and becomes institutionalized, in conditions where authoritative value systems that provide meaning and clarity are more and more attenuated. Overall, risk consciousness understood this way reflects 'the difficulty that society has in bringing meaning to uncertainty', explains Furedi (2011, p. 92).

The insight that risk consciousness expands and gains traction in conditions where value systems are weak is one of the most important for understanding parenting culture. This point is elaborated as follows:

> The estrangement of contemporary western culture from a grammar of morality means that threats and dangers are unlikely to be conveyed in an explicit moral form. Moral regulation has an amorphous form and is often promoted indirectly through the language of health, science and risk. (Furedi, 2011, p. 96)

In a similar vein, Hunt has explained:

> [I]ncreasingly morality has come to function through proxies, not in its own voice, but in and through other discursive forms, the two most important and closely related being the discourses of 'risk' and 'harm'. (Hunt, 2003, p. 166)

The contention is thus that responses to problems of concern are now rarely conceptualized in terms relating to general systems of values or beliefs. Rather, perceived problems are most likely to be represented as such because they 'increase the risk of harm', that is, they are somehow threatening to the 'wellbeing' of the individual. This way of thinking inevitably means that the bodies we (and our children) inhabit, and the minds inside each one of our heads, *individually* become the focus for attention. Thus the solution to this individualized problem of being 'at risk' is perceived to rest in 'risk management strategies'. Reducing and managing risk emerges as the temporary stand-in for a crisis of meaning and morality, and in this way a particular form of morality – risk management, which has 'keeping us safe' as its prime value – attains dominance.

This development can be readily identified when it comes to children; it is now entirely routine for parents to be warned about a wide variety of risks and dangers which threaten the health and well-being of their children, particularly those for which they are responsible (for example, feeding a baby formula milk, disciplining a child 'the wrong way', or letting them watch too much television).

Hunt, however, also makes the following very important observation about this development:

> The point that needs emphasis in explicating the thesis that moral discourses function through proxies is that the moral dimension is not excluded, rather it becomes subsumed within discourses whose characteristics have a utilitarian guise ... The most striking feature of the hybridization of morals and risk is the creation of an apparently benign form of moralization in which the boundary between objective hazards and normative judgements becomes blurred. (Hunt, 2003, p. 167)

For Hunt, then, the development of a way of looking at the world in which dangers and problems are identified as risks does not mean this interpretation lacks moralizing power. On the contrary, it acts to generate powerful codes of conduct for behaviour but in a way which places the focus squarely on the individual and their way of life.

For example, to return again to the topic of feeding babies, this is now an activity with pronounced moralized connotations. What mothers do is surrounded (and influenced) by precepts and ideas about what they *should* do. However, the 'should' is very rarely articulated in conventional moral terms (for example, making explicit reference to the alleged sacredness of the child at the breast). Rather, the message 'mothers should breastfeed' is routinely justified on the grounds that 'medical evidence shows' and that 'experts know' as if there is no other way of thinking or speaking about what counts when it comes to feeding a baby that might be relevant, other than specialist knowledge.

The abandonment of a 'grammar of morality' is, in this light, a development with very significant implications. The possibility of opening up for debate the question 'how might we as adults best approach the task of raising the next generation?' is closed down. Only one sort of answer becomes possible; we go by what 'the evidence' says about how the individual parent should 'parent' their child, and debate the issues in these terms.

(4) *Demoralization and policing*

The fourth key area that scholarship about risk consciousness highlights is the effect of this attention on individual behaviour for formal systems of regulation – that is, policing. With reference to the work of American sociologist Howard Becker, Furedi notes that the link between moralization and policing has been long recognized; this is, for example, central to the exploration of 'moral panics' and is true also of the widespread use of term 'pregnancy police' associated with the moral regulation of pregnant women. Furedi notes, however, that while the terms now used to describe risk and what we should fear are rarely explicitly moral, they have a powerful effect for the policing of behaviour:

> [R]isk society appeals are oriented towards regulating personal behaviour and are no less prescriptive than traditional moral crusades. Indeed, fear entrepreneurs often self-consciously assert the moral authority of their enterprise. (Furedi, 2011, p. 99)

Hunt (2003), following a similar line of thought, notes in a comment very relevant for our interests here, that harm is 'medicalized' in advice given to people – and in particular, pregnant women – about drinking alcohol. As we detail further in Part II of this book, the warning from officialdom is that 'drinking when pregnant may harm your unborn baby', but this is backed up more or less explicitly by policing. In the US this can mean legal sanction (Armstrong, 2003; Golden, 2005) and in Britain admonition by health professionals if a pregnant woman admits she has breached the 'no drinking' rule.

The implications of this development can be thought about at the level of the individual. How does one experience life as a parent when one's everyday behaviour is placed under scrutiny in this way? It can also be thought about more widely, at a social and cultural level. What are the costs for the wider public life when an answer to the question 'what is right and what is wrong?' is increasingly sought *only* at the level of individual behaviour? The movement to risk consciousness feeds off, and encourages, the demise of thinking that can pose questions of right and wrong in a more generalized, social sense. For this reason it also constitutes the basis for the turn to viewing 'parenting' as the cause of, and solution to, social problems. In conditions where ideas about how to effect wider social change are elusive, change is envisaged only where it seems possible to enact it, for example, in the management of the small-scale relations between individuals, especially those between parent and child.

As noted above, with reference to Stearns' (2009) analysis of American culture, risk consciousness appears to have grown since the 1970s. The precursor – the idea of the child as 'vulnerable' and 'precious' – is thought to have been in existence for at least a century (Stearns, 2009), and earlier precedents can no doubt be found. However, a range of studies about a variety of issues detect that during the 1970s there was an important shift in emphasis, towards focusing on 'risks' to the child (Armstrong, 2003; Best, 1993a), and that since then, risk conscious-ness associated with children has expanded and spread at a remarkable pace (Guldberg, 2009). In this light, the other area of scholarship that has proved important for our study of parenting culture is that which suggests a way of thinking about how risk consciousness emerges and develops. For this reason, our work, drawing on that of others referred to above, is strongly influenced by a **constructionist perspective**.

'Parenting' as a social construct

> Risk provides a major form in which many aspects of life are prob-lematized ... The identification of risks provides one form in which problems are experienced, grasped and articulated. Risk problema-tization brings into play a discursive formation that provides a way through which the future is framed and which connects some anxiety-inducing feature of the present to the fear of future harm. (Hunt, 2003, p. 173)

In this extract, Hunt indicates that risk talk (a 'discursive formation') provides a way of 'grasping' or 'framing' aspects of life through which they are given meaning; they are 'problematized' in a particular form. He also makes the very important point that this way of constructing the *present*, in which events or experiences are connected to the pos-sibility of danger, leads to a distinctive view of the future, one which is influenced by 'fear of future harm'. A projection forwards, predicated on a sensibility of possible harm, plays back into a way of living and organ-izing life in the present, which maximizes safety as its central objective. The question this raises, however, is 'how has this 'discursive formation' arisen and come to exert such a high degree of influence?' This is a question that we seek to address in a range of ways through the chapters that follow, but we offer a few preliminary comments here.

Our general orientation is towards an analysis that understands 'problematization' as a process of social construction (Best, 1993a, 1993b, 1995, 2001; Figert, 1996; Loseke, 1999). This way of thinking about social problems has been summarized by Best, with reference to the case made in the 1970s by Spector and Kitsuse:

> Constructionists intentionally define social problems broadly, as a general process: according to the best known definition, social problems are 'the activities of individuals or groups making assertions of grievances and claims with respect to some putative conditions' [Spector and Kitsuse 1977, p. 75]. (Best, 2011, p. 44)

The merits of this approach have been indicated by work that has proved valuable in trying to think through puzzles posed by contemporary culture and society. One such puzzle is how best to understand and explain a situation where there is a manifest disparity between the *incidence of a phenomenon* and *expressed concern about it*. Examples of this kind include:

- Teenage pregnancy and motherhood, which became from the 1970s onwards an ever-increasing focus for expressed concern and policy-making in Britain and the US, when pregnancy and early motherhood rates were *stable* or *declining* (Arai, 2009; Luker, 1996).
- Child abduction, which is statistically very rare, but which has been a consistent feature of discussions about threats to children in recent decades (Best, 1993a).
- Fetal Alcohol Syndrome, a rarely occurring and complex birth defect, which has come to be represented as a general threat to all children (Armstrong, 2003).

We agree with Best's (2011) proposition that phenomena like these are not captured well by the concept 'moral panic'. This is because, first, there is less a 'panic' about them that comes and goes, than a consistent, expansive discussion and concern. Secondly, the form in which concern is expressed is, as we noted above, often something other than 'moral', at least in the sense in which this term is conventionally understood. In this light, our preference is to think about the development of risk consciousness and its relation to the way we think about children, parents, and the wider society, as a *process* that involves the accumulation and expansion of *sets of claims*. These claims draw our attention to risks and dangers, and seek to persuade people (especially policymakers) that they should take a putative threat seriously. These sets of claims may sometimes compete and enjoy relatively greater or lesser success.

This is a process that, as Best indicates, has come to be viewed as wide in scope involving a diverse range of social actors:

> As the constructionist literature has evolved, analysts have come to appreciate that claims making is a multifaceted process, that while its domain certainly includes activists demonstrating to draw attention to troubling conditions, it also encompasses scientists and physicians making claims about conditions, news and entertainment coverage of such claims and conditions, policymakers seeking to devise formal methods of addressing such conditions, the various workers who must implement those policies and all of those who evaluate or criticize policies in operation. (Best, 2011, p. 44)

The questions this raises include: Who is it that develops a particular language or way of representing a problem in a particular way? On what existing cultural resources do they trade? What is the response of others to the claim, and how does it fare as wider endorsement is sought? At what point and how does a claim come to be taken seriously by institutions including the media and government departments? In the essays that form Part II of this book, we discuss in detail some particular examples of parental determinism and try and provide some insights in response to these questions.

This type of approach has been criticized on the grounds that it suggests a relativistic orientation to social problems (Best, 1993b). The sense in which problems are understood as 'constructs' has been taken to mean that social constructionists believe there to be no 'reality' or 'underlying cause' that can explain why phenomena come to be so strongly viewed as something to be anxious about and act against. In response we would first suggest that in many instances (at least those that we have researched) the gulf between a consciousness of risk attached to a phenomenon and the sense in which it could plausibly be deemed 'risky' by merit of what could properly be called evidence *is* what demands the most critical attention. For example, we would suggest this to be true of feeding a baby with formula milk in industrialized countries or drinking alcohol at low levels in pregnancy. The real issue to explain is why formula feeding, or drinking when pregnant, has become so strongly associated with *danger* when babies born to women who do these things thrive.

On this matter, we also accord with Hunt's analysis that risk-based claims can achieve a high degree of success by default, rather than by the merit or logic of the case presented. Risk consciousness can become institutionalized, he suggests, in conditions where there is no alternative focus regarding action and activity in institutions, and particularly in policymaking circles:

> A proliferation of single-issue movements have developed their own expertise through which they dispute traditional forms of state and professional expertise and act as what may be usefully referred to as 'risk-promotion' movements. Such movements not infrequently succeed in effecting 'regulatory capture' of expert systems, in that it is often easier for them to 'go along with' the risk entrepreneurs of such risk-promotion movements than to fight them. (Hunt, 2003, p. 170)

Conditions can prevail (and we would suggest they now markedly do) in which 'risk entrepreneurs' can gain an unprecedented degree of success for their claims because there is no focus or will to 'fight them'. For example, we discuss this in the second part of this book in relation to claims about 'neurons' and 'synapses' now routinely made by risk entrepreneurs warning of the harm done to children's brains by 'poor parenting' (Wall, 2004; Wastell and White, 2012; Wilson, 2002). Despite the unscientific nature of these claims, they have attained a remarkable level of 'regulatory capture'. The general proposition, then, is that risk consciousness grows and develops, finding new foci in circumstances where there is very little to act as a countervailing force. It becomes orthodoxy more by default than by merit.

While there is a 'newness' about risk consciousness focusing on children that needs to be brought to the fore, there is also a much longer standing cultural precept of which it has come to feed. This is a presumption of *parental incompetence*, which long pre-dates the 1970s. Indeed, the questioning of parental authority has a very long history. This is engagingly discussed by Hays (1996) with regard to ideas about American mothers, and central to her case regarding the 'intensification of motherhood' is the observation that expert questioning of maternal capabilities has been built into modern American society from the outset. Similarly, Furedi shows how the 'targeting' of parental authority is a core theme in discussions of 'the problem of family' from at least the nineteenth century.

However, this pre-given insistence on the 'problem of parents' intensifies and becomes more strongly stated in the context of risk consciousness. A pre-existing cultural context that views parents as inadequate in the face of the task of 'building tomorrow' develops into parental determinism as a consciousness of risk is expansively applied to children. This reaches its logical conclusion in the situation we discuss in Chapter 4. The recognition that some adults may harm children has become transposed, in the form of society-wide regulatory projects regulating inter-generational contact, into the sensibility that *all* adults should be screened in case they *might* pose a danger to children. In this way, the presumption of generational responsibility that has historically underpinned childrearing becomes disorganized, with adults positioned as both the omnipotent protectors of children and the ultimate cause of all of their problems.

A note on the structure of this book

We have structured this book in two parts. Part I aims to review and discuss key components of parental determinism, and Part II takes a set of examples to discuss how this way of thinking has developed recently in specific areas. Overall, the chapters are built out of reviewing and offering a commentary on what we consider to be the most interesting and helpful literature for the study of parenting culture.

As we have already indicated, work by Sharon Hays and Frank Furedi is foundational, but we have drawn upon a large literature from across the disciplines to write what follows. As much as anything else, we intend all of the chapters in the book to provide a guide to reading, for those interesting in teaching about or writing about the issues and problems this book addresses. For this reason we have also provided a note about 'key readings' at the end of each chapter. Four people have written this book together, and in this sense it is very much a joint project. As the text indicates, however, particular chapters are the work of an individual.

Charlotte Faircloth has written the opening chapter, which discusses the core contention of both Hays and Furedi, that parenthood has become increasingly 'intensive'. Hays' term 'intensive motherhood' has inspired and influenced a whole body of scholarship globally about the contemporary experience of motherhood, some of which Faircloth discusses here. Furedi's term is 'parenting on demand', suggesting that fathers are not excluded from recent developments, but in common with Hays he draws attention to the way that what parents do, and are expected to do, has become both more demanding of time (despite increased participation of mothers in employment) but also of *emotion*. This aspect of parenting culture – preoccupation with the emotional connectedness of parents and their children – is the area Faircloth examines further in the second part of the book, through her discussion of the problematization of 'detachment' and the rise of 'attachment' and 'bonding' as social problems. Here, she also provides a commentary on what research suggests about the 'intensification' of fatherhood.

Faircloth's discussion in Chapter 1 also offers a commentary about the changing social construction of childhood; indeed, following Hays and Furedi, a central point she explores is how parental determinism is contingent on, and exists in relation to, the rise of the idea of the child 'at risk'. It is also very clear from the analysis offered by Hays and Furedi that understanding this redefinition of childhood is inseparable from an exploration of claims made by 'experts'.

The preoccupation of experts with childhood in modernity, and the ramifications of this for parents and the family, is the subject of Ellie Lee's contribution in Chapter 2. In Part II of the book, Lee continues her assessment of the relation between 'expert' definitions of risk and parental determinism through an exploration of pregnancy, focusing on drinking in pregnancy.

The relation between expert-generated 'codes of conduct' for parenting and policymaking is the subject matter of Chapter 3 by Jan Macvarish. The development, over the past decade and half, of a distinct and historically unprecedented preoccupation by policymakers with 'parenting' is, as Furedi indicated in *Paranoid Parenting*, especially marked in Great Britain. The themes of policy, however, are global, in particular the case for 'early intervention', and indeed as the literature suggests, have their origins in the US. Macvarish's contribution explores how a particular construction of both the child (as exquisitely vulnerable in the face of what parents do) and the project of policymaking (to intervene in the relation between parent and child in the early years to prevent harm) characterize current policy thinking. Macvarish's essay in Part II draws attention to the importance of 'brain based' claims-making for the further development of this policy approach.

One of the most important ideas we have taken from *The Cultural Contradictions of Motherhood* and *Paranoid Parenting* is that contemporary parenting culture drives the privatization and individuation of parenting. Parents, as Furedi notes, raise children in a context where solidarity between them, other parents, and other adults is undermined. The relation between parents and the wider community of adults is the subject of Chapter 4, written by Jennie Bristow. This chapter explores the way that the intensification of parenting has proceeded through a process of distancing adults in general from the task of relating to new generations. The essay she has written for Part II considers this issue further through the specific example of the so-called 'cotton wool kid' and 'helicopter' parent.

Overall, this book can be thought of as a guide to Parenting Culture Studies. The rationale for writing it arises not simply from the isolated research interests of the authors; rather it comes from our experience over recent years of finding a large, growing, and eager audience of students and colleagues in universities (and many thinking people outside the university) who want to understand better why 'parenting' has become such a moralized, politicized, and contentious topic. The need the volume seeks to satisfy is thus educational in its broadest sense. In our conclusion, we set out some thoughts on how the study of parenting culture might proceed, and hope this book encourages others to take forward this area of scholarship.

Note

1. The authors of this book all work with the Centre for Parenting Culture Studies (CPCS). The Centre is based in the School of Social Policy, Sociology, and Social Research at the University of Kent but has Associates at many universities in the UK and other countries. The idea for the Centre was first discussed at an international conference held at the University of Kent in May 2007, called 'Monitoring Parents: Childrearing in the age of intensive parenting'. From that point onwards, those now involved with CPCS exchanged ideas, developed collaborative research and writing projects, and further events. In 2010 CPCS was established formally as one of the University of Kent's many research centres. Our website is: http://blogs.kent.ac.uk/parentingculturestudies/.

Part I
Parenting Culture

1
Intensive Parenting and the Expansion of Parenting

Charlotte Faircloth

In her introduction to *Parenting Out of Control* the US sociologist Margaret Nelson describes how childrearing has changed in the last 40 years:

> When I was raising my children in the 1970s, there were no baby monitors to help me hear them cry in the middle of the night, no cell phones to assist me in keeping track of their whereabouts at every moment, and no expectation that I would know any more about their educational success than they, or a quarterly report card, would tell me. Indeed, although I thought of myself as a relatively anxious parent, I trusted a girl in the third grade to accompany my five-year-old son to and from school, and when he was in first grade, I allowed him to walk that mile by himself ... In retrospect, and from the vantage point of watching my younger friends and colleagues with their children today, my parenting style seems, if not neglectful, certainly a mite casual. (Nelson, 2010, p. 1)

Nelson is far from alone in her observation that expectations around, and experiences of, how we raise our children have shifted in fairly fundamental ways over the last half-century (Furedi, 2002; Hays, 1996; Nelson, 2010). This chapter focuses on this development, the rise of what has been called 'intensive parenting', and looks at how childrearing (particularly in the US and the UK, but also beyond) has expanded in recent years to encompass a growing range of activities that were not previously seen as an obligatory dimension of the task. We argue that the extension of 'parenting' is not down to material changes in the health and safety of children (if anything, they are healthier and safer than ever before). Rather, we suggest that our perception of children themselves has shifted.

Children are today seen as more 'vulnerable' to risks impacting on physical and emotional development than ever before. As a corollary, parents are now understood – by policymakers, parenting experts, and parents themselves – as 'God-like', and wholly deterministic in an individual child's development and future. This has inflated the social importance of the parent role, precipitating a range of 'intensive' styles of parenting (readily understood through such tags as 'Gina Ford', 'Tiger Mothers', 'Attachment', or 'Helicopter parenting'). In turn, these parenting styles have themselves become a lens through which many adults (mothers in particular) derive their sense of identity, in a form of 'identity-work' akin to a vocation (Faircloth, 2013).

Intensive parenting

One of the earliest – and still most influential – observers of the changes in parenting culture was the US sociologist Sharon Hays, in her 1996 book *The Cultural Contradictions of Motherhood*. She noticed that many mothers she worked with were going to extreme lengths in the course of raising their children:

> Why do so many professional class employed women find it necessary to take the kids to swimming and judo and dancing and tumbling classes, not to mention orthodontists and psychiatrists and attention-deficit specialists? Why is the human bonding that accompanies breast-feeding considered so important that elaborate contraptions are now manufactured to allow children to suckle on mothers who cannot produce milk? Why are there copious courses for babies, training sessions in infant massage, sibling-preparedness workshops, and designer fashions for two-year olds? Why must a 'good' mother be careful to 'negotiate' with her child, refraining from the demands for obedience to an absolute set of rules? (Hays, 1996, p. 6)

Hays recognizes that children need an extended period of physical care to make the transition from infancy to adulthood. But as she says, 'modern American mothers *do much more* than simply feed, change and shelter the child until age six. It is that 'more' with which I am concerned' (Hays, 1996, p. 5; emphasis in original). This 'more' involves devoting large amounts of time, energy, and material resources to the child. There is a belief that a child's needs must be put first and that mothering should be child-centred. This 'more' is also almost always done by the mother – these messages about parenting are more strongly internalized by women, so that even where fathers are very 'involved', ultimately the buck stops with the mother, says Hays. And finally, the 'more' requires that a mother pay attention to what experts say about child development. It is not enough to 'make do' and do what seems easiest.

Hays coins the term 'intensive motherhood' to describe an ideology that urges mothers to 'spend a tremendous amount of time, energy and money in raising their children' (Hays, 1996, p. x). According to this ideology, 'the methods of appropriate child rearing are construed as *child-centred, expert-guided, emotionally absorbing, labor intensive,* and *financially expensive'* (Hays, 1996, p. 8). But as she says, 'the ideas are certainly not followed in practice in by every mother, but they are, implicitly or explicitly, understood as the *proper* approach to the raising of a child by the majority of mothers' (Hays, 1996, p. 9). So rather than being a uniform set of practices, intensive motherhood is best thought of as 'the normative standard ... by which mothering practices and arrangements are evaluated' (Arendell, 2000, p. 1195).

Hays is particularly puzzled by the emergence of the ideology of intensive motherhood at a time when women (in the US at least) make up over 50 per cent of the workforce (*Economist*, 2009). One might expect that, as women work longer hours, motherhood becomes less time-consuming – yet this does not appear to be the case. In fact, according to time-use studies, in the case of two-parent families, today's children are in fact spending substantially *more* time with their parents than in 1981 (Gauthier *et al.*, 2004; see also Sayer, 2004). This is despite an increase in female participation in work, attendance at day care and preschool by children, and an increase in time spent with children by fathers.

Perhaps it is not surprising, then, that the mothers with whom Hays worked talked about being tired, overstretched, and 'torn', when the worlds of work and home have both become so demanding. Not only are parents spending *more* time with their children but also the *quality* of that time has become far more intense.

The 'new momism', total motherhood, and the 'mommy wars'

Numerous scholars have picked up on Hays' concept of 'intensive motherhood' to describe the contemporary experience of parenting in Euro-American settings (Arendell, 2000; Bell, 2004; Douglas and Michaels, 2004; Freely, 2000; Hochschild, 2003; Maher and Saugeres, 2007; Ramaekers and Suissa, 2012; Umansky, 1996; Warner, 2006) and elsewhere (Faircloth *et al.*, 2013).

Douglas and Michaels focus in particular on the idealistic portrayal of motherhood in the US media, where motherhood is presented as ultimately fulfilling for women. They refer to this as the 'new momism';

> [the] insistence that no woman is truly complete or fulfilled unless she has kids, that women remain the best primary caretakers of children, and that to be a remotely decent mother, a woman has to devote her entire physical, psychological, emotional, and intellectual being, 24/7, to her children. The new momism is a highly romanticized and yet demanding view of motherhood in which the standards for success are impossible to meet. (Douglas and Michaels, 2004, p. 4)

They take particular issue with 'celebrity mom' spreads in glossy magazines, where the mother in question expounds on the joy of intensive childrearing (whether that be natural birth, breastfeeding, or one-on-one time with their child) while magically still managing to appear on catwalks and in blockbuster movies (a combination for which an army of behind-the-scenes helpers is presumably required). These idealized images do not chime with the experience of most working mothers who are more likely to feel tired, harassed, and less than sleek. What their work demonstrates is how this 'new momism' acts as an *idealistic* standard, which – although recognized to be ridiculous (by them as much as by other mothers) – retains a powerful hold over women as they go about imagining their own identities in relation to motherhood. Indeed, they show how these representations can induce strong feelings of failure when mothers do not manage to live up to them.

These representations are often manifested as antagonistic portrayals of working mothers in conflict with stay-at-home mothers, in what has been termed the 'mommy wars' (Douglas and Michaels, 2004). Hays recognizes here that while not all mothers will be working mothers, the cultural contradiction between the worlds of work and home is one that affects all parents. She notes that there is an irony, in that we live in a society where childrearing is generally devalued, and the emphasis is on the world of work, while at the same time holding up motherhood as an almost sacred endeavour. This means that people have to undertake what she calls 'ideological work' to make their own positions liveable. (In fact, contends Hays, people are forced to make their decisions around childcare in circumstances that are often beyond their control – although this rather pragmatic recognition does not sell newspapers so well.)

What is clear, then, is that whether women work or not the day-to-day practices of motherhood have become the subject of public, even of political debate (Freely, 2000). What parents feed their children, how they discipline them, where they put them to bed, how they play with them: all of these have become politically, and morally, charged questions. As Lee *et al.* note: 'What were once considered banal, relatively unimportant, private routines of everyday life for children and families ... have become the subject of intensive debates about the effects of parental activities for the next generation and society as a whole' (Lee *et al.*, 2010, p. 294).

Wolf (2011), writing about motherhood in the US, links this public interest to a broader argument around risk-consciousness and an emergence of a 'neo-liberal' culture, where dangers are redefined as risk and individuals hold themselves ever more responsible for managing risk and ensuring the safety of themselves and of those who are dependent on them (Lupton and Tulloch, 2002; Nelson, 2008). Wolf therefore talks about 'total' motherhood to characterize the experience of contemporary mothers. She notes that mothers are expected to become experts on all aspects of childrearing – making sure that those meal times, stories, and playing are not only safe, but also optimal for infant development: 'lay paediatricians, psychologists, consumer products safety inspectors, toxicologists, and educators. Mothers must not only protect their children from immediate threats but are also expected to predict and prevent any circumstance that might interfere with putatively normal development' (Wolf, 2011, p. xv).

Echoing Hays and Furedi, Wolf draws attention to the way in which this focus on risk frames good motherhood as totally child-centred, with no cost considered too high for mothers to bear. Since children are vulnerable and unable to protect themselves, mothers are charged with reducing (or avoiding all together) any risks to their children's health and well-being. This frames the mother–child relationship in an antagonistic way:

> Total motherhood is a moral code in which mothers are exhorted to optimize every aspect of children's lives, beginning in the womb. Its practice is frequently cast as a trade-off between what mothers might like and what babies and children must have ... When mothers have 'wants' – such as a sense of bodily, emotional, and psychological autonomy – but children have 'needs' – such as an environment in which anything less than optimal is framed as perilous – good mothering is defined as behaviour that reduces even infinitesimal or poorly understood risks to offspring, regardless of the potential cost to the mother. The distinction disappears between what children

need and what *might enhance* their physical, intellectual, and emotional development. Mothers are held responsible for matters well outside their control, and they are told in various ways that they must eliminate even minute, ultimately ineradicable, potential threats to their children's well-being. (Wolf, 2011, p. xv)

Furedi draws attention to the 'army of professionals' who now colonize parenting, as it is increasingly understood to be too important a task to be left up to parents. Instead, the view of policymakers (in both the US and the UK) is that parents should be 'enabled' to parent well, on the basis of 'research about the characteristics of effective parenting' (Johnson, 2007). Edwards and Gillies (2013) back up this analysis. In their research on the differences between parenting in 1960s and 2010s Britain – what would have been considered standard parenting practice (leaving children unsupervised to play, letting them go out at night alone, or asking older children to supervise younger ones, for example) would be considered neglectful today. The expectation more latterly is that parents should be constantly present to monitor their children, and protect them from 'risks', both known and unknown. Organizations such as the British Medical Association (BMA) have even gone so far as to abandon the use of the term 'accident' in favour of 'unintentional injury' in order to emphasize that what were once seen as random and unavoidable exposures to adversity for children can in fact be monitored, predicted, and prevented (British Medical Association, 2001, in Jenkins, 2006, p. 379). These shifts in the perception around risk have literally changed the physical landscape children inhabit – from the style of playground now being built to daily commutes children take (Franklin and Cromby, 2009; Stearns, 2009).

Nelson (2010) therefore highlights the way in which technologies themselves (and specific brands thereof) now characterize the experience of contemporary parenthood. In their wish to be ever-present, constantly attuned parents (and who would risk the accusation of being otherwise, when so much is at stake?), parents have embraced technologies such as baby monitors and cell phones to adopt a state of 'hypervigilance'. The irony is that not only are these technologies financially expensive (in line with Hays' outline of intensive motherhood) but they also do little to alleviate anxiety, and if anything they extend and intensify it (Nelson, 2008, p. 524). Interestingly, Nelson shows that while this is particularly acute in infancy, this vigilance extends beyond childhood, even to the point of leaving home to go to college. Many of her undergraduate students report being in contact with their parents several times a day, with parents being heavily involved with their children's academic life (in contact with tutors by phone, email, and in person). Nelson draws on Lareau's term 'concerted cultivation' not only to describe the constant work of making sure children achieve their potential (Lareau, 2003), but also points towards some of the potential negative effects of this hyper-vigilant involved parenting culture – recounting the example of parents who stay in their children's room during the first week of college for fear that they cannot cope without them. This phenomenon has been termed 'helicopter parenting', and we discuss it further in our essay in Part II of this book.

What each of the scholars cited above point to is that within this new style of 'parenting', a specific skill-set is denoted: a certain level of expertise about children and their care, based on the latest research on child development, and an affiliation to a certain way of raising a child and a particular educational strategy. There are, of course, many ways of caring for children 'intensively' (such as with methods that advocate the strict timetabling of feeding, sleeping, and so on, as well as the more 'attachment'-based parenting models that I explore in my essay in Part II). But whichever way one does it, it is clear that there is a broader cultural logic around intensive parenting, which holds that parents are wholly responsible for their children's outcomes.

This has interesting implication for the subjectivity of parents. Being well-educated is a requirement for participation in these choices between parenting models, as is a certain access to economic resources which enable parents to consume the material goods that in turn come to define the various methods of infant care. But this is also about adopting a certain sort of identity:

> Most of all [parenting] means being both discursively positioned by and actively contributing to the networks of ideas, values, practices and social relations that have come to define a particular form of the politics of parent-child relations within the domain of the contemporary family. (Faircloth *et al.*, 2013, p. 2)

Different performances of the cultural script

The ideology of intensive parenting described above does not, of course, affect all parents equally, and certainly not all parents today in the US (or the UK) are 'intensive parents'. However, it remains an important 'cultural script' or 'ideal' to which parents respond in negotiating their own practices. Particular lenses that have been used to explore the ideology of intensive mothering include 'work-life balance'

(Johnston and Swanson, 2006; Milkie *et al.*, 2004); gender differences in mothering and fathering (Dermott, 2008; Shirani *et al.*, 2012; Wall and Arnold, 2007); risk (Lee *et al.*, 2010); health (Lupton, 2012c); class (Gillies, 2006; Parsons Leigh *et al.*, 2012); teenage parenting (Duncan *et al.*, 2003); infant feeding (Avishai, 2007; Faircloth, 2013; Knaak, 2006; Kukla, 2006; Lee, 2007a, 2007b, 2008; Murphy, 2000, 2003; Wolf, 2011); consumption patterns and performativity (Pugh, 2005; Clarke, 2007); disability (Landsman, 1998); attitudes towards childcare (Riggs, 2005; Vincent and Ball, 2006); non-traditional families (Layne, 2013); global fluctuations in parenting culture (Faircloth *et al.*, 2013); and family leisure (Shaw, 2008). We look at three of these themes in particular, as a means of signposting issues for further discussion.

Gender

As Hays observed, perhaps the most obvious difference in response to this ideology is in terms of gender. While some recent research has shown how men increasingly see 'good fathering' as about being 'involved' with and emotionally present for their children (Dermott, 2008), mirroring the 'intensive' mothering model to some extent, other research has shown that they also continue to hold on to more traditional ideas about fathering. Shirani *et al.* (2012), for example, show that men (in the UK) are more likely to question expert advice about parenting, reject the need for hyper-vigilance, and limit material consumption as a means of contesting the competitive aspect of contemporary parenting culture.

Similarly, Shaw's (2008) work on family leisure draws on work with parents in North America, to explore gender differences in response to this ideology. In an era of 'intensive' parenting there has been a shift in family leisure patterns towards maximizing children's health and well-being, she observes (rather than on adult-oriented activities, for example). Parents are expected to act as pseudo-teachers, optimizing their children's intelligence through a range of extra-curricular activities. Shaw notes that it is women who act on these discourses, both self-consciously and in more invisible ways. Much of the work of enabling a child-centred approach to family time (the scheduling and planning) falls to women, says Shaw, echoing Dermott's (2008) observations on the gendered split between 'caring about' and 'caring for' children, or what Lupton (2012c, p. 13) refers to as the 'invisible mental labour' of mothering.

Class

Nelson's work in particular draws attention to the classed differences in the internalization of the 'intensive' parenting ideology (2010; see also

Gillies, 2009; Lareau, 2003). For the professional middle-class parents with whom she worked, who demonstrated the 'intensive' parenting style, she sees a desire to extend and protect childhood. For the working-class parents, the impetus to do this was constrained by material, financial necessity that children earn their own living as quickly as possible. Thus: 'within what I have called the professional middle class, parents do, indeed, adopt a style of parenting that has as its key features constant oversight, belief in children's boundless potential, intimacy with children, claims of trust and delayed launching' (Nelson, 2010, pp. 174–175). By contrast, in 'the working class and middle class ... parenting styles draw on concerns about concrete dangers, an awareness of youthful indiscretions, and a desire to see children mature sooner, rather than later' (Nelson, 2010, p. 175). In short, material necessity has a direct impact on one's cultural orientation towards parenting.

Cultural variation

In a recent collection, Faircloth *et al.* (2013) collated a series of chapters to explore the spread of 'intensive' parenting in a cross-cultural perspective. Several of the contributions looked at the experience of immigrant parents, who are forced to 'straddle' two competing cultures of parenting (that of their home and their host cultures).

Jaysane-Darr (2013) in particular looks at South Sudanese refugee responses to the US intensive parenting discourses, and particularly at the 'culture of expertise' that defines contemporary American parenting. She shows how a local non-profit organization's parenting workshops try to structure South Sudanese parent–child relationships in a way that replicates a middle-class American way of understanding infancy, childhood, and the individual person, even as they ignore the socio-economic and racial realities that structure diasporic life (thus chiming with Nelson's comments on 'Class', above). Through analyses of conversations and interactions with volunteers from the non-profit organization, as well as childrearing practices in the home, she shows how South Sudanese seek to glean knowledge about how to raise their children in American society, at the same time as they strive to reshape the parenting sessions according to South Sudanese ideals of socio-centricity, hospitality, and respect.

Parenting out of control?

Thus responses to this cultural script are far from stable. A common theme of the observations above, however, is that this intense anxiety and uncertainty around childrearing is not only negative for adults but is also negative for the next generation. With examples like those from Nelson's undergraduate students, some critics have even declared that we are breeding a 'nation of wimps' (Marano, 2008).

The American author Judith Warner (2006), for example, has written about her experience of motherhood in Paris (as has, more recently, Druckerman, 2012). On her return to her native country Warner noticed how distorted the culture around mothering had become. Where in France, women were encouraged to lead a 'balanced' life to avoid falling into 'excessive child-centredness' (Warner, 2006, pp. 10–11), in the States, she saw mothers who had 'turned into a generation of perfectionist control freaks, more concerned with creating the perfect playgroup or tracking down the last gram of trans fat in their kids' crackers than in running or changing, or even participating in, the larger world' (Warner, 2006, p. 4).

Warner diagnoses this as a problem of control – echoing work on risk-consciousness, discussed in the 'Introduction' to this book that positions women as ultimately responsible for harm to their children. Yet as she puts it, 'It's about how that feeling of being out of control drives them to parent in ways that are contrary to their better instincts, their deepest values and the best interests of their children' (Warner, 2006, p. 7). That is, while mothers perhaps recognize that this over-scheduling, hyper-vigilant culture is not necessarily ideal for children, there is a sense of motherhood as a 'winner takes all' game. With the expansion of college education, places in good schools have become ever more competitive, meaning that you do not want to be the one not to put your child in music or swimming class, for fear of jeopardizing their chances of getting into *that* school, college, job, and so on. This in turn brings us back to Lareau's idea of concerted cultivation.

There has, however, been some backlash to the manifestations of intensive parenting culture. Skenazy (2009), for example, recognizes that parents have lost all perspective on safety and danger, over-analyze the significance of everyday decisions, and ultimately do more harm than good by neither teaching nor modelling good judgement for their children. Instead, she endorses what she calls 'free-range' parenting. Others have implied more explicitly that it is parents themselves who are at fault for raising a generation of 'cotton wool kids'. We discuss this backlash further in Part II of the book, in Jennie Bristow's essay on 'The Double-Bind of Parenting Culture: Helicopter Parents and Cotton Wool Kids'.

Here, it is worth examining the proposed solution to the excesses of intensive parenting. This most often takes the form of instructing parents to 'relax' – though usually with the help of expert-led training

(Layard and Dunn, 2009). But this is to miss the point. As Lee *et al.* (2010) argue, these measures would have little impact on a broader cultural script, in which parents are cast as deterministic in the outcomes of their children. Even models of parenting which apparently advocate building children's resilience (by encouraging them to take risks, for example) share in the principles of intensive, involved mothering:

> [T]hrough her exploration of the themes in parenting advice about fostering resilience, Hoffman argues it can be understood as not an alternative to what has come before, but rather 'yet another approach to parenting that encourages intensive parental investment and involvement in children's lives'. (Lee *et al.*, 2010, p. 296)

Ramaekers and Suissa (2012) concur that telling parents to 'relax' will not solve anything, although they recognize that the genie is out of the bottle to the extent that there is now an appetite for support and information on the part of parents.

A different solution to the problem comes from feminist academics, such as Hochschild, who see that the answer lies in getting fathers and partners more involved in childcare, thereby easing the intensive burden that women largely shoulder alone:

> Why has the cultural revolution that matches women's economic revolution stalled? When rapid industrialization took men out of the home and placed them in the factory, shop or office, a corresponding ideological revolution encouraged women (middle-class white women, especially) to want to tend the home and care for the children. Hochschild argues that we now need a new ideological revolution encouraging men to want to cook, clean and nurture children, and encouraging employers and the state to want to provide for child care, job sharing and parental leave. (Hays, 1996, p. 5)

Hays, by contrast, remains unconvinced that 'involving' fathers further would be a solution to a much broader social contradiction between the worlds of work and home. Rather, she proposes that we radically rethink the way we see children:

> [W]hat Hochschild suggests – that we shift the focus from intensive mothering to intensive *parenting* – is only a partial solution to the contradiction between the demands of home and work, and one that does not begin to address the larger cultural contradictions. If men and

women shared the burden that Rachel [one of her interviewees] now bears primarily, the larger social paradox would continue to haunt both of them and would grow even stronger for men. Given the power of the ideology of the marketplace, a more logical (and cynical solution) would be an ideological revolution that makes tending home and children a purely commercial, rationalized enterprise, one in which neither mother nor father need be highly involved. Why don't we convince ourselves that children need neither a quantity of time nor 'quality time' with the mothers or their fathers? (Hays, 1996, p. 5)

As Lee *et al.* (2010) indicate, the strategies outlined above, which encourage individual parents to find ways of resisting the excesses of intensive parenting through relaxing, building resilience in children, or reorganizing gender roles so that fathers can take more of the burden of childcare, all implicitly endorse the core message of intensive parenting culture: that parental actions should be organized around what is presumed to be best for the individual child, in isolation from wider family or social considerations. By a similar token, these strategies endorse the conceptualization of childrearing as a highly privatized, rather than a generational, responsibility.

In Chapter 4 of this book, we discuss the extent to which contemporary culture encourages the privatization of childrearing through exacerbating parental anxieties about the dangers that may be posed to their children by other adults. We also indicate how this disruption of the idea that childrearing is a generational responsibility, which needs to be shared by adults in general, brings with it the growing regulation and surveillance of the activities of both adults and children.

These developments can be understood as implying the emergence of a historically distinct way of thinking about children and childhood. Today, a growing distance has been placed between children and the adult world; children, by and large, have less to do than they used to with ordinary adults in communities. Yet this distance by no means leads to children being left to 'do their own thing'. Children are not freer or more autonomous beings by merit of their increased estrangement from adults. On the contrary they are, as we have indicated, both more overseen in their activities by their parents, and the subject of more intervention and social control in other ways too. As the sociologists of childhood Allison James, Chris Jenks, and Alan Prout have commented:

Children are arguably now more hemmed in by surveillance and social regulation than ever before ... parents increasingly identify the world outside the home as one from which their children must be shielded and in relation to which they must devise strategies of risk reduction ... On the other hand, both public and private spaces are increasingly monitored by closed circuit television to contain the threat that unsupervised groups of children and young people are thought to potentially pose. Even the boundaries of the family are held to be at risk of penetration by insidious technologies like video and the Internet which could pose serious moral threats to our children's childhoods. (James *et al.*, 1998, p. 7)

The emergence of this particular sort of childhood – its distinct social construction – can be considered the underpinning of contemporary parenting culture. Centring on the definition of children as 'at risk', it is this way of thinking about children, what they need, and the problems of how adults relate to them, that makes 'paranoid parenting' possible. We therefore now discuss briefly, first, what it means to think of childhood as a 'social construct'.

There is a very large literature – indeed a subfield of sociology – relevant to this area and we cannot do justice to it here. Rather, our aim is to highlight the central points of this way of thinking about childhood that are relevant for our discussion. We then comment on the present social construction of childhood with its emphasis on vulnerability and being 'at risk', before returning to explore in more detail the relation between this and 'parenting'.

A social history of 'childhood'

Childhood has always been as much about the imagination and actions of adults as it is about physical children. Hendrick's (1997) history of childhood in English society draws on Prout and James (1990, p. 8) to note that 'childhood':

'[A]s distinct from biological immaturity, is neither a natural nor universal feature of human groups but appears as a specific structural and cultural component of many societies' ... In other words, though biological immaturity may be natural and universal, what particular societies make of such immaturity differs throughout time and between different cultures. So we say that it is socially constructed. (Hendrick, 1997, pp. 9–10)

Certainly, across space and time, societies have had different ideas about children, which in turn shapes how parents are expected to behave towards them. If children are considered inherently good, for example, society is assumed to need to change to enable this 'natural' purity to unfold; whereas if they are assumed to be inherently bad, it is children who must be shaped by society (Gittins, 1993, p. 22).

For the historian Philippe Ariès (1968 [1962]), author of *Centuries of Childhood*, one of the seminal and most widely debated studies of this area, the idea of childhood did not even exist in medieval times. However:

> [T]his is not to suggest that children were neglected, forsaken or despised. The idea of childhood is not to be confused with affection for children: it corresponds to an awareness of the particular nature of childhood, that particular nature which distinguishes the child from the adult ... In mediaeval society, this awareness was lacking ... as soon as the child could live without the constant solicitude of his mother, his nanny or his cradle-rocker, he belonged to adult society. (Ariès, 1968 [1962], p. 125 in Gittins, 1993, p. 27)

What Ariès sees is much less differentiation between children and adults; children were seen simply as small adults and came to 'belong' to adult society at a very young age. Many historians demonstrate this by giving the example of children put to death for crimes such as theft, according to the general law of the time.

Ariès also believed that children were treated with emotional indifference because parents could not afford to invest in them too highly, due to high rates of infant mortality. Other historians disagree – arguing that there was good evidence that parents were interested and invested in children. Cunningham, for example, sees 'anguish and a struggle to make sense of their loss' (Cunningham, 2006, p. 70) in the writings by parents about their deceased children at the time. That said, he agrees with Ariès that youth was seen as an unenviable life-stage, rather than as something to be 'cherished', more common today. Indeed, the idea of 'childhood' demarcated by its own clothes, toys, games, literature, or education would have seemed utterly foreign to the average medieval parent (Guldberg, 2009, p. 48).

This picture started to change, around the eighteenth century. Postman's *The Disappearance of Childhood* (1994) argues that this shift owed much to the birth of the printing press, for in a literate society, 'adulthood has to be earned. It became a symbolic, not a biological achievement' (Postman, 1994, p. 36). Children became seen not as mini-adults, but 'unformed adults' (Postman, 1994, p. 41) who must be educated into maturity. This different conceptualization of children was intimately related to wider changes of the period:

> The Enlightenment brought about a radically new conception of human beings: the idea that individuals are autonomous and rational, should have rights and responsibilities, and are capable of participating in political life, came to fruition during this time. It was this conception of human beings that brought about the distinction between adults and children. (Guldberg, 2009, pp. 49–50)

This emergent *separation* of adults and children was a new and very significant development. What it meant was that *adulthood* must also come to be redefined, with the questions posed of how adults should socialize, educate, and relate to children, through the distinct period of *childhood*.

The posing of questions about adults and their relation to children is reflected in the writing of the philosophers John Locke (1632–1704) and Jean-Jacques Rousseau (1712–1778), who held very different views of children. For Locke, children arrived in the world as a *tabula rasa*, or 'blank slate' needing to be 'filled up' with knowledge via education, and generally civilized by the adult world. Rousseau, by contrast, held a more romantic vision of children – highlighting their charm, purity, and need for protection, as outlined in his seminal text *Émile* (1762).

Prioritizing the child's needs, Rousseau argued that maternal practices should 'follow from the development of a child's inner nature, rather than from adult interests, and that children should be cherished, treated with love and affection, and protected from the corruption of the larger society' (Rousseau [1762], in Hays, 1996, p. 26). This represented a novel challenge to traditional parental authority. As Frank Furedi indicates in the Foreword, Rousseau was sceptical about parents' ability to meet the needs of the child so defined. Indeed, Rousseau was particularly scathing about the selfishness of mothers who used wet nurses to feed their babies, interpreting this as a clear example of the failure to recognize the child's needs and 'inner nature'.

As Guldberg writes, although the Lockean and Rousseauian views are often presented as being in contradiction, what is important is 'that both present an image of children as different from adults' (Guldberg, 2009, p. 50). Most historians agree, however, that this intellectual shift towards differentiating or 'constructing' childhood did not translate into a time in life that could be called 'childhood' for all children in the eighteenth or nineteenth centuries – many people 'had little choice but to treat children as little adults,' writes Guldberg (2009, p. 51). It was not until the nineteenth and twentieth centuries that the basic definitional features of 'childhood' as we might think of it today began to emerge for the mass of children.

In part, the shift was a product of fertility decline which itself was a product of wider economic changes. As life expectancy generally started to improve families started having fewer children, meaning they could invest more highly in each child, and – for middle- and upper-class families at least – those children would not need to work to help support such a large family unit. These shifts influenced (and were influenced by) changing conceptions of both childhood and work; as Wise puts it: 'The term child labor is a paradox, for where labor begins the child ceases to be' (Wise, in Zelizer, 1994, p. 55).

Indeed, central to the construction of childhood in its modern sense is the physical removal of children from 'labor', and the development, instead, of schooling as the socially recognized and legitimated occupation for all children. This, more than anything else, acts to make real the distinction between childhood and adulthood.

In England, an important moment in this development came in 1833, when the government passed the Factories Act, which prevented children under nine years of age from working, with limits on the number of hours for children under 18. It also provided for two hours a day of schooling. Towards the end of the century the state took on responsibility for the education of all children between 5 and 12 years of age through the Education Act (1870).

As Cunningham (2006) observes, however, another factor was critical in this emergence of 'childhood' – not directly linked to education or work, but to the experience of childhood as an end in itself. Zelizer (1994) argues that as children ceased to be economically valuable, as they came to play less and less of a part in earning money for the family, they became 'emotionally priceless', or 'sacralized'.

As she explains it, discussing the United States:

> Between the 1870s and 1930s, the value of American children was transformed. The twentieth-century economically useless but emotionally priceless child displaced the nineteenth-century useful child. To be sure the most dramatic changes took place among the working class; by the turn of the [twentieth] century middle-class children were already experienced 'loafers'. But the sentimentalization of childhood intensified regardless of social class. The new sacred child occupied a special and separate world, regulated by affection and education, not work or profit. (Zelizer, 1994, p. 209)

Childhood in crisis?

If modern 'childhood' was invented, and 'sacralized', in this way it has more recently come to be seen as a period of life under threat. Postman (whose book *The Disappearance of Childhood* was first published more than 30 years ago) is one of a number of critics expressing concerns that childhood is no longer distinguishable from adulthood. Just as literacy meant that adulthood could be achieved by 'children' in the past, today, that literacy is being replaced by media which (he argues) requires no skills to master, so childhood as a category is disappearing. Postman claims that there is evidence that children are no longer playing games, eating food, or wearing clothes specifically designed for them, and contends they lack respect for their elders, and also lack a sense of shame (discussed in Cunningham, 1995, p. 179). His concerns have come to be widely echoed in academic and media discourse:

> On 13 September 2006 a national newspaper in the UK, the *Daily Telegraph*, launched a campaign to halt the death of childhood. Warming up Postman's (1982) [1994]) lament on the 'disappearance' of childhood 24 years earlier, 'Hold on to Childhood' was supported by 110 academics, writers and medical experts, collectively calling for a public examination of children's lives. Their much-publicized letter in the *Telegraph* asserted that children have been 'tainted' by over-exposure to electronic media, lack of space to play and an over-emphasis on academic testing in schools. A recent Unicef report (2007) on the well-being of children and young people in 21 industrialized countries ranked the UK at the bottom of the table in their assessment of child well-being and the US second from bottom. The report focused on six areas: material well-being; health and safety; educational well-being; family and peer relationships; behaviours and risks; and young people's own perceptions of well-being. (Kehily, 2010, pp. 173–174)

Indeed, the claims that childhood is 'at an end', 'under threat', 'in crisis' and now made 'toxic' are frequently made and very visible. This notion that adult culture and society today is forcing children to grow up too fast, treating them too much like adults, and robbing them of their childhood, is considered further in Part II.

Whatever assessment is made of the demands today's culture places on children, it seems clear, however, that there is no simple process of the 'disappearance' of childhood, through which children simply become again like their medieval predecessors; treated just like adults. While it is now the (disturbing) case that signs can easily be found of the erosion of boundaries between adulthood and childhood, for example, children being charged with adult criminal offences (Furedi, 2013a; Keating, 2007), it is also clear that there has been an *expansion* of childhood. This takes a number of forms, from the extension of the time that most children spend in secondary education to the increased parental supervision of their grown-up children in higher education and employment (a point discussed in Jennie Bristow's essay on 'Helicopter Parents' in Part II).

The sociologist of childhood Alan Prout also identifies this paradox or contradiction in the way childhood is presently socially constructed:

> On the one hand, there is an increasing tendency to see children as individuals with a capacity for self-realisation and, within the limits of social interdependency, autonomous action; on the other, there are practices directed at a greater surveillance, control and regulation of children. (Prout, 2000, p. 304)

Cunningham (2006) concurs, observing that at no other time in history have we been quite so concerned about children and their safety. He says that children are more monitored today than ever before, because they are viewed as endangered by engagement with the adult world (a point explored in Chapter 4). There has been an evacuation of public spaces formerly seen as the domain of children, such as local parks; and a turn towards new forms of child entertainment (indoors and online, which are then subject to the anxieties Postman voices). In sum, Cunningham suggests that childhood in Western societies today has four overriding characteristics:

(1) The child is set apart as different from adults (see also Elias, 1998);
(2) The child is said to have a special nature and be associated with nature;
(3) The child is innocent, but corruptible;
(4) Today, the child is vulnerable and 'at risk'.

In relation to the last of these points, Stearns (2009), writing about American childhood over the course of the twentieth century, notes that our current ideas about children as 'at risk' and emotionally fragile are prefigured by cultural representations from the 1920s. During this period, he writes, using examples from the burgeoning area of childrearing literature, there was already a growing emphasis on children's vulnerability:

> The new breed of childrearing manuals began speaking more frequently of the 'problems of childhood' with the child him- or herself seen as a 'delicate organism'. 'Helplessness' was another term frequently used, and soon whole books, such as those authored by Renz (1935) gained titles like 'Big Problems on Little Shoulders'.... the dominant mood, particularly among popularizers, promoted a tone of growing concern about the many difficulties children almost inevitably encountered, if left to their own devices. (Stearns, 2009, pp. 39–40)

There was an assertion that children were emotionally vulnerable – both to their parents and to themselves. A new language emerged to express this fear: '"Festering" was a term applied to the potential damage children suffered from emotions that were almost inevitable yet which could not be managed by children on their own' (Stearns, 2009, p. 40). The responsibilities of the good parent became magnified as mothers were tasked with recognising this incapacity on the part of their children, and protecting them from any factors which might exacerbate it.

For Stearns, the basic cultural logic that emerged in the 1920s has largely persisted, as '[d]ominant cultural symbols still emphasize the preciousness of children but also their vulnerability and lack of capacity' (Stearns, 2009, p. 45). Certainly, soon after the 1920s, expert studies in this field built on, and cemented, the concern with psychological vulnerability during infancy. It was during the post-World War II period that psychological and cognitive child development theorists also came into an ascendency, with Freud, Erikson, and Piaget[1] publishing their studies of childhood, associating childhood experience with adult development.

What united these studies was the assumption of the absolute necessity of a mother's loving nurture. 'Attachment theory', which is discussed in the essay on 'The Problem of "Attachment"' in Part II of this book, claimed that the constant presence of a loving and responsive attachment figure – typically the mother – was the foundation for lifelong mental health. On the basis of his research with children in institutional settings, the psychiatrist John Bowlby wrote:

> What is believed to be essential for mental health is that the infant and young child should experience a warm, intimate and continuous relationship with his mother (or permanent mother-substitute)

in which both find satisfaction and enjoyment ... A state of affairs in which the child does not have this relationship is termed 'maternal deprivation'. (Bowlby, 1995 [1952], p. 11)

It was along the same lines that the wealth of experts we know today (Dr Benjamin Spock, Penelope Leach, and Thomas Berry Brazelton, to name three of the most popular experts to emerge in the second half of the twentieth century) produced the first editions of their books designed to help parents 'parent'. As we discuss in Chapter 2, the underlying paradigm developed by parenting experts – that experience in early infancy has lifelong implications and that this period of life is one entailing enormous risk – is now so taken for granted as to be unremarkable in contemporary parenting culture (Hays, 1996).

As we indicated in the Introduction, and emphasize throughout this book, it is the presumption of children as, *de facto*, vulnerable, and at risk, which is the most distinct and important aspect of the social construction of childhood today. This has profound implications for the definition of the mothering and fathering roles.

The inflation of the parenting role

Risky parents

As Lee *et al.* (2010) note, it is hard to overestimate how far the concept of the 'at risk' child has expanded when applied to the area of parenting. Children are cast as particularly vulnerable in today's culture, with their health and safety seen as compromised by a 'toxic' social environment. Because of this, parents are, in effect, seen as risk-managers, tasked with optimizing their children's outcomes in conjunction with expert advice (Lee *et al.*, 2010). The corollary of this is that parents who themselves indulge in 'risky' behaviour are increasingly framed as a danger to their children:

> Attention has been drawn to the distinctiveness of a culture that now routinely represents 'parenting' as the single most important cause of impaired life chances, outstripping any other factor ... the idea that *parents themselves* constitute an important, and according to some perhaps the most significant, risk factor in children's lives. (Lee *et al.*, 2010, p. 295)

This logic applies to the 'obvious' candidates for the label of 'risky parents' – the father who smacks (BBC, 2012), the woman who drinks or smokes during pregnancy (Hinton *et al.*, 2013; Lowe and Lee, 2010a, 2010b) or the mother who formula feeds (Knaak, 2010; Lee, 2007a, 2007b; Murphy, 2004), for example. But what is more interesting, perhaps, is the way it now appears to apply to *all* parents:

> It has also been noted that the risk parents present to children is not only considered significant when parents are considered to be 'bad'. Parenting is also problematized where parents are construed to be 'unaware' or 'out of touch'. This happens for example in discussions about the alleged threat represented to children by technologies parents do not understand (such as the Internet), or in the debate about parental 'lack of awareness' of how much exercise their children take or of the calorie content of the food they feed their children. (Lee *et al.*, 2010, p. 295)

The developmental paradigm, now so firmly established as fact, is one of the key reasons parents are seen as a determining force in how their children turn out. The flipside to the 'vulnerable child' is the risky parent: or, as Furedi puts it, 'Omnipotent parenting is the other side of the coin of child vulnerability' (Furedi, 2002, p. 58). For Furedi, these two important 'myths' result in a highly skewed understanding of adult–child relationships:

> The interlocking myths of infant determinism, that is, the assumption that infant experience determines the course of future development, and parental determinism, the notion that parental intervention determines the future fate of a youngster, have come to have a major influence on relations between children and their parents. By grossly underestimating the resilience of children, they intensify parental anxiety and encourage excessive interference in children's lives; by grossly exaggerating the degree of parental intervention required to ensure normal development, they make the task of parenting impossibly burdensome. (Furedi, 2002, p. 45)

The idea that children are at risk from their parents has a long and established history. As Christina Hardyment's (2007) historical study of childcare advice 'from John Locke to Gina Ford' explains, from the Enlightenment onwards, 'scientific' approaches to childrearing have continually put traditional parental authority into question, setting it against whichever 'modern' method is in vogue. Today, however, the strength of assumptions about parental determinism and the need for parenting 'expertise' means that 'now almost every parenting act, even the most routine, is analysed in minute detail, correlated with a negative or positive outcome, and endowed with far-reaching implications for child development' (Furedi, 2002, p. 65).

With experts stressing the importance of the early (even pre-conception) environment for infant development (see, for example, Gerhardt's (2004) book *Why Love Matters*), providing children with the right kind of environment turns normal activities of parenting into a series of tasks to be achieved. Touching, talking, and feeding are no longer ends in themselves, but tools mothers are required to perfect to ensure optimal development. Lee *et al.* (2010) give the example that playing with a child is no longer simply an enjoyable activity for adult and child; it is perceived as an instrumental way of ensuring positive 'long-term outcomes'. Rose has even argued that 'love' can be used to promote a certain type of self-understanding in children, and is duly emphasized for mothers: increasing confidence, helpfulness, dependability at the same time as averting fear, cruelty, or any other deviation from the desired norm (Rose, 1999, p. 160). The conversion of 'love' from a spontaneous sentiment manifested in warm affection into a parental function or skill is one of the key reasons why mothers are now routinely told to 'enjoy their baby', with almost magical powers ascribed to 'unconditional love' (and disastrous consequences to its absence) (Furedi, 2002, p. 79).

Intensive parenting and adult identity

This inflation of the role of the parent has meant that parenting has become an increasingly important part of adult identity. As Furedi says, 'Adults do not simply live their lives through children, but in part, develop their identity through them ... parents are also inventing themselves' (Furedi, 2002, p. 107).

This point became clear in my own research (Faircloth, 2013), where an affiliation to an 'attachment' parenting philosophy emerged as central to some mothers' sense of identity. I worked with networks of mothers in London and Paris who breastfeed their children 'to full term'. This means that a mother breastfeeds until her child outgrows the perceived need to do so – which can be at any point between a year and eight years old, though is typically between two and four years. In line with the 'attachment' philosophy, which values long-term maternal-infant proximity as a means of optimizing child development, other typical practices include breastfeeding 'on cue', 'bed-sharing', and 'baby-wearing'. As I explore further in the essay on 'The Problem of "Attachment"' in Part II, these women practice a form of infant feeding that is unusual, but validated by wider policy directives emphasizing the risks associated with formula milk use. However, their 'identity work' (their narrative processes of self-making and accountability, now so familiar to contemporary parenting culture) is less straightforward than may be expected.

The widespread moralization of infant feeding practices (and parenting more generally) appears to have amplified tensions between various 'tribes' of mothers, who often feel the need to defend themselves in vociferous and highly judgmental terms. In terms of risk consciousness and total motherhood, the mothers in these networks are in a double bind: on the one hand, their marginal position is affirmed through recourse to risk reduction, while on the other, their non-conventional practices are left open to the charge of 'riskiness' with respect to the social and emotional development of their children. They are therefore in the position of having to carry out the 'ideological work' as described by Hays about the benefits of their chosen style of mothering. The same logic could equally be applied to other 'deviant' parents (such as the formula feeder who insists that a less stressed mother is better for a baby).

This is echoed in recent work by Villalobos (2009), which extends Hays' assertion that mothering these days is 'child-centred', to highlight that it might, in fact, be better described as 'mother–child centred'. Indeed, on the basis of her research with mothers from a range of demographics in the US, Villalobos positions her research at the apex of the trend towards intensive motherhood (Hays, 1996), and the emergence of a 'culture of fear' (Furedi, 1997) to show how mothers often focus on micro/everyday practices of mothering as a way of counteracting broader social/macro insecurities (such as under- or un-employment or greater fluidity in relationships). Mothering is then both about protecting and immunizing children from an insecure world *and* a source of meaning for many women: they attach themselves 'vehemently' to the mother–child relationship to counter their own psychic insecurity (Villalobos, 2009, p. 7).

One explanation Furedi offers for this investment in particular parental 'tribes' is linked to the 'emptying out' of adult identity more broadly:

> The moral significance of the child today is directly linked to the emptying out of adult identity. When the desire for recognition lacks an obvious outlet, the validation of the sense of self through one's child acquires a new importance. When in previous eras adults lived through their children, they did so as members of at least outwardly relatively stable families and communities. The child was used as a

means of self-realization and sometimes as an instrument of family advancement. Today, the child has been transformed into a far more formidable medium for the validation of the adult self. At a time when very few human relations can be taken for granted, the child appears as a unique emotional partner. (Furedi, 2002, p. 120)

Similarly, Layne's (2013) work with 'Single Mothers by Choice' (SMC) in the US has explored the contradiction between child-centred approaches to parenting, where children are seen as the 'unique emotional partner' and the parental couple-relationship. Using the case study of Carmen, a well-educated, middle-class mother of three children conceived using *In Vitro* Fertilization (IVF) via donor sperm, Layne highlights how an 'intensive' commitment to one's children is arguably more feasible when one does not have a partner to contend with. While recognizing the lack of material and structural support most single mothers face, for Carmen, who has resources to draw upon, a husband would be an unnecessary distraction from the business of raising her children in the 'Tiger Mom' fashion for which she has opted. This obviously points to some interesting observations around the primacy of the mother–child 'dyad' in an intensive parenting ideology, and the pressure this puts both on that relationship and other family dynamics.

Conclusion

This chapter has shown that even though there are important differences of class, gender, and ethnicity, a particular parenting style has emerged in Euro-American contexts that is widely considered 'ideal'. It is broadly one that is child-centred, expert-guided, emotionally absorbing, labour intensive, and financially expensive (Hays, 1996, p. x). What we suggest is that this has not emerged 'from below' or spontaneously from parents themselves, but rather as a product of cultural developments and influences at the levels of expertise, policy, and intergenerational transmission. These points are explored in the next three chapters, beginning next with discussion of the role and place of experts in the intensification of parenting.

Chapter summary

- The 'intensification' of parenting is the process by which, in recent years, childrearing has become a much more labour-intensive, demanding task for contemporary adults.

- This is premised on an acceptance of the 'infant determinism' paradigm, which attributes lifelong outcomes to infant experience, highlighting children's vulnerability and thereby inflating the importance of the parental role.
- The cultural turn towards intensive parenting has not been uniformly experienced by all parents (race, gender, class, and geography all shape its internalization); but it remains an idealized standard against which many parents assess themselves.
- The inflation of the parenting role can have negative implications for society more broadly, both in encouraging over-involvement in children's lives, and in corroding the bonds between parents themselves, who have become increasingly 'tribalized'.

Notes

1. For example:
   Freud, S. (1977 [1910]) 'A Special Type of Choice of Object Made by Men (Contributions to the Psychology of Love 1)', in A. Richards and A. Dickinson (eds), *On Sexuality: The Penguin Freud Library, vol. 7* (London: Penguin Books), pp. 227–242.
   Erikson, E. (1959) *Identity and the Life Cycle* (New York: International Universities Press).
   Piaget, J. (1955) *The Child's Construction of Reality* (London: Routledge and Kegan Paul).

Further reading

Douglas, S. and Michaels, M. (2004) *The Mommy Myth: The idealization of motherhood and how it has undermined all women* (New York: Free Press).
This is a useful book for those with an interest in popular and media representations of mothering. Douglas and Michaels examine the cult of the 'new momism', a trend in western culture (and particularly the US) that suggests that women can only achieve contentment through the perfection of mothering. They point out that the standards of this ideal remain out of reach, no matter how hard women try to 'have it all'.

Lareau, A. (2003) *Unequal Childhoods: Class, race, and family life* (Berkeley: University of California Press).
Drawing on the in-depth observations of black and white middle class, working class, and poor families, this study explores the fact that class does make a difference in the lives and futures of American children and offers a picture of childhood in the twenty-first century. Lareau's term 'concerted cultivation' has been widely picked up in the study of parenting culture to explain the work that parents put into ensuring optimal outcomes for their children.

Nelson, M. (2010) *Parenting Out of Control: Anxious parents in uncertain times* (New York and London: New York University Press).
This is a book based on Nelson's research in the US, examining the realities of what she terms 'parenting out of control'. Analyzing the goals and aspirations parents have for their children as well as the strategies they use to reach them, Nelson discovers fundamental differences among American parenting styles that expose class fault lines, both within the elite and between the elite and the middle and working classes.

Zelizer, V. (1994) *Pricing the Priceless Child: The changing social value of children* (Princeton: Princeton University Press).
This is a very important book for those with an interest in the history of childhood. In this book, Zelizer traces the emergence of the modern child, at once economically 'useless' and emotionally 'priceless', from the late 1800s to the 1930s. This provides an analytical foundation for the 'expansion' of parenting culture explored in this chapter.

2

Experts and Parenting Culture

Ellie Lee

> A vast industry of childcare advice has arisen. Bookshop shelves groan under the weight of warring theories about the best way to bring up baby, guides for fathers, grandmothers and even aunts ... Parents spill out intimate details of conflict in the kitchen and crises in the bedroom in magazine columns, blogs and internet forums. Information overload is turning parenthood into a nightmare of anxiety and stress. (Hardyment, 2007, p. 283)

The above comment appears at the start of the final section of *Dream Babies*, Christina Hardyment's influential history of childcare advice in Britain and North America. Her account begins in 1750, indicating that the issuing of 'childcare advice' is certainly not new. However, the present seems notably different to the past. The volume and scope of childcare advice today is remarkable, as is the extent to which 'intimate' matters which were previously not the subject of public discussion have 'spilled out'. Hardyment gave the final chapter of her book, which examines the years from 1981 to 2001, the title 'Spotlight on Parents', suggesting that, in particular, *the parent* has become the target of advice in a distinct way.

This chapter sets out an account of what is specific about childcare advice in the present, in the context of its long history. Our aim is not to provide a comprehensive history of 'parenting experts' and their messages (some of our favourite works that provide excellent historical accounts looking at North America and England are listed at the end of the chapter). Rather, we compare what emerges from a comparison of three points in time, the late nineteenth century, the mid-twentieth century, and the present, with the aim of throwing into relief what is distinct about today.

Our commentary is informed by two general insights from the literature. The first is that what experts have had to say in both the past and the present can be understood as a reflection of the wider cultural context. The psychologist William Kessen has made this point as follows:

> [T]he child is essentially and eternally a cultural invention and ... the variety of the child's definition is not the removable error of an incomplete science ... not only are American *children* shaped and marked by the larger cultural forces of political maneuverings, practical economics, and implicit ideological commitments ... *child psychology* is itself a peculiar cultural invention that moves with the tidal sweeps of the larger culture. (Kessen, 1979, p. 615, emphasis in original)

Not only are children influenced in their experience by 'larger cultural forces' but also are theories and schools of thought which set out claims about what children are and what they need. In Kessen's example, child psychology can thus be thought of less as an enterprise that emerged and has developed in reflection of ever-better scientific knowledge, than as an 'invention' reflecting the 'tidal sweeps of the larger culture'.

This is not to dispute that genuine, important insights have emerged from, for example, developmental psychology, paediatrics, and other specialisms concerned with child development and child health. They surely have, and such insights have contributed enormously to the health and welfare of children. Rather, it is to show how theories about children change, and to recognize their relation to the wider society and culture in which they are found.

A common characteristic of society at the points in time discussed in what follows is dislocation, flux, and a sense of uncertainty about the future. The nature of social dislocation – associated for example with urbanization and industrialization in the nineteenth century, and the effects of the World War II in the mid-twentieth century – varies. However, we suggest that the messages that experts have communicated to parents can only be made sense of when viewed as an aspect of the problem of uncertainty that arises as a result of social dislocation, whatever its specific cause. In this light, contemporary 'parenting expertise' can be similarly understood as a manifestation of the uncertainty that pertains in the present.

A second, related, point raised by Kessen concerns boundaries; where the line is drawn between disinterested, scientific investigation of *the child*, and efforts to address perceived social problems through changing *how parents relate to their children*. Throughout history, this line between the 'is' of the child, and the 'ought' of the parent, between *descriptions* of children and *prescription* of parental action and attitude, has proved porous. As Kessen suggests, however, the general trajectory has been towards the 'ought':

> [T]he implication *in all theories of the child* is that lay folk, particularly parents, are in need of expert guidance. Critical examination and study of parental practices and child behavior almost inevitably slipped subtly over to advice about parental practices and child behavior. The scientific statement became an ethical imperative, the descriptive account became normative … whatever procedures were held to be proper science at the time, were given inordinate weight against poor old defenceless folk knowledge. (Kessen, 1979, p. 818, emphasis in original)

The de-legitimation of 'folk' or 'tacit' knowledge about how to understand and relate to children in this way is common to the different points in time explored in this chapter. However, there are shifts in the balance between the imperative to prescribe on the one hand (the 'ought'), and the upholding and validation of 'folk', or what could also be termed 'instinctual', understanding on the other. Thus while it is true to say that, from the late nineteenth century onwards, there is a distinct turn towards calling into question 'folk' knowledge, this tendency co-exists until fairly recently with some validation of 'instinct' as a guide which is as good as any other. One conclusion to emerge from the discussion that follows is that perhaps the single most distinctive feature of expert commentaries and statements about today's parents is the tendency to reposition 'instinct' as either mythical or problematic. The transformation in expert discourse of the relationship between a parent and a child into a set of skills that has to be learned and acquired, and for which instinct provides no satisfactory guide, stands out as a defining feature of today.

The rise of the child expert in the nineteenth century and the search for order

Most investigations of the history of parenting experts and parent education point to the importance of the nineteenth century; notably, literature exploring England, the United States, and other countries including Canada and Australia identifies similar themes and developments. Centrally, these studies highlight the relation between the activities of 'child experts' of various kinds and the construction of childhood during this period. As noted in Chapter 1, while ideas about childhood predate this period by a considerable stretch, the relation between urbanization and industrialization, the problem of social order, and efforts to delineate the world of the adult from that of the child (for example, through restrictions on child labour and mandatory education for all children) characterize this time. Hence, although most studies of 'modern' parenting experts begin in the 1700s, the 1800s are identified as the most important starting point in understanding the pre-history of the present.

Explorations of the nineteenth century highlight a process whereby the authority of the mother, specifically, is unseated. Hays thus points to a shift in expert discourse in America away from a positive validation of the special attributes and contribution of the mother, towards calling into question quite where her instincts might lead if left 'uneducated'. The overall context, she suggests, was the growing fissure in society between the public world of commerce, economy, and politics, and the private world of 'the home'. In the early 1800s, this gave rise to claims about 'moral motherhood'; at this time, she explains, 'a mother's role in child rearing began to take on new importance', and mothers emerged 'as the keepers of morality', within a portrait of 'moral mothers raising virtuous children' (Hays, 1996, p. 30).

The expansion in the number of childrearing manuals at the time signalled the development of an interest in influencing parent–child relations. However, explains Hays, the overall tone of the commentary in them was of the sacralization and glorification of the home, and of motherhood. The domestic sphere was thus the 'empire' of the mother. 'To rule this empire, a woman's "passion" had to be repressed, but her "affections" were now understood as a positive and crucial force for the good of all', summarizes Hays, as the key message of the time (1996, p. 30). This meant that '[a]lthough the father was still the ultimate authority, the mother had a much larger and valued role to play in shaping the child' (1996, p. 32). While in expert messages, 'the fear of maternal indulgence persisted, and notions of women as lacking in reason lurked in the background' (1996, p. 34), there was a distinct message of reverence for the mother and the family home she created.

However, argues Hays:

Toward the end of the nineteenth century middle-class child-rearing ideologies took a somewhat curious turn. A mother's instincts, virtue and affection were no longer considered sufficient to ensure proper child-rearing. She now had to be 'scientifically' trained ... mothers' status as valorised, naturally adept child nurturers was diminished at the same time that affection and sentimentality lost favour ... The prominent child experts of this era ... were all interested in making child rearing a scientific enterprise; none thought it should be left to untrained mothers. (Hays, 1996, p. 39)

This turn away from the validation of 'a mother's instincts, virtue and affection' towards childrearing as a 'scientific enterprise' is widely discussed as central to the roots of modern American parenting culture (Apple, 1995; Stearns, 2003). Stearns thus suggests that there was a 'huge contrast' between the nineteenth-century manuals and those that came later. The former were short and confined to discussion of a small number of topics, for example, piety and obedience, authored by 'proponents of moral common sense' (usually clergymen or their wives or daughters). By contrast the latter, written by men of medicine or psychology, 'encompassed a huge range of topics, now usually phrased as problems', which suggested that '[p]arental obligations could be met, but imposed major demands' (Stearns, 2003, p. 19).

Similar perceptions and messages also characterized Victorian England. As Hardyment puts it, with reference to the arguments of the influential early twentieth-century child expert Ellen Key:

The confident early-nineteenth-century years, where mothers had enjoyed the responsibility of motherhood, were past ... the hallmark of motherhood was now anxiety, an anxiety produced in large part by the systematic demoralization of mothers concerning the quality, or even the existence, of their maternal instinct in the face of the united front presented by the state, by doctors and by manual writers, on their inadequacies. (Hardyment, 2007, p. 116)

In this way, the relation between the parent (primarily the mother) and the child, as it appears in accounts from experts, moved from expressions of optimism regarding a mother's contribution to the future given by her love and commitment to her child, towards by the late nineteenth century, far greater scepticism about her instinctive childrearing capacities. This period showed more marked efforts by experts to educate and influence the mother, and make her 'instinct' secondary to their 'science'. We can see this shift as a reflection of the sense in which social elites, by the late nineteenth century, were more and more

preoccupied with how to address problems of order and social disinte-
gration, and looked to 'science' and the apparent certainty it offered to
find a resolution to this problem. As Hays explains:

> Two related social phenomena ... may in part explain the shift in
> ideas about appropriate mothering. On the one hand there was
> increasing concern with the effect on the nation of the exponential
> rise in the number of new immigrants, the growing ranks of the
> urban poor, and the striking increase in labour unrest. On the other
> there was a new belief in the possibility of discovering scientific,
> technical, expert-guided, and state-enforced solutions to such social ills.
> (Hays, 1996, p. 41)

Others make a similar case, explaining the orientation to scientific
solutions within the context of a perceived problem of order and
instability. It has been argued that the rise in America and England
of 'Social Darwinism' crystallized this development, by drawing direct
parallels with the Darwinian theory of evolution in nature and the
organic development of society, positioning the development of the
child as the microcosm of this process. In their seminal study of
'experts' advice to women', Ehrenreich and English thus depict the
rapid decline of rural pre-industrial society in the context of economic
change, where:

> It was as if the late Victorian imagination, still unsettled by Darwin's
> apes, suddenly looked down and discovered, right at knee-level, the
> evolutionary missing link ... in the child lay the key to the *control* of
> human evolution. (Ehrenreich and English, 1979, p. 168)

The child undergoing the process of development towards adulthood
came to be seen, they suggest, as the link from the past to a new indus-
trial future: 'This child is conceived as a kind of evolutionary proto-
plasm, a mean of *control* over society's not-so-distant future' (Ehrenreich
and English, 1979, p. 172). Kessen called Charles Darwin 'the father of
child psychology', with his ideas about human evolution initiating 'a
long and continuing line that has preached from animal analogues, has
called attention to the biological in the child' (Kessen, 1979, p. 816).
The idea was thus that the child and her development could be fully
understood through the application of science, with her development
both analogous to that found in the animal world, and also capturing,
in microcosm, evolution from past to future. Understanding the child

and controlling and ordering her development would, for this reason, provide a key to the problem of social order as a whole.

To leave the child to the vagaries of maternal instinct, from this perspective, was tantamount to leaving the future to fate; far better to take control over social evolution through the exertion of scientific knowledge and influence. The problem that needed to be addressed, according to the renowned American paediatrician Luther Emmett Holt, author of the 1894 manual *The Care and Feeding of Children*, was that, 'instinct and maternal love are too often assumed to be a sufficient guide for the mother' (Ehrenreich and English, 1979, p. 181). This required, necessarily, that parents would come to be represented in a new way by those proclaiming their leadership of the new 'study of the child'. Parents had 'new evolutionary responsibilities' necessitating that they would rear their children under the guidance of scientific insight, rather than folk or everyday custom (Ehrenreich and English, 1979, p. 171). The idea of the child as the key to the future in this way brought with it a clear message: 'To say that the child alone held the key to social change was to say that the present generation of adults did not' (Ehrenreich and English, 1979, p. 170). (Notably, Holt was also a proponent of eugenics, arguing in his 1913 address to the American Association for the Study and Prevention of Infant Mortality (AASPIM): 'We must eliminate the unfit by birth, not by death. The race is to be most effectively improved by preventing marriage and reproduction by the unfit, among whom we would class the diseased, the degenerate, the defective, and the criminal' (Holt, 1913)).

The burgeoning enterprise of 'child study' that developed in America from the late nineteenth century into the twentieth century was one influential outcome of this shift towards an agenda of child-focused change (Hulbert, 2004; Lupton and Barclay, 1997). Ellen Key was best known for designating the twentieth century in England as 'The Century of the Child', advocating the need for the generalization of what she considered to be scientifically based ideas about children, to shape their rearing, and so build a better future. Some historians have noted, also, a change in assumptions about the behaviour and role of fathers in this context. Efforts to encourage mothers to follow the agenda of science did not mean that 'the father role' was immune to concern. Lupton and Barclay suggest, by contrast, that the new science of the child included expressions of concern about the 'over-feminisation of boys', and the 'development by experts of a model of ideal fatherhood' (Lupton and Barclay, 1997, p. 40).

American commentaries indicate that the de-authorization of the parent as part of this growing emphasis on the child as the key to the future was most marked in immigrant working-class families, who were considered to be the most distanced from the new urbanized world (Ehrenreich and English, 1979; Hays, 1996). Investigations indicate significant similarities between the US and England in this regard, in that the strongest preoccupation in England, too, was with the childrearing practices of the urban poor (Hendrick, 1997).

The range and differing perspectives of the social actors involved are wide (including social purity campaigners and child savers, public health officials, eugenicists, imperialists, law enforcers, and educationalists). Overall, however, it is clear that the explosion of concern with the 'health, welfare and rearing of children' was 'linked to the destiny of the nation and the responsibilities of the state' (Hendrick, 1997, p. 39). To 'save' the child was to make secure the future of the nation. Interpretations of the perceptions of working-class mothers are more or less critical of the arguments of those who sought to 'save children' by making the working-class family more 'hygenic' and less 'neglectful' (Hendrick, 1997; Lewis, 1980; Ross, 1993). There is a common recognition, however, that mothering practices were considered deficient, leading to, for example, mother-craft education and the promotion of mothering skills through health and welfare systems, and legislative change through maternity and child welfare laws.

The relevant research detects important ambiguities in this period, however. First, it is argued that the developments of this time involved more than oppression. According to Hays, for example, they also 'demonstrated a profound belief in the importance of mothers and children': who, after all, were presented as the key to the future (Hays, 1996, p. 43). Thus, '[m]iddle class women also stood to gain from this new cultural model: it did after all promise to elevate their child-rearing and domestic duties to the status of a scientific profession' (Hays, 1996, p. 43). Ehrenreich and English (1979) and Hulbert (2004) also emphasize on how this period gave rise to a new middle-class 'mothers' movement'; women who 'refused to see child raising as something instinctive' (Ehrenreich and English, 1979, p. 185) and who enthusiastically embraced the idea of becoming educated in the science of childrearing, working together with child experts.

A second important aspect of the reorganization of authority in favour of those knowledgeable in the 'science of the child' was its ambiguous relationship to 'the family' – for the Victorians, the most sanctified institution of all. Hence, architects of the child study movement and authors of childcare advice manuals held the view that '[t]he

vagaries of casual stories about children, the eccentricities of folk knowledge, and the superstitions of grandmothers were all to be cleansed by
the mighty brush of scientific method' (Kessen, 1979, p. 817). Yet there
was a tension between this openly critical approach to 'folk knowledge',
and the sacralization of motherhood and family. As Kessen puts it, talking of the past at least: 'Strangely at odds with the theme of rational
scientific enquiry has been the persistence of the commitment to home
and mother' (1979, p. 818).

An important feature of the late nineteenth and early twentieth
century, then, is the coexistence of the questioning of the efficacy and
acceptability of certain parental practices, with the upholding of home,
family life, and 'the mother' in a particular form. For this reason, intervention by experts, campaigners, and the state into working-class and
immigrant communities and families took place in the context of the
sanctification of the middle-class family as a private institution.

Experts, attachment, and child-centredness

On the surface, what experts had to say in the 1950s and 1960s seems
very different to the late nineteenth century. In the earlier period, literature on childrearing:

> [W]as directed at the inculcation of self-discipline and self-control in
> children, qualities that became increasingly important in the wake of
> industrialization and what was considered to be a subsequent break-
> down in the regulation of individuals by the family and community.
> (Lupton and Barclay, 1997, p. 39)

By contrast, the economic depression of the1930s followed by the catas-
trophe of the World War II, gave rise to a different emphasis:

> It was ... during this period that the categories of psychological and
> cognitive child development that had first come into vogue in the
> Progressive Era were elaborated ... These theories in turn were popu-
> larized in child-rearing literature. (Hays, 1996, p. 47)

In this era, it was the 'inner world' of the child's mind that became the
focus of growing interest. Emphasis shifted from advising on how to
develop attitudes that were considered most in line with the needs of
early twentieth-century society, to ensuring that childhood anxieties
did not lead to abnormal development. Drawing on ideas about 'stages'

of child development (following Freud and also Piaget) the message became that:

> [G]ood parents, like good educators, recognize and build upon these stages ... Taken together the popularized versions of these theories suggested that parents needed to guard against a wide variety of childhood fears and anxieties by carefully fostering a basic sense of trust between parent and child, that infancy and early childhood were the stages most critical to the child's overall development, and that good parents would 'naturally' want to acquire further knowledge of cognitive and emotional development. (Hays, 1996, p. 47)

Despite this important shift in emphasis, however, continuity remained in the ambiguity between the privileging of expert authority and knowledge (now about the inner world of the child) and the upholding of the importance of motherhood and of family values. This was apparent in the arguments made by the figure most closely associated with this period, the British psychiatrist John Bowlby, and the growing preoccupation with the problem of 'attachment' (Riley, 1983; Urwin and Sharland, 1992; see also Part II of this book).

In 1951, Bowlby provided a report for the World Health Organization (WHO), which had as its context widespread concerns about 'the effects of institutionalization on children' in the light of the experience and aftermath of the World War II (Richardson, 1993, p. 43). The experience of parents and children in this war is now difficult to comprehend. Vast numbers of British children were orphaned by the war, or separated from one or more parents for long periods of time, because of their evacuation from cities to the countryside and, in some cases, overseas. Evacuation policies, which began in September 1939, with the official declaration of war by the British Government in response to the threat of the aerial bombing of large cities in the end involved over 3.5 million people. In the first three days of evacuation over 800,000 school-age children and over 500,000 mothers with children under five were moved. At the end of the war there was, understandably, concern about those children left without one or both parents or made homeless.

In the book *Child Care and the Growth of Love* which resulted from his report, Bowlby set out his argument that 'the early attachments, or bonds, a child forms are crucial to her future mental health', and that 'in order that the process of maternal bonding could take place ... the child needed to experience a warm, intimate and continuous relationship with the mother, in which both found satisfaction and enjoyment'

(Richardson, 1993, p. 43). By merit of this emphasis on the need of the young child for nurture and intimacy as a precondition for normal psychological development, Bowlby is widely seen as one of the founding figures in the turn to 'child centredness'.

The ambiguity of this new version of 'child science' has been commented on, with a tension identified between an emphasis on what is 'natural' and 'instinctual' and the place of the expert or professional. Richardson (1993) thus draws attention to the centrality of 'instinct' for Bowlby, noting that in his approach, '[b]eing a good mother meant adopting a positive and loving attitude towards one's infant. All a mother had to do to achieve this was just to act naturally'. She emphasizes the way Bowlby assessed the problem of 'maternal deprivation' in infancy, resulting from institutionalization: '[I]n discussing children who have been severely deprived of "normal maternal love and care during infancy", Bowlby states that, "... it is exactly the kind of care which a mother gives without thinking that is the care which they have lacked"' (Bowlby, in Richardson, 1993, p. 18). Similarly, explain Lupton and Barclay:

> Bowlby insisted upon the importance of the attachment between mother and child in promoting caring behaviour from the mother, protecting the infant from harm and ensuring the development of the child ... he took an evolutionary approach seeing infants as possessing innate signals such as crying and smiling responses such as sucking which elicited appropriate genetically programmed responses from the mother ensuring physical closeness. (Lupton and Barclay, 1997, p. 42. See Charlotte Faircloth's essay on 'The Problem of "Attachment"' in Part II for further discussion of this point.)

The logic, then, was that anything that impaired 'bonding' was problematic, but that bonding is 'instinctual'. Additionally, as Hendrick (1997) discusses, the effect of focusing attention on the detrimental effects of the separation of the child from her mother was also to create an argument that the World War II showed the need for 'the family' to be placed at the heart of welfare, and far more should be done to guard against the breakdown and disruption of the family as a unit.

Richardson (1993) also emphasizes the influence of the arguments of Bowlby's contemporary, the psychoanalyst Donald Winnicott, who coined the term 'the good-enough mother' to encapsulate the message that, 'A woman becomes an ordinary devoted mother just by being herself' (Richardson, 1993, p. 45). Notably, in his 1964 work *The Child, the*

Family and the Outside World, Winnicott also warned explicitly against the disruptive and destructive effects of professional intervention in families. According to Richardson, the idea that mothers need to be educated about 'what is best for their children' is, in this way, contested by the much more ambiguous message that, 'Mothers did know best, although it seemed they still needed experts to tell them "what it all meant"'. The best known of all post-war parenting experts, Dr Benjamin Spock, also set out a version of this approach (Knaak, 2005). Famously, he opened his bestselling parenting manual *Baby and Child Care* with the line 'Trust yourself, you know more than you think you do', suggesting that mothers will know 'what is best' through instinct (so long as experts draw this fact to their attention).

The literature exploring the claims of experts in this period detects at least two contradictions in what is said about 'instinct'. Hays draws attention to the coexistence in the 1950s and 1960s in the US of claims regarding both the absolute necessity of mother-love and nurture, and a perceived problem of maternal overprotection (a contradiction between maternal instinct and overprotectiveness that Stearns (2003) suggests first emerges in expert discourse in the 1920s). Hays suggests that John Bowlby's theory of maternal deprivation and the critical significance of bonding between mother and baby was the exemplar of the former way of thinking, but it was accompanied by expert-communicated fears about mothers who 'love too much': '[T]hese theorists of maternal attachment and maternal hostility seemed to say that while maternal affection was absolutely necessary ... It could easily slide into dangerously unwholesome forms' (Hays, 1996, p. 48). Mental illness and social disruption could allegedly result from *either* under- or over-nurture, posing the need for the expert or parent-educator, as the mediator between the 'instinct' of the parent and the 'needs of the child', in the process of childrearing.

Secondly, the precept that 'mother knows best' was called into question through the working through of 'child centredness'. Hays points to this development as follows:

> Throughout the nineteenth and early twentieth centuries the explicit goals of child rearing were centred on the good of the family and the good of the nation; the emphasis was on imprinting adult sensibilities on children from the moment of birth; and it was the making of a proper adult that was understood as the basis for the training of the child. By contrast, the most striking feature of permissive-era advice is the idea that the natural development of the child and the fulfilment of children's desires are ends in themselves and should be

the fundamental basis of child-rearing practices ... *The child (whose needs are interpreted by experts) is now to train the parent.* (Hays, 1996, p. 45, our emphasis)

Thus, while it was held to be the case that the mother may 'instinctually' meet the child's needs in some respects, it was also held that she may lack the insight and knowledge to comprehend fully what the child's needs are. Expert interpretations of the 'needs' of the child, in particular with the realm of emotion, led to a reconstruction of the role of the expert. In the late nineteenth century, an expert desire to mould the child into a model citizen led to the displacement of folk knowledge by scientific insight. In the second half of the twentieth century, the expert view held that the future society should be moulded around the (presumed) physical and, especially, emotional needs of the child, with parents trained to participate in this task.

In the more recent era, the insistence that parental instinct cannot be relied upon and that parents need to be trained to identify and fulfil the basic criteria of rearing children, has become especially marked. It is to this explicit focus on 'the parent' that we now turn.

Parenting experts in the twenty-first century

Who are the experts?

Hardyment suggests one feature of the present is the expansion and diversification of parenting advice. Today, a variety of experts and 'brands' of parent training compete for attention: 'No one great thinker's name dominates', she observes (2007, p. 286). She also notes that an interesting development is the emergence of the parent-parenting expert; that is, parents (often celebrities) who present their 'journey' to becoming a parenting expert as one that began with their own experience, and led them to 'share' what they had come to understand to help others. For example, British 'parenting expert' Sue Atkins describes herself this way:

Hi, my name is Sue Atkins and I am the founder of Positive Parents. I'm not a Super Nanny or a Mary Poppins. I'm just like you ... I'm a parent. No matter what's happening with your child I know that you, like me, have had at some time or other a challenge with raising your children. That's why I wrote my best-selling book 'Parenting Made Easy – How To Raise Happy Children'. So whether your child has a small problem or a big problem, I can help you because I, like you, know that even the smallest of problems for a child is the biggest problem for you their parent. So stop worrying and click on the links below for *the* answers because your kids deserve to have a happy, relaxed and positive home. (Atkins, n.d; emphasis in original)

Through her study of pregnant women, focussing on their experiences of addressing their anxieties about how to disclose the fact of, and manage the reality of, pregnancy in the workplace, Gatrell (2011) also draws attention to this feature of parenting advice and expertise today. Her study examined responses and advice given to women online in Internet chatrooms and via websites, and detected the fluid and expansive nature of what now constitutes 'expertise'. 'Expert opinion', in her study, thus included examples like the website 'Verybestbaby.com' and the 'What to Expect' website. It also comprised other opinion emanating from mothers who have re-styled themselves as advisers and experts. Overall, this innovative look at how pregnant women go about and experience finding advice about a perceived problem begs the question what is the foundation or basis for the expertise purportedly on offer?

The emergence, in this way, of self-styled 'parenting experts', individuals who self-consciously use this term to describe and promote themselves on this basis but for whom the grounding of their claims to be 'expert' is unclear, is a notable development of the past decade. 'Parenting expertise', in this form, has nonetheless become a marketable commodity, sold by a particular type of person, both to parents individually and also to the media (many 'parenting experts' advertise themselves as available for media appearances and comment). Indeed, the daily appearance of 'parenting experts' debating a range of issues and parenting practices, across the digital and print media, speaks to the development of context different to that of the past.

In identifying what is specific about the present, we can also look to the terms used by these experts themselves. First is the ubiquity of the term *parenting* in their description of the work they do. The starting point for their claim to 'expertise' lies not in their understanding 'the child', but of 'parenting': as noted above, in contrast to the twentieth century, the focus today is clearly upon the actions, behaviours, and feelings of the parent. The advocacy of a particular 'parenting style' by such experts is notable as part of this focus (Sue Atkins, as well as many other 'parenting experts' advocates a style called 'positive parenting'). Unlike the 'child expert' of the past, the project of the 'parenting expert' is not simply to alert parents to what 'expert opinion' considers to be the most up-to-date insights from science about what a child needs in specific areas. Rather, it is to promote the need for a general orientation of a certain kind on the part of parents towards their children – for example, a 'positive' one. In doing so, the focus on 'parenting' more or less explicitly calls into question the actions and approach of the parent as they presently stand, and advocates their replacement with an allegedly coherent and consistent 'style' (Reece, 2013).

The other part of the new terminology is the widespread use of the word *expert* (or alternatively 'trainer', 'coach', or 'educator') as the prefix to the verb 'parenting'. This suggests that 'parenting' can be understood as the acquisition of a set of skills or theories about which the purported expert is 'expert', through which a work of 'parenting' can come to be performed more effectively. It is in this area that the break with the past becomes most apparent. While it is not always made explicit, the conceptualization of the development of *the relationship* between parent and child as a process that happens *through acquiring and implementing a skill set* suggests a decisive break away from instinct or intuition as a desirable basis for the development of this relationship.

Two researchers who examined the advice given to parents on Internet sites about how to talk to children about terrorism, following the terrorist attacks of 9/11, 2001, identified this shift in the following way:

> A causal link is established between the advice and psychological outcomes for the child, with parents discouraged from relying on their own intuition and experience. (Dolev and Zeedyk, 2006, p. 468)

'Advice' (alternatively termed 'training' or 'education') from an expert is represented as the best, and indeed only reliable, route to maximize 'outcomes'. A distinct difference with past, then, is that the previous ambivalence about the extent to which parents should be encouraged to look to expert advice, rather than instinct or intuition has shifted decisively, in the direction of the presumption that all parents should always look to the experts for guidance about how to raise their children.

An important development discussed further in Chapter 3 is the formalization of what it means to be a 'parenting expert' through official parent-training programmes. In Britain, for example, the government has over the past decade established what it calls a 'parenting workforce', made up of 'parenting experts and practitioners'. In one document about this new sector of so-called professionals, the British Department of Education (DfE) states that:

> Parenting Experts and Practitioners are responsible for the delivery of evidence-based parenting programmes to parents of children

considered to be at risk of poor outcomes ... Parenting Experts and Practitioners specifically target the parents of children and young people whom local agencies ... agree are at risk of poor outcomes. (DfE, 2010)

In this account, certain features of contemporary parenting experts are crystallized. First, it is claimed that there is a reliable base of 'evidence' underpinning their work; second, that the utilization of that evidence by the 'experts' who understand it can improve 'outcomes' for children; and third, that government agencies can, and should, 'target' certain parents and their children whom they assess to be 'at risk'. The increasingly intense official focus on targeting certain groups of parents (usually those with low incomes) is common to many countries (see, for example, Romagnoli and Wall, 2012). Its effect for the redefinition of social problems and for the experience of those parents subject to such interventions is discussed later in this book. This articulation of the work of the 'parenting expert' is clearly bound up with perceptions of *particular* parents held by policymakers (those whose children are deemed to be 'at risk' of 'poor outcomes'). The ideas underpinning it, however – that 'parenting' is decisive in 'outcomes' for children and that there is a body of knowledge about parenting understood by particular 'experts' – are framed as being generally relevant for *all* parents.

From the scholarly literature which has examined 'parenting expertise', 'psychologist' emerges as a common status-invoking term used to underpin the claim to be a 'parenting expert' or 'expert on parenting matters'. The rise of interest from this quarter in 'parenting' is discussed by Lupton and Barclay, following Erica Burman's critique of developmental psychology:

> At the end of the twentieth century, the focus of developmental psychology *has shifted from the actions and behaviour of the child to the mother and more lately the father* ... The child has remained the primary subject of developmental psychology, in terms of interest directed at its physical, intellectual and moral development, needs and welfare, but *the gaze of researchers has moved from investigating the child to investigating the parent.* (Lupton and Barclay, 1997, p. 42, our emphasis)

The purpose of research, this suggests, has become less about illuminating aspects of child development than emphasizing the influence and contribution of *parenting activities* in 'healthy child development'. This has the inexorable effect of generating evidence about 'what parents should do'. In a similar vein, Kanieski identifies a shift in the emphasis of psychologists who research attachment, from 'the identification and treatment of attachment disorders in children' in the 1930s and 1940s, to 'greater emphasis on the parents, particularly mothers, monitoring themselves in the promotion of secure attachment in their children' (2010, p. 335).

Literature that interrogates contemporary claims about 'experts' interested in 'parenting' does not, however, focus only on the field of psychology. An increasing propensity to focus on the 'ought' of what the parents should do, rather than the 'is', of the child is detected in studies of a range of childcare issues. Arnup's widely cited work takes as its staring point the questions she asked herself when she first became a mother. As she emerged from 'the fog of new motherhood', she explains, she was, 'shocked by the degree to which expert advice had taken hold of my life. I scarcely took a move without consulting a manual'. Gradually, however, 'I began to ask questions. Where has all this advice come from? How did these experts know they were right?' (Arnup, 1994, p. xii). One insight to emerge from Arnup's search for answers to these questions is that parenting has become more and more professionalized, with commentary on what parents ought to do disseminated by 'officials in various levels of government and members of the medical, nursing, and psychological professions' (1994, p. 6).

Joan Wolf, author of the book *Is Breast Best?* (2011), subtitled this work 'taking on the breastfeeding experts'. Wolf discusses what is said to mothers about how they should feed their babies by paediatricians, policymakers, global organizations (for example, the WHO) and single-issue advocacy organizations (for example, La Leche League International (LLLI)). In the collection of essays titled *Mother Knows Best: Talking back to the 'experts'* (Nathanson and Tuley, 2008), contributors discuss claims made by those working in a wide array of medical specialties: psychologists specializing in the study of 'attachment'; campaigning organizations (for example, those advocating alcohol abstinence in pregnancy, or exclusive breastfeeding); and advocates of attachment parenting. Armstrong's (2003) study about claims made regarding the danger of drinking alcohol when pregnant highlights the activities of 'medical entrepreneurs' (that is, doctors who work to establish themselves as the authoritative voices on this topic) and single-issue campaign groups, primarily the National Organization on Fetal Alcohol Syndrome (NOFAS): a campaign that began in the US but subsequently developed in the UK, and has had a significant policy impact, as discussed in Part II, in my essay 'Policing Pregnancy: The Pregnant Woman Who Drinks'.

Emerging from these various studies is the observation that a dominant belief is held across this numerically large, varied, and socially influential sector of people who commonly advise on 'parenting'. This is the conviction that parents will not only 'parent' better, but also in fact can *only* be expected to parent effectively, if they bring up their children in concert with experts. Indeed, the belief that 'coping' with 'parenting' is too much to ask of parents is at the very centre of the ethos of the parenting expert. As Furedi puts it, comparing the present moment with previous eras:

> Although experts [in the past] believed that there were limits to what parents could do, they assumed that with sound advice most problems could be solved. Today's experts take a radically different approach. They assume not only that parents haven't a clue but also that they are unlikely to be able to cope on their own. Informing parents that they can't cope alone and that therefore they should seek support is a central theme of contemporary child-rearing literature. (Furedi, 2008a, p. 177)

We turn now to discuss the construction of 'support' as an essential prerequisite for 'parenting'. We indicate that the claim that parents need support co-exists with claims about need for 'greater awareness' (predicated upon the assumption that 'parents haven't a clue'), and that these two set of claims together comprise the main planks justifying the need for expert, rather than informal, tacit knowledge about childrearing today.

Warnings and instructions/the case for 'support'

Warning over middle class parents' alcohol habits; too many middle-class parents are drinking excessively as a way of coping with the demands of family life, a report suggests. (Richardson, 2012a: *BBC News Online*, 8 October)

Warning: tiny amount of alcohol during pregnancy can harm child's IQ. (Smyth, 2012: *The Times*, 15 November)

Smacking or shouting at your children 'raises their risk of cancer, heart disease and asthma later in life'. (*Daily Mail*, 2012: 12 November)

Playground children having more accidents because parents too busy playing on their smartphones; experts blame the sharp rise on parents being distracted by text messages and emails. (Borland, 2012: *Daily Mail Online*, 23 November)

Limit children's screen time, expert urges. (Richardson, 2012b: *BBC News Online*, 9 October)

Parents must fight the 'sound bite' urge; stressed parents should take time to chat' to their children. (Spurr, 2012: *Sunday Telegraph*, 4 November)

Parents today are rarely informed that they worry too much, that the situation for their children is better than they might think it is, and they are doing a perfectly fine job of rearing their children (Furedi, 2002/2008a; Guldberg, 2009; Kukla, 2008). The stories above all made the mainstream news media in England over a two-week period in 2012, warning parents about their drinking habits (both in pregnancy and afterwards); their discipline practices; their use of technology (in the playground and in the form of TV and computer screens at home); and their general lifestyle (too busy to talk to their children).

There are two notable features of these claims about parenting. The first is that the typification of the 'problem parent' is not restricted to welfare claimants. As we noted above, policymakers focus particularly on the 'parenting' practiced by low-income families. However, as the above extracts suggest, professional or middle-class parents are also subject to criticism from experts. The second point to note is the connection made by those who warn parents between 'modern society' and 'parenting'. Phenomena of modern society (for example, computer technology, or the greater availability of consumer goods) are presented as risks to child well-being, but the risk is to be managed by the parent (and their present failure to manage the risks is, we are told, endangering children). Hence, 'mobile phones' or 'screens' are threatening because of the way parents use them. An important feature of expert claims today is that they draw attention, in this way, to purported threats to children emanating from parental deficiencies in the management of risk.

In most circumstances, however, warnings of this kind do not simply issue a direct instruction to parents to change their behaviour. Rather, parents are admonished in a way that presents itself as non-prescriptive and above all 'supportive'. 'Modern-day experts insist that they are not in the business of judging parents and prescribing formulas', notes Furedi. 'Their advice is often conveyed in a nondirective, nonprescriptive form ... Parenting programmes are deliberately packaged to come across as non-authoritarian'. Indeed, Furedi observes that expert messages about the problems parents allegedly need to take on board are best understood as a project of 'creating demand for support' (2008a, p. 176). Hence, what is presented to parents as 'information' or 'evidence' about how to manage that are deemed (by experts) to face children is better understood as a claim or argument that parents need parenting professionals.

The other important aspect of claims about parents' 'need for support' is the emphasis placed on parental feelings. The rationale for support is not only that this will lead to 'better outcomes' for a child, but also that it has a therapeutic value for the parent themselves. As Lupton and Barclay observe, the arguments made by professionals about modern fatherhood:

> [T]ypically portray fatherhood as an overwhelmingly problem-atic experience, thus requiring the close attention and help of professionals ... Such terms as 'stress', 'strain', 'role transition' and 'psychological disruption' are frequently used in the literature. (Lupton and Barclay, 1997, p. 48)

They note that as part of this emphasis on fathers' vulnerability, 'pre-parenthood' as well as parenthood itself comes to be represented as a time when men require 'support':

> Men are positioned as requiring much in the way of expert help in terms of preparing themselves for fatherhood, getting through pregnancy and birth unscathed ... the primary intention of such literature is to ensure that men conform to the expectations of 'appropriate' fatherhood as they are designated by experts. The focus on the need to counsel men ... is typical of the contemporary impor-tance placed in self-expression and therapeutic practice. (Lupton and Barclay, 1997, p. 50)

Warnings and instructions on one hand, and the case for support on the other, can appear contradictory, with the former appearing mani-festly authoritarian and the latter self-consciously non-authoritarian. However, both share a common starting point. This is the belief in the profound significance for the child of parental action, and a presump-tion that the parent is inadequate in the face of this responsibility. Whether this is expressed through an attempt to appeal to parents on the basis of fear (parents' own perception that if they get parenting 'wrong' it will have devastating consequences), or an appeal to feelings of inadequacy, unpreparedness, and the need to 'talk through' how best to be a parent, the underlying claim is the same. It is that there is a direct link between parenting style and 'outcomes' for the child, and that for this reason, the parent cannot be left to their own devices to 'parent'.

The crystallization of a belief that what parents do leads directly to measurable 'health' or 'wellbeing' 'outcomes' in the child – the parental determinism that we describe in the introductory chapter – is at the centre of the world view of contemporary parenting experts. Indeed, this idea of the 'parent as God' emerges from Furedi's analysis as the flipside of the dominant construction of the 'vulnerable child'. The most distinct feature of 'parenthood' as it is now constructed, then, is of a role defined by both its profound significance for the future of individual children and also society as a whole. However, the parent-God is a deity of a particular kind; he or she is a God who, as well as being all-powerful, is inadequate in the face of the task for which he or she is responsible. He or she has power, but should only use it under the tutelage of the expert. It is to this feature of parenting culture, termed by Furedi 'shared authority', that we now turn.

Parental determinism and the problem of shared authority

As the discussion earlier in this chapter indicated, commentaries about children, their development, and what they need, can be viewed as metaphorical statements about how the relationship between the present and the future is perceived and understood. In previous eras, the particular ways in which the nature of 'a good childhood' and 'good childrearing' was imagined reflected perceptions of the present and future in more general terms. The present preoccupation with 'parent training' can be similarly understood as reflective of a wider sensibility about tomorrow and its relation to today. Furedi describes this sensibility this way:

> The future is seen as a terrain which bears little relationship to the geography of the present. Since the process of change appears unresponsive to human management, its future direction becomes more and more incomprehensible. (Furedi, 1997, p. 61)

The context for the rise of expert oversight of 'parenting', from this perspective, is a narrowed field of vision. How change can be brought about is presently viewed as 'incomprehensible', with 'human management' considered unlikely to be an effective way to bring about change. As a result, the minutiae of parent–child relations become a far greater preoccupation. Limiting risk becomes the dominant substitute for efforts to bring about purposeful change, and exerting control over the area of life where it seems most possible to do so arguably attains far greater attraction than in the past. In an era where wider society offers little possibility for action and intervention, a relatively easier project seems to be that of 'intervening early' in the development of the child through influencing the parent to behave in a particular way. The individuation of the process of change in this way – what has been termed 'the politics of behaviour' (Furedi, 2005) – is not restricted to parent–child relations, but finds a potent expression in this area of life.

According to Furedi, a central problem for parents generated by this development is that it contributes to making bringing up children an 'intensely unsettling and trying task'. His diagnosis is that this experience results from the fact that authority in childrearing has become more and more contested, and yet has become increasingly understood as 'shared'. He makes this point as follows:

> Effective child rearing relies on authoritative parenting ... That is why the prerequisite of effective parenting is self-confidence and belief in their role. Without this confidence, the exercise of parental authority is fraught with problems ... The literature on childrearing is surprisingly silent on the potential problems caused by the sharing of parental authority ... It is not possible to share some of this authority hitherto accorded to the parent without weakening this authority overall ... Those who are uncertain about their authority are likely to find child rearing an intensely unsettling and trying task. (Furedi, 2008a, p. 182)

Following this line of analysis, the way parents now experience their role is directly connected to this sharing of authority. In response, suggests Furedi, it becomes necessary to ask more searching questions about what is meant by the term 'expert' and on what basis the claim to authority can legitimately be made. As he puts it:

> [I]t is worth asking from what the experts involved in these projects derive their expertise ... Parenting expertise is one of those mysterious arts seldom asked to account for itself. (Furedi, 2008a, p. 175)

Most clearly of all, the notion that *the relationship*, as it develops over years, between parents and their children can be grasped and helpfully influenced through the learning of 'skills' from an 'expert' is, he suggests, an unwarranted and illegitimate expansion of the meaning of expertise. This point is explored through the following defence of experiential, as opposed to formal, expert-generated learning:

> The issue is not whether parenting needs to be learned but whether it can be taught. Everyday experience suggests that not everything that has to be learned can be taught ... in the end, people learn through their interactions with the other party in the relationship ... Parents learn what is right for their children through interacting with them ... They certainly don't gain such understanding through books and parenting classes. Until they have a child, even basic parenting questions remained unfocused and unspecific. (Furedi, 2008a, p. 193)

Underlying the claim to be a 'parenting expert', this suggests, is a central myth, which construes the development of a relationship with a child and the process of coming to understand their needs, to be a form of activity about which there can be a genuine 'expert knowledge'. In contrast, the alternative view is that while there most certainly are specific problems (for example, well-identified diseases of childhood about which experts have knowledge and parents do not), more general claims to 'expertise' become questionable.

In this light, the case emerges for insisting on a clear boundary to define where expertise or professionals do, and do not, have a useful role to play. In other words, it is to define and specify in what circumstances the exercise of professional authority is legitimate and when it is not. Furedi explains the distinction between genuine expertise and the authority it rightly commands, compared to that of the 'parenting expert' this way:

> In these encounters [with genuine experts], most sensible adults do not presume a relationship of equality. They seek out experts precisely because they trust their knowledge and authority ... Matters are different when it comes to the relationship between a parent and a parenting professional. This relationship involves a direct conflict of authority about who knows what's in the best interests of a particular child. (Furedi, 2008a, p. 181)

We now turn to consider the arena of policymaking, in which the courting of the parenting expert and the encouragement of shared authority is very apparent. The next chapter thus considers how the growing influence of what might be termed the pseudo-expertise has been encouraged and facilitated by policymakers and the emergence of a new definition of family policy. This new politics of the family, we suggest, has given considerable weight to the development of contested and unclear authority.

Chapter summary

- The 'expert' is a key figure throughout the history of the modern family, indicating that the ability of the parent to raise the child in an effective way has been continually called into question. The messages of experts regarding what is wrong, and what needs to change in the way children are raised, reflect the wider social and cultural context of the time.
- The contemporary field of 'parenting expertise' and the 'parenting professional' is distinguishable from that of the past in the following ways:
  - ○ This field is more diffuse, varied, and extensive;
  - ○ Less emphasis than in the past is placed by experts on the importance and value of 'instinct', and effective parenting is instead said to rely on acquired or learned skills;
  - ○ The focus of the contemporary expert is clearly on the parent and their behaviour;
  - ○ Messages from experts to parents contain both warnings to parents about the riskiness of the parenting practices, and insistence that they should seek support and expert guidance to manage risk;
  - ○ The context for contemporary parenting expertise is not a particular identifiable social upheaval giving rise to concerns about the future, but rather an absence of ideas about how to make the future, leading to a greater focus on individual behaviour.
- The rise and influence of efforts to change how parents relate to their children has made authority in childrearing unclear and contested.
- Distinctions can, and should, be made between genuine expertise, where it is true to say the expert 'knows best', and much of what is said by contemporary 'parenting experts', whose opinions are merely opinions.

Further reading

Ehrenreich, B. and English, D. (1979) *For Her Own Good: 150 years of the experts' advice to women* (London: Pluto Press).
   Chapters 6 and 7 of this book, 'The Century of the Child' and 'Motherhood as Pathology', are most directly relevant for the study of parenting culture. They

form part of a larger study of the relation between experts' advice and women, which stands as the seminal feminist history of the relation between scientific expertise and gender.

Hardyment, C. (2007) *Dream Babies: Childcare advice from John Locke to Gina Ford* (London: Francis Lincoln).
This is the most recognized 'must read' for those who want to find out about the history of advice to parents. While written for a wider market, it contains both excellent historical material going back to the eighteenth century, and social analysis.

Hulbert, A. (2004) *Raising America: Experts, parents, and a century of advice about children* (New York: Vintage).
This work focuses on twentieth-century America, and provides a very detailed account of experts, their arguments, the context, and the response from parents at different points in time. It provides an excellent account of the 'famous names' and what they had to say, but its great strength lies in its contextualization of expert opinion in wider scientific, social, and cultural developments.

Kessen, W. (1979) 'The American Child and Other Cultural Inventions', *American Psychologist* 34(10), 815–820.
This short journal article is by William Kessen, Professor of Psychology and Paediatrics at Yale University. Kessen was a genuine expert, whose pioneering contribution to understanding early child development is widely recognized, as was his work exploring the nature of developmental psychology as a field of research and its relation to the wider culture.

Wolf, J. (2011) *Is Breast Best? Taking on the breastfeeding experts and the new high stakes of motherhood* (New York: New York University Press).
This recent work explores a specific area of parental experience – feeding babies – and provides two sorts of analysis. One is an account of the scientific literature and what it does actually tell us about the relation between health and breast or bottle feeding. In this respect it shows us the value of science, properly defined. The other is a sociocultural account of why expert claims about how a baby should be fed, centring on 'breast is best', depart so widely from what science actually tells us. This account rests primarily on an analysis of how we have come to think about risk, and is invaluable for those wanting to understand this concept better.

3
The Politics of Parenting

Jan Macvarish

The family has been the object of political attention for many decades. However, the form that this attention has taken – in particular, the relation presumed to exist between the family and the state – has undergone important changes over time. This chapter examines the relation between the family and state that has developed in the present era, in the context of the wider historical and political trends discussed so far.

From the mid-nineteenth century onwards, and particularly since the emergence of the welfare state in post-war Western societies, the modern state has increasingly taken responsibility for the well-being of children (Richter and Andresen, 2012). As Smeyers points out:

> The State has always intervened in this realm, whether through general legislation concerning human and children's rights or in more specific ways through tax regimes and all sorts of regulations concerning schools. (Smeyers, 2010, p. 265)

Others have described how, over a similar period, the child has also been politically significant in a symbolic sense. For example, Kessen argues that from the late nineteenth century in the US, '[t]he child became the carrier of political progressivism and the optimism of reformers. From agitation for child labor reform in the 1890s to Head Start, American children have been saviours of the nation' (1979, p. 818).

According to Davis, for the past 200 years, 'the earliest years of children's lives' have been associated with 'peculiar prestige and aura' (2010, p. 285), meaning that:

> Infancy is then vouchsafed within this symbolism as a state in which all of society's hopes and ideals for the young might somehow be

enthusiastically invested, regardless of the complications that can be anticipated in the later, more ambivalent years of childhood and adolescence. (Davis, 2010, p. 286)

Supporting this account of a growing political interest in children in the late nineteenth and into the twentieth century, Hays suggests that the US state sought to resolve the tensions of race and class manifest in issues relating to immigration and labour force unrest, through an increased involvement in the project to improve American citizens in their infancy (Hays, 1996, p. 67). Moving forward to the late twentieth and early twenty-first centuries, Parton suggests that greater moral and existential uncertainty has led to children becoming a 'prime site for trying to control the future' because they are 'unfinished' (Parton, 2006, p. 173). British sociologist Nikolas Rose concurs, describing how, because childhood is linked to the 'destiny of the nation and the responsibilities of the state', it has become 'the most intensively governed sector of personal existence' (Rose, 1999, p. 121). Rose goes on to point out that because, by and large, the young are cared for within families, political attempts to 'conserve and shape children' require the 'petty details of the domestic, conjugal and sexual lives of their parents' to be brought in to public view, scrutinized, and evaluated (Rose, 1999, p. 123).

The degree to which parents *themselves* have been the object of child-centred politics, however, has varied over time and place, but Daly (2013) explores the present trend across most of Europe towards the provision of 'parenting support' as a discrete area of policy 'offering services to parents around the way that they parent' (Daly, 2013, p. 163). The task of this chapter is to identify the particular features of this most recent intensification of the 'politicization of parenting'. We have chosen to concentrate on policy and political developments in the UK since the late 1990s, as this reveals a particularly rapid shift in political attention towards early childhood, with an attendant focus on what parents do and what parents ought to do, forming an increasingly coherent and relatively uncontested, ideological framework; as Daly argues, since 1997, 'England could be said to be in some ways an archetype in that it has put in place the most elaborate architecture anywhere for parenting support' (Daly, 2013, p. 164).

This particularly intensive period of policy development has drawn much of its inspiration and authority from prior developments in the US over a longer historical period. As Furedi (2001) and Welshman (2008, 2010) have noted, prior to the 1990s, ideas emphasizing 'cycles of poverty', 'dysfunctional' communities or family cultures, or failed individual behaviour gained little political traction in the context of political contestation over structural conceptualizations of economic problems and social inequality. Welshman describes how in 1972, when British civil servants were invited by the President of the Ford Foundation to observe the Head Start early intervention programme (which targeted the education, health, and parenting of children in low-income families), they returned to Britain unconvinced that 'cycle of poverty' explanations deserved a prominent place in social policy because of their emphasis on 'individual traits and behavioural deficiencies' (Welshman, 2010, p. 92).

While the efficacy of policy solutions to reduce poverty in the form of 'early intervention' to 'break the cycle of disadvantage' has been argued over in the US since the mid-1960s, they have only really taken off in a British context since the late 1990s. As Clarke points out, initiatives by the New Labour government from 1997 onwards 'drew on a number of programmes in the US which had been established in the 1960s' as part of President Johnson's 'war on poverty' (Clarke, 2006, p. 706). Clarke draws particular attention to the influence of the US Head Start programme and the HighScope Perry study: the latter claimed to show that preschool interventions prevented crime, violence, and educational underachievement over a 40-year period, thereby saving public money in the long term.

Head Start was directly imitated in Sure Start, Labour Prime Minister Tony Blair's flagship preschool early intervention initiative, indicating that 'cycle' ideas had became entrenched across the political spectrum in the UK:

> What seems to have had the greatest impact on policy at the birth of Sure Start was the research into childhood disadvantage and intergenerational transmissions of economic status, which was quickly adopted in Treasury documents and the annual poverty reports. (Welshman, 2008, p. 82)

The international transmission of policy thinking from the US to the UK is a theme running throughout this chapter. The process that sociologists have described as the 'diffusion of social problems' (Best, 2001) helps to explain the dominance, across Anglo-American culture, of particular ideas about family policy. This concept is also useful in indicating how policy developments in the UK can illuminate processes that begin, or occur concurrently, in the US and elsewhere in Europe, despite the apparently large differences in the relationship between state and society in these countries.

From 'implicit' to 'explicit' family policy

One way of understanding what Parton describes as the increasing 'intensity of the government of childhood' (Parton, 2006, p. 187) is to conceptualize policy as moving from an 'implicit' to an 'explicit' way of operating (Clarke, 2006; Lewis, 2011; Wasoff and Dey, 2000). Seeking to understand US family policy, Bogenschneider (2000) restates and expands upon on Kamerman and Kahn's (2001) distinction between implicit policies, which are 'not specifically or primarily intended to affect families but having indirect consequences on them', and explicit policies, which are 'designed to achieve specific goals regarding families' (Bogenschneider, 2000, p. 1137). Daly traces a distinctive UK trajectory in family policy, in contrast with more statist European nations, arguing that historically, the UK lacked 'institutional or *sui generis* family policy':

> Hence, while financial and service supports were in place for families and Child Benefits were universally paid for all children, policies oriented to the protection and support of family as a social institution (such as existed in France or Germany, for example) never developed in the UK. (Daly, 2010, p. 433)

Daly attributes the prior absence of explicit family policy in the UK to a 'strong liberal heritage' which determined that 'the prevailing ideology was that the family works best when the state and other institutions intervene only in cases of need or crisis' (Daly, 2010, p. 433). This liberal heritage necessitated the negotiation of a delicate balance between efforts to improve the well-being of children and to rescue children in dire conditions of abuse or neglect, and the equally strong imperative, noted in Chapter 2, to preserve or 'sanctify' the middle-class family as a private place where parental autonomy and intimate relationships could be sustained.

However, many authors, including Daly, have observed that in political rhetoric and policy practice since the late 1990s, the balance has been definitively tipped in the direction of increasing state intervention, with the UK having 'discovered something of a new policy domain in early childhood education and care', leading to a 'major restructuring' in policy, with the result that 'the UK has more family in its policy portfolio than ever before' (Daly, 2010, pp. 433–434). This concurs with Lewis' assessment of the most recent developments in UK family policy, suggesting that, since the late 1990s, the UK's implicit policy has undergone a transformation:

> Family policy became more explicit under successive New Labour governments and increasingly included a focus on family relationships and on programmes that addressed parenting, in addition to family arrangements such as childcare. (Lewis, 2011, p. 107)

Lewis goes on to argue that this development was not arrested by the end of the New Labour administration and the election of a new Conservative/Liberal-Democrat coalition government in 2010, noting that, 'Members of the Coalition government also signalled their interest in "early intervention", which includes parenting programmes, both before their election in May 2010 and since' (Lewis, 2011, p. 107).

The particular novelty of policy developments since the first New Labour administration in 1997 has been explored at length by many scholars of social policy. All identify the period from 1997 onwards as marking a significant turning point in policy thinking and implementation, which put children and parents at the centre of the agenda to address inequality, now reconceptualized as social exclusion (Gillies, 2005; Levitas, 1998).

The first ever National Childcare Strategy was issued in May 1998 in the Green Paper 'Meeting the Childcare Challenge' (DfEE, 1998). The innovative character of this development was acknowledged by policymakers themselves in the government consultation document *Supporting Families* (1998). It was, according to the then Home Secretary Jack Straw (who was also Chairman of the Ministerial Group on the Family), 'the first time any government' had 'published a consultation paper on the family', and as such was 'long overdue' (Home Office, 1998, p. 3). In *Paranoid Parenting*, Frank Furedi described this set of proposals as representing 'so far, the most ambitious project designed to politicize parenting' (2001, p. 179). Looking back at the report today, *Supporting Families* can be said to have established a policy agenda in Britain that has remained essentially unchanged since. This is despite three different Prime Ministers: Tony Blair (Labour), Gordon Brown (Labour), and David Cameron (Conservative); and four changes of administration (New Labour under Tony Blair in 1997, re-elected in 2001, with a change of leadership to Gordon Brown in 2005, and finally the Coalition government between the Conservatives and the Liberal Democrats in 2010).

Henricson identifies this 'preoccupation with the governance of parenting, its support and control' as a 'distinctive feature of the New

Labour project which has taken root, manifested in something of a national consensus across the political spectrum' (Henricson, 2008, p. 150). However, the development of a political consensus around the notion that parenting is of legitimate government interest is evident beyond, and prior to, New Labour. Bogenschneider (2000) argues that in the US, there was growing policy interest in the family from the 1970s, culminating in the 1980 White House Conference on Families, which was 'instrumental in putting families on the political agenda' (Bogenschneider, 2000, p. 1136). Despite this, however, there was generally low political interest in children and families, in part because discussions of the family 'proved so politically contentious' that federal policy developments were 'stymied' for almost a decade (Bogenschneider, 2000, p. 1136). It was not until the Clinton administration of the 1990s, with its 'Third Way' approach (later to be adopted by New Labour in the UK) that family policy was able to transcend oppositional party politics, ceasing to be 'Republican, or Democrat, conservative or liberal', allowing concern with the family to be seen as a vote-winner in a less ideological political landscape (Bogenschneider, 2000, p. 1138).

In the European context, such developments have also become increasingly evident. In 2007, the Council of Europe published recommendations concerning 'positive parenting' which addressed 'the core issues related to positive parenting and non-violent upbringing, with particular emphasis on parents' entitlement to support from the state in parenting' (Council of Europe, 2007). 'Positive parenting', as Reece (2013) explains, is a strategy that parents are increasingly advised by official sources to use in disciplining their children, which relies on the use of 'positive reinforcement' in place of punishment. While the cross-border promotion of such orthodoxies as 'positive parenting' suggests a universalizing of concern to support and direct parents in the intimate choices they make with their children, other examples demonstrate considerable national variation in approach. For example, whereas Henricson (2008) points out that the New Labour government sought to avoid an explicit statement of parental responsibilities and attendant rights, Ramaekers and Suissa give the example of Flanders in Belgium, which has introduced a pledge of commitment by parents, explicitly to compensate for the decline of civil marriage (Ramaekers and Suissa, 2011, p. 202).

From 'the family' to 'families': de-moralizing family policy

Sociologists have noted the shift in British politics at the end of the twentieth century, moving 'beyond left and right' towards the formulation of a post-ideological 'Third Way', referred to above in the context of the US (Furedi, 2005; Giddens, 1994, 1999). This shift allowed 'the family' to move away from being an inevitable site for contestation over traditional versus progressive values of family type or sexual behaviour (Goldson and Jamieson, 2002; Jensen, 2010). This was in marked contrast to the polarizing family politics of the 1990s, most notably in the UK, the failed 'Back to Basics' campaign launched by the Conservative Prime Minister John Major. 'Back to Basics' attempted to 'turn back the clock' on sexual politics and family change, notoriously by attacking single mothers and homosexuality, but instead it provoked a campaign of ridicule and hostility by the press, who took it upon themselves to expose the peccadilloes and hypocrisies evident in the personal lives of certain government ministers and other politicians (Duncan, 2007; Fox Harding, 2000).

A new approach to politicizing the family was evident in the choice of words in the title of New Labour's first family policy consultation document, referred to above. The fact that the document was called *Supporting Fam*ilies rather than *Supporting the Family* suggested from the outset a greater acceptance of diverse family forms. The report self-consciously states that, 'There never was a golden age of the family. Family life has continually changed – and changed for good reasons as well as bad'. The report argues that changes such as divorce and single parenthood were to be accepted rather than railed against, because 'Government could not turn the clock back even if it wanted to do so' (Home Office, 1998, p. 2). However, as Gillies notes, the apparently relaxed approach to family form and the 'diversification of families' coexisted with a 'greater anxiety about the quality and management of relationships and family practices' (Gillies, 2011, para 9.1). It was clear in the new proposals that the family was conceived of as being in greater need of assistance than ever before and that this assistance was of a new kind to that offered in the past.

A recurring theme in policy literature since *Supporting Families* has been that there are new and increasing pressures on family life: both parents are now holding down jobs outside the home; parents are often caring simultaneously for children and elderly parents; new technology introduces new risks to childhood and relationships become harder to sustain. The family is cast as fragile and as bearing the brunt of the fast-moving modern age. Vansieleghem describes this outlook as widespread:

> The notion that we are living in a complex and permanently changing society pervades the prevailing discourse in academic

contexts as well as in the popular media and contemporary politics. (Vansieleghem, 2010, p. 341)

She argues that this discourse of disorienting change and the idea that we have broken the possibility of historical continuity in family practices legitimize greater recourse to expertise and the expansion of measures to manage the inner life of families. This de-moralizing of intergenerational relationships determines that:

> Upbringing is thus no longer understood in terms of a general transfer of norms and values from one generation to another; rather, it appears to be a process of skilfully generating solutions to (self-actualization) problems produced by our so-called permanently changing society. (Vansieleghem, 2010, p. 344)

It was against this backdrop of a concern about the vulnerability of families to the pressures of modern life, and the assumption that families, in all their forms, needed to be helped to become 'competent' (Gillies, 2011) in the project of raising citizens for the twenty-first century, that the New Labour government developed its rhetoric of 'supporting families'. The government's reluctance to criticize unmarried, divorced, or single parents, and its desire to embrace a number of diverse family forms, went hand in hand with developing new ways to 'evaluate the internal quality of the relationships between the individuals within the family' (Gillies, 2011, para 9.1).

Policy innovation: parenting the parents to break the cycle

In his 1999 'Beveridge' lecture, named in honour of William Beveridge, the social reformer and economist credited with the creation of the British welfare state, the then Prime Minister Tony Blair spoke of his government's commitment to eradicating child poverty within a generation and to the breaking of what he called the 'the cycle of disadvantage', 'so that the children born into poverty are not condemned to social exclusion and deprivation' (Blair, 1999, p. 16). This indicated that the language of 'cycles', with its connotations of cultural and behavioural rather than structural explanations for poverty, was judged to have found a new resonance in British politics.

A prominent theme in the social policy literature discussing this development is that problems that would once have been conceived of as structural in origin, such as poverty, inequality, poor educational progress, or the ill health associated with social deprivation, have now come to be attributed to parental behaviour (Churchill and Clarke, 2009; Gillies, 2011; Jensen, 2010). The targeting of parental behaviour as the key to unlocking children's potential was central to the reframing of inequality as 'social exclusion'. As Clarke explains:

> The idea of social exclusion as a trans-generational phenomenon has repeatedly found practical expression in interventions that aim to change parenting practices in poor families and to provide poor children with high quality early education, in order to counteract the effects of their poor social and physical environment and produce a better future generation of adults. (Clarke, 2006, p. 701)

The presumption gained strength after 1997, that parents in straitened circumstances will inevitably find it harder to deliver the kind of parenting children need. It has become commonsense to suggest that without additional support, economically poor parents must be capable only of 'poor parenting'. *Supporting Families* set out a vision for the governance of the post-traditional family which included considerable policy innovation and institutional change in this direction (Daly, 2010): for example, a new National Family and Parenting Institute was established to bring together research and expertise in 'parenting' best practice. However, the most-discussed, and arguably most popular, parenting initiative launched by New Labour was Sure Start.

Announced in 1998 as the central element in New Labour's strategy to counter social exclusion, £540 million was allocated to build Sure Start centres in areas of high social deprivation and to train a new 'early years' workforce. But besides delivering resources for playing and learning directly to children and providing low-cost childcare to parents, Sure Start centres and the professionals trained to work in them were also charged with changing parental behaviour. Targets were set for reducing smoking and raising breastfeeding levels amongst new mothers and fathers; 'healthy eating' was promoted in shopping and cookery lessons; and parents were taught how to relate to their children in particular ways by receiving supervised guidance in playing with their babies, being encouraged to talk, sing, and read to them, and by adopting 'positive parenting' approaches to discipline (Churchill and Clarke, 2009, p. 43).

This approach was not without its critics, even from within the world of policymaking. In a later assessment of Sure Start, the eminent psychologist and government adviser Professor Michael Rutter expressed his continued resistance to attempts to deal with poverty at the level of individual behaviour:

> To see this as a way of dealing with child poverty was naive... It's the structural effects that are much more important in relation to poverty and we have a real dilemma in how best to deal with that. (Rutter, 2011, p. 6)

However, despite the presence of such doubts and inconclusive findings of efficacy in the first Sure Start evaluation (Belsky *et al.*, 2007), there was, from 2006, a renewed push on tackling social exclusion through targeting the parenting of young children and strengthening the claim that the arguments for early intervention were 'backed up by evidence and academic research' (Welshman, 2008, p. 83).

Over the same period of time, alongside the reorganization of UK services to families around the presumption of a universal need for support and guidance were more overtly disciplinary features, developed in conjunction with the justice service. Although blaming particular parents for delinquency was not new, Goldson and Jamieson observe a shift from 'finger pointing to explicit finger-wagging' in policies designed to hold parents responsible for their children's behaviour (2002, p. 88). Back in 1996, the Labour Party discussion paper, *Tackling the Causes of Crime*, had linked parenting with antisocial behaviour (Furedi, 2001, p. 179); and once elected, New Labour brought in measures to discipline the parents of disorderly children as part of the Crime and Disorder Act 1998.

These developments were expanded in the Anti-Social Behaviour Act (2003) and Criminal Justice Act (2003). Parenting orders were introduced, which usually consist of two requirements that can last up to 12 months: that the parent(s) attend a parenting programme and that they demonstrably change their child's behaviour, for example, by ensuring that the youngster observes a curfew or attends school (Lucas, 2011, p. 189). If the parent(s) fail to bring about the prescribed change of behaviour in the child, they can be fined up to £1000. Parents can even be rehoused, with their children, in heavily monitored accommodation, until their parenting is judged to have improved. Welshman (2008) and Clarke (2006) demonstrate, on this basis, how the argument that antisocial behaviour, in parallel with social exclusion, is caused by 'poor' parenting, has recast poverty and inequality as a problem of social order and social integration rather than a problem of social justice.

The expanding scope of policy

Although Furedi noted back in 2001 that '[a]t present, the authoritarian impulse in public policy is focused on a small group of "irresponsible parents"' (2001, p. 183), by the mid-2000s, policy attention was directed at a broader range of parents – and children. The increasing emphasis on early intervention has meant that ever-younger children have been drawn into policy purview (Lewis, 2011, p. 109). New Labour's initial Sure Start strategy was to focus services on the under-eights, but this was rapidly modified to focus on younger children because it was felt that this was where the biggest gap in service provision was located and because, it was argued, there was stronger evidence for more successful outcomes if interventions happened at the age of four and under (Clarke, 2006). According to Clarke, the move to concern with younger children:

> Represents an important shift of resources to a section of the population, children under four, whose needs had previously been seen as almost entirely the private responsibility of their parents, and, in practice, primarily their mothers. (Clarke, 2006, p. 716)

The reach of policy is thus both increased, by including a wider age range of children, and transformed, by extending to preschool children who will have to be accessed in the home, at specialist centres alongside their parents, or by separating infants from their parents in formal early education settings. Parents and the intimate world of family relationships are therefore more explicitly located as 'the problem'. In addition to Sure Start, two further initiatives in Britain – *Every Child Matters* (ECM) and the Family Nurse Partnership – express the expanding scope of family policy, and the kind of parents (and parenting methods) deemed problematic and we briefly review these examples of explicit policy next.

Every Child Matters

The 2003 ECM report was produced in response to the Laming Inquiry into the horrifying abuse and eventual death of eight-year-old Victoria Climbié at the hands of her guardians (her great-aunt and great-aunt's partner), and marked an intensified policy emphasis on 'prevention', characterized by a strong emphasis on risk, monitoring, and surveillance (Parton, 2006, p. 176). The overall approach was on 'shifting the focus from dealing with the consequences of difficulties in children's lives to preventing things from going wrong in the first place'

(DfES, 2004, p. 2). As such, it sought to increase collaboration between child protection services, health services, and the police in order to prevent a recurrence of what had happened to Victoria Climbié.

ECM also set out an approach which seemed to have relatively little to do with preventing such extreme and rare cases of child abuse. As Parton notes, while the ECM Green Paper 'was presented as a direct response to the public inquiry into the death of Victoria Climbié', in fact it 'was much more than this', encapsulating a far wider set of ideas about sub-optimal parenting (Parton, 2006, p. 139). Enforced by the Children Act 2004, the ECM recommendations targeted the well-being of *all* children from birth and set out five key outcomes it hoped the services would help children attain: 'being healthy, staying safe, enjoying and achieving, making a positive contribution to society, and achieving economic wellbeing' (ECM, 2003). Parton explains the expansive scope of ECM as follows:

> It aimed to take forward many ideas about intervening at a much earlier stage in order to prevent a range of problems later in life, namely those related to educational attainment, unemployment and crime, particularly for children seen as 'in need' or 'at risk'. In this respect it aimed to build on much of the research and thinking [developed after 1997] and the policies introduced by New Labour in relation to childhood, where child development was seen as key and children were conceptualised primarily as future citizens. (Parton, 2006, p. 139)

Others have noted, along similar lines, that a significant feature of policy since the late 1990s has been the attempt to join up different areas of policymaking. According to Smith, 'a radical and qualitative shift is taking place in the UK with regard to direct state intervention in parenting', which is evident in the increased joining up of services to children and families:

> We should note that the title of Department for Children, Schools and Families, which partly replaces departments of state in whose title the simple word 'education' used to figure, itself indicates the preparedness of the state to intervene in the lives of parents more widely than simply by ensuring educational provision for their children, and indicates too the importance now attached to 'joining up' the various agencies whose job it is to care and intervene. (Smith, 2010, p. 358)

Approaches which look at family policy through the lens of risk culture, as described in the introductory chapter to this book, offer insights into the expansion of policy concern and the drive to create comprehensive strategies of prevention typified by ECM. The preventive and predictive focus of risk culture does not just create an imperative to prevent the most extreme incidences of harm but also leads to a redefinition of what harm means. Parton exemplifies this by tracing the changing terminology and expanding scope of child protection in the UK, arguing that, 'In the late 1960s the object of intervention was "the battered baby syndrome", in the 1970s "non-accidental injury", in the 1980s "child abuse", and by the late 1990s the child's "safety and welfare"' (Parton, 2006, p. 173).

The categories of 'abuse' and 'neglect' now include behaviour which would once have been regarded as within a normal range of family experiences, such as children becoming overweight or parents getting angry and using moderate physical chastisement. The development of the category 'emotional abuse' means that evidence of abuse or neglect cannot just be 'read off' from bruises, broken limbs, or poor health in the child's body, but must either be interpreted from the child's behaviour or predicted on the basis of the way in which the parent is judged to relate to the child. Parenting professionals in the UK are now instructed to record and measure the relationship between new mothers and their babies for evidence of 'attachment', 'attunement', 'sensitivity', 'positive parenting' or for maternal depression (Department of Health, 2008, p. 6). Wrennall goes as far as to suggest:

> The term 'Child at risk' used to mean, at risk of abuse or neglect, but it has now been redefined to mean, a child at risk of not meeting the government's objectives for children. (Wrennall, 2010, p. 310)

Dodds (2009), Macvarish (2010a, 2010b), and Parton (2006) have pointed to the ways in which the policy remit has expanded and now seeks to identify not just children that are being, or have been harmed, but those who are at risk of future harm or disadvantage. Smeyers (2008, p. 729) and others have commented on the significance, in this respect, of cases where the parents of overweight children have been accused of neglect and in some cases, the children have been taken into state care, based on a projection of the risks to the child in their future health as adults.

The Family Nurse Partnership

The Family Nurse Partnership is an early intervention programme which, like Sure Start, originated in the US (where is it is called the

Nurse Family Partnership programme). The scheme relies on intensive, health-led home visiting during pregnancy and the first two years of life and claims to improve outcomes for both mother and child, particularly in those families categorized as most 'at risk'. This programme, which in the US, concentrates on poor, first-time parents, but in the UK targets teenage parents, engages pre-emptively with parents-to-be identified as vulnerable. However, the programmes are not designed to prevent abuse, rather they aim to train parents, identified as possessing certain 'risk factors' (such as being aged under 20), in recommended ways of parenting. Parents are 'supported' in achieving 'healthy behaviour' during pregnancy, in establishing 'positive' relationships with their partners and families, and in engaging with their baby in ways that are deemed appropriate.

This extremely high degree of state involvement in the intimate relationships of a targeted group has been legitimized by a prior consensus formed around the presumptions that, by virtue of their age alone, teenage parents are inherently 'vulnerable', that their children are inherently 'at risk' of inherited deprivation, and that 'good parenting' is capable both of being taught and of solving social problems.

The amplification of teenage parenthood as a social problem in the UK, despite evidence of fewer teenage pregnancies than in the past, has been explored most thoroughly by Arai (2009) and Duncan *et al.* (2010). As these authors make clear, in 1997 New Labour moved teenage pregnancy to a central position as part of its agenda to tackle 'social exclusion', not only raising its profile as a <u>marker</u> of continued inequality but targeting it as a <u>cause</u> of poverty and deprivation (Arai, 2009; Carabine, 2007; Dodds, 2009; Duncan *et al.*, 2010; SEU, 1999). The 'teenage mother' became the exemplar of 'poor parenting' and, with the popularization of the idea that teenage mothers beget future teenage mothers, of the idea of the 'intergenerational transmission' of poverty through deficient parenting (Macvarish, 2010a, 2010b; Macvarish and Billings, 2010).

Prioritizing teenage pregnancy as a social problem susceptible to political mobilization had proved itself to be a consensus issue in the US, and commentators on the earlier US discussion offer many valuable insights (see, for example, Furstenberg, 1991; Geronimus, 1997; Luker, 1997; Vinovskis, 1988). While President Clinton, in his January 1996 'State of the Nation' speech, spoke of the need to continue lowering the rate of teenage pregnancy in order to 'restore the family', a notable feature of the later UK discourse was that it was less overtly moralistic in traditional terms (Macvarish, 2010a, 2010b; Macvarish and Billings, 2010).

In the UK's social exclusion framing, it was the mother's age, not her unmarried status, that was emphasized, and her sexual behaviour was framed as negatively affecting her and her baby's health and life chances, rather than as threatening the moral standards of the nation. The children of teenage mothers were cast as socially and biologically 'vulnerable': a relationship was drawn between young maternal age and low birth weight babies, higher rates of infant mortality, a higher likelihood of being exposed to 'risky' antenatal behaviour such as unhealthy diets, smoking, and lower rates of breastfeeding. It was claimed that low birth weight (in fact only associated with the very youngest mothers) is associated with low IQ. Young mothers were also claimed to be more prone to post-natal depression, which was said to undermine maternal bonding and which in turn was claimed to affect the baby's neurological and emotional development. Thus, both the body and the brain of the baby were constructed as being 'at risk' from the mother's age (Macvarish, 2010b).

We can see here the power of ideas about parental determinism when they are enacted in policy. The expansion of the category of problematic parental behaviour was anticipated by Furedi in 2002:

> In the past, politicians were only interested in indicting the so-called problem parent. The main concern was with the problem posed by a small group of marginalized poor families. Later, the weakening of the institution of marriage and the apparent decline of the family led some politicians to represent single mothers as the symbol of moral decay. During the 1990s, the deadbeat dad became the subject of moral concern. Gradually, with the intensification of moral uncertainties, other parents were brought into the frame. The yuppie parent who was more concerned about career than family life soon joined the working mother. Today, political scrutiny is no longer fixed on a specific group of mothers and fathers. All potential parents face the attention of policy makers. (Furedi, 2002, p. 192)

Parent training for all

If deficient parenting is perceived to be the problem, then it is not surprising that explicit attempts to 'retrain' parents have become a feature of family policy, in particular, of those measures claiming to address social inequalities (Churchill and Clarke, 2009). As Lucas notes, 'In the UK instruction of parents became a key plank in policy responses to social exclusion through parenting orders (POs), parenting early intervention pilots, parent support advisors, respect parenting practitioners, and the role of parenting experts in local authorities' (Lucas, 2011, p. 182). As Lewis describes, however, services have expanded from problem families to universal provision:

> Initially such programmes were provided for parents whose children's bad behaviour had already come to the attention of the authorities (usually social workers or the courts). However, parenting programmes have become part of a much wider package of 'parenting support' – a term that gives expression to the state's desire to work 'in partnership' with parents – and from the mid-2000s they have taken their place alongside a range of services such as 'stay-and-plays', drop-in centres, health visiting and (in some local authorities) family nurses, and home/school programmes that are funded by central government and offered by local authorities ... Thus, parenting programmes have been made available both for group work with referred and self-referred parents, and for intensive, preventative work on a one-to-one basis with children deemed to be at risk of offending and socially excluded families. By 2010, access to parenting programmes on a voluntary basis had become universal, while parents of children whose behaviour had come to the notice of the authorities could be ordered to attend such programmes. (Lewis, 2011, p. 107)

Gillies (2011), Lucas (2011), and Lewis (2011) all place parenting re-education programmes within the long history of childcare advice, but all concur that the recent period has seen a massive expansion in the scale and reach of such programmes. Gillies talks of 'the emergence of a whole new industry and matching workforce with the aim of promoting "good parenting" across the state and the third sector' (Gillies, 2011, para 6.2). Parenting programmes currently being trialled in the UK include Triple P (Positive Parenting Programme), which originates in the University of Queensland, Australia, but is now a global enterprise operating in 25 countries; the Incredible Years programme, originating from Carolyn Webster-Stratton in the US; and FAST (Families and Schools Together), again originating in the US, but brought to the UK by Professor Lynn MacDonald of Middlesex University.

In 2011, a new pilot scheme was announced by the British Conservative-Liberal Democrat Coalition government, entitling 50,000 parents to £100-worth of parent-training sessions (We discuss this scheme further in the concluding chapter to this book). Called 'CANparent' (Classes and Advice Network), the scheme was partly rationalized as a way of de-stigmatizing help-seeking – vouchers were to be distributed through a commercial pharmacy chain, were likened to antenatal classes (which have a wide take-up), and it was mooted that employers might incorporate parenting classes into employee benefits packages (suggesting that respectable, working families require training like anybody else). While this could be seen as a tactic to avoid stigmatizing 'problem' families and thereby discouraging those often labelled 'hard to reach' from seeking help, there is a genuine belief in policy circles that all families need support at some time and that parenting requires a set of skills which all parents can enhance.

The increasing certainty of policy: what constitutes 'good parenting'?

In the early days of the UK's explicit family policy, it was claimed that good parenting was a protective factor against social disadvantage, but over time, the claims have become more strongly deterministic, arguing that 'poor' parenting actively, if unintentionally, *causes* disadvantage. Thus a 2006 document produced by the Department for Education and Skills (DfES) claimed that:

> We know that parents are the major influence on a child's life. Parenting in the home has a far more significant impact on children's achievement than parents' social class or level of education. (DfES, 2006, p. 4)

In 2010, the report *The Foundation Years: Preventing poor children becoming poor adults*, produced for the new Conservative-Liberal Democrat Coalition government by Labour Member of Parliament Frank Field and the Independent Review on Poverty and Life Chances, further strengthened the parental determinism claim and revealed its cross-party appeal:

> A healthy pregnancy, positive but authoritative parenting, high quality childcare, a positive approach to learning at home and an improvement in parents' qualifications together, can transform children's life chances, and trump class background and parental income. (Field, 2010, p. 16)

Alongside the increasingly forceful argument that good parenting prevents social disadvantage while poor parenting causes it, as articulated above, run ever-more certain claims that what constitutes 'good parenting' can now be scientifically known. By 2006, a report by the DfES states that 'We *know* the key principles of effective parenting' (DfES, 2006, our emphasis). As Gillies points out:

> The notion that there could and should be consensus over what counts as good parenting is increasingly justified through reference to scientific research. Emphasis is placed on assessing the evidence base for particular interventions to ensure successful programmes are reproduced, with little discussion of how 'success' might be defined across diverse cultures and values. (Gillies, 2011, para 6.2)

The most recent way in which claims to certainty are made has been through the appropriation of 'brain science' by early intervention advocates: a phenomenon that we discuss in detail in Part II of this book. Although 'brain claims' began to enter UK social policy from 2006, it has been widely noticed that such arguments for early intervention have become a defining feature of family policy since the election of the Coalition government in 2010. Picking up on the prior development of this trend in the US, Furedi anticipated the priority given to the infant brain by the popularization of parental determinism back in 2002. More recently in the UK, Wastell and White (2012) have begun a critique of what they see as the re-moralization of family life, albeit in the 'softened and medicalized' language of neuroscience (Wastell and White, 2012, p. 408). They describe how 'The mythological version of the infant brain is fast becoming part of the policy and practice of child welfare, easily invoked to profound rhetorical and material effect' (Wastell and White, 2012, p. 409).

A qualitative shift in approach

Ramaekers and Suissa note an 'unprecedented burgeoning of policy initiatives in the area of families and parents' (2012, p. viii). They identify this as representing not just 'a simple increase in the level of public intervention into the realm of the family' but a 'subtle but significant shift in the way in which parents are conceptualised and talked about in policy and popular discourse on "parenting"' (Ramaekers and Suissa, 2011, p. 201). This qualitative change in family policy was also identified by Hays (1996), in her description of a shift, from the 1970s in the US, towards a concern with certain emotions as the basis for social order. According to Hays, this development led childcare experts to teach people how to relate to the child with love and empathy and to pay attention to children's emotional and cognitive development as the solution to social problems. Others have talked of this as the 'therapeutic turn', a dynamic by which the inner world of the individual is increasingly opened up to public scrutiny and governance (Furedi, 2004; Illouz, 2007; Lasch, 1977, 1979; Nolan, 1998; Rose, 1999) and, as Jensen explains, social action increasingly becomes orientated towards 'cultural and intimate conduct' (Jensen, 2010, p. 11).

Gillies describes how the 'contemporary attentiveness to the personal' has produced a 'huge surge in the significance attributed to feelings and introspective analysis as a means of understanding and addressing long standing social issues and problems' (2011, para 2.3). However, according to Furedi, this apparent validation of the private and the desire to make it more central to public life is actually driven by a profound mistrust of what might go on 'behind closed doors'. In his book on this trend, *Therapy Culture*, Furedi argues that 'By the 1970s, the private sphere, particularly family life, had acquired overtly negative connotations' (Furedi, 2004, p. 70). Furedi explains:

> The revision of social attitudes towards the private sphere has gone hand in hand with the emergence of a new consensus that regarded family life as *the* source of individual emotional distress. This shift in attitudes represents probably the single most important alteration to the value system of western societies in the past two decades. (Furedi, 2004, p. 70)

This jaundiced view of private life is articulated by Clem Henricson, a policy analyst within the Family and Parenting Institute, when she writes that, 'Too much of what is the underbelly of humanity goes on behind net curtains even in the twenty-first century' (Henricson, 2008, p. 153). What seems to be apparent in family policy is that parents' abilities to provide love and emotional support to their children have become the object of considerable concern, fuelled by an anxiety that the emotional development of individuals underpins social and even economic formations.

Justifying increased intervention in the intimate domain of emotional life requires the renegotiation of an important tenet of liberal democracies – the privacy and autonomy of the family home and of interpersonal relationships. Jacques Donzelot's classic (1979) study *The Policing of Families* indicates the extent to which the boundary between the principle of parental autonomy and the obligation to protect children from harm at the hands of their parents has generated much philosophical discussion and requires rigorous legal procedures to override it.

Ramaekers and Suissa identify the sensitive nature of the balance between the state and parents' rights and obligations towards children:

> A great deal of literature in philosophy of the family, political philosophy and philosophy of education on parents and children has been concerned with precisely this question of the limits and justification of parents' freedom to bring up their children as they wish, and the relationship between this freedom and, on the one hand, the rights of children and, on the other, the rights and obligations of the (liberal) state *vis-à-vis* children. (Ramaekers and Suissa, 2012, p. 100)

Parton (2012), along similar lines, tells us that social work has always played 'a key role in "governing the family" in advanced Western societies', but that a balance had to be struck between protecting the child from 'significant harm' while at the same time recognizing that 'it is also important that the privacy of the family is not seen as being undermined' (Parton, 2012, p. 87).

However, it is identified that an important shift towards the de-validation of 'the privacy of the family' has taken place in policy. Broadhurst *et al.* point out that the increasingly 'child-centric' focus of family policy has intensified the tension between the 'sanctity of the birth family and the need for intervention to protect children' (2010, p. 1050). According to Smeyers, the balance has tipped in favour of statutory involvement, driven in part by demand provoked by the high profile of family cruelty and neglect *causes célèbres* such as the Fritzl case in Austria 2008, the case of Marc Dutroux in Belgium 1996, and the death of 'Baby P' in the UK in 2007 (Smeyers, 2010, p. 265). Gillies describes how up until the late 1990s, 'conceptions of "the family" were characterized by a strongly bounded notion of privacy' – but the advent of New Labour marked a significant shift in this balance, and a 'remarkably aggressive attempt to re-position family life as a public rather than a private concern':

> Previous legislation and sensibilities which placed everyday personal and family life as largely outside the remit of state intervention have been explicitly challenged through a moral focus on children as the most important constituents of family life. (Gillies, 2011, para 5.1)

The growing view that privacy is problematic and should be dispensed with has become overt in less than two decades. Back in 1996, Labour

MPs Jack Straw and Janet Anderson authored a Labour Party discussion paper on parenting. Straw, then Shadow Home Secretary, wrote in the foreword what has now become a familiar refrain when he described parenting as the 'most important task any of us ever undertake' (Straw and Anderson, 1996). Less familiar today is the need felt by Straw to justify even raising the issue of parenting, describing how when he first did so, in 1994, he 'did so initially with great trepidation'. Setting the scene for one of the arguments in *Supporting Families* (1998), Straw states, 'No one wants to be preached at – particularly by politicians' but says that 'almost everyone I have spoken with wants to break the taboo on public discussion of parenting' (Straw and Anderson, 1996).

In *Supporting Families* (1998), there is similarly an explicit recognition that government intervention into the family is contentious, although the wording suggests the primary concern is with avoiding the *appearance* of moralizing:

> … governments have to be wary about intervening in areas of private life and intimate emotion. We in Government need to approach family policy with a strong dose of humility. We must not preach and we must not give the impression that members of the Government are any better than the rest of the population in meeting the challenge of family life. They are not. (Home Office, 1998, p. 5)

In 2005, however, it was clear matters had changed. The then Prime Minister Tony Blair made a speech 'on improving parenting' in which he acknowledged the shift in sensibility from a cautious approach to family intervention to a far less apologetic case for earlier and harsher measures:

> You know a few years ago probably the talk about sort of parenting orders and parenting classes and support for people as parents, it would have either seemed somewhat bizarre or dangerous, and indeed there are still people who see this, is this an aspect of the nanny state, or are we interfering with the rights of the individual? And I think the point is this, we need to give people that support, and we need to do that particularly in circumstances where if we don't give people that support, and also put pressure on them to face up to their responsibilities as a parent, they end up having an impact on the whole of their local community. So it is not something we can just say well that is just up to you as to whether you do this properly or don't do it properly, because unfortunately the way that you do it makes a difference to the lives of other people. (Blair, 2005)

Here we can see that the change in language employed by politicians reveals a significant shift in ideas about the relationship between the family and the state. In a few short years, politicians went from talking hesitantly about the need to 'break the taboo' on treating everyday matters of family life as legitimate arenas for public policy, to making the case stridently for intervention in the family as an expected part of the policy agenda. Part of this rhetorical shift, of course, may be seen to indicate a concern with impression management rather than an acknowledgement that there may be legitimate arguments for limiting intervention in order to preserve the privacy of the family. However, the speed at which policymakers were able to discard even their rhetorical commitment to 'approach[ing] family policy with a strong dose of humility' reveals that the qualitative shift from implicit to explicit family policy was complete in the UK by the early years of the twenty-first century.

Conclusion: 'collateral damage' – the consequences of broader and deeper intervention

Some have raised concerns about the potential that this wider and deeper intervention has to cause 'collateral damage' to the custom, conduct, and quality of family life. Smeyers suggests that intervention risks endangering 'benign forms of interaction customary in the private sphere of the family' (Smeyers, 2010, pp. 265–266); indeed Furedi warned of precisely this effect in *Paranoid Parenting*:

> By legitimizing the professionalization of parenting, public policy can have the unintended consequence of disempowering parents further. It is evident that one of the main causes of parental paranoia is the way in which intimate family relations have become subject to public scrutiny. Such pressure, whether in the form of helpful advice, periodic health warnings, or the intervention of professionals or of politicians, continually erodes parental confidence. (Furedi, 2001, p. 181)

A further call for a more cautious approach to intervention is founded on the concern that by generalizing the supervisory gaze to incorporate all families, policy risks diverting resources from those children and families who really need help. Discussing early intervention programmes such as Nurse Family Partnership and Head Start in the US, Chaffin comments:

> The possibility needs to be considered that prevention programs may expend effort inefficiently by targeting far too many parents

who will never maltreat their children anyway, while failing to provide sufficient focus and intensity for those who are truly at-risk.
(Chaffin, 2004, p. 583)

Smeyers also asks if attention to extreme cases of child abuse displaces
resources from other social problems. Beyond that, he questions
whether the cases of extreme cruelty and neglect which tend to dominate media discourse and create demands for more intervention are
even susceptible to effective intervention at all: 'It is clear that cases
such as these present us with real problems, but it is important to ask
whether state remedies will ever be able to prevent these sorts of abuses
from taking place' (Smeyers, 2010, p. 265).

Furedi suggests that the generic tensions and problems of family life
are too delicate to be improved by state intervention. 'State policy is too
crude an instrument to deal with the management of the intimate emotional relationship between parent and child', he explains. 'Parental
anxieties and the complex relations between adults and children are not
problems that are susceptible to public policy solutions. Why? Because
the problems of human relationships are too specific and too personal
to be tackled by policies, which are by definition general in character'
(Furedi, 2001, pp. 180–181).

Others have fleshed out the possible consequences of the application
of external, public criteria to the internal, private world of the family.
In the late 1970s, the American social theorist Christopher Lasch (1977)
warned that the market and public institutions were invading the family, with the values of instrumentalism and individualism undermining
familial bonds: a point later developed by Hays (1996). This chapter
suggests that the move away from a concern with family form has
opened up family life to external scrutiny of its inner workings. A new
conformity is thus required, not to traditional morality, but to a new
morality of appropriate practices and attitudes. For Vansieleghem, the
danger lies in the fact that these new norms are free floating, bureauc-
ratized, and technologized rather than moral:

Just as traditional norms have in the past, parental services are
now normalizing individual behaviour; only these parental services
technologies and monitoring systems are not related to an existing
order ... By codifying and prioritizing behaviours in terms of potential risk, these monitoring systems and services bypass actual parental behaviour as a source of immediate information and create new
standards for legitimating or normalizing intervention into parenting

practice. Through parental services, norms and rules are established in the very act of judgement itself. (Vansieleghem, 2010, p. 354)

These commentators are raising the issue that the interpersonal world of the family is transformed by the demand that it submit itself to a new system of evaluation and scrutiny. What Smeyers (2010, p. 266) describes as the idea that standard practice can be identified, justified and enforced means that, as Clarke explains, the child's home is reduced to 'its role in producing a particular outcome in the child's scores on a variety of scales' (Clarke, 2006, pp. 709–710).

In a special issue of the journal *Educational Theory* (2010), edited by Paul Smeyers, a number of contributors raise concerns with these developments. In particular, they discuss the impact of de-moralizing parental decision-making and the subsequent impoverishment of intimate life. The editorial suggests that 'the diversity that could enrich parents' choices in dealing with their children' is replaced by 'narrow outcomes, recommended pathways' (Smeyers, 2010, p. 266), and that by 'removing practical judgement from parenting', the task of raising children is turned 'into a skill'. This in turn risks 'bureaucratizing childrearing', opening it up to 'the laws of the market' which leads to the erosion of the 'practices of the community' (Smeyers, 2010, p. 266).

Similar concerns about the development of a dehumanizing dynamic within social work have been raised by Broadhurst *et al.* (2010), who suggest that there is 'professional discontent with the formalisation of practice through systems of risk management and audit' (2010, p. 1047), whereas '[a]t the heart of the *humane* project of social work are a range of informal, moral rationalities concerning care, trust, kindness and respect' (Broadhurst *et al.*, 2010, p. 1047). They argue that in parallel with the family, 'the terrain of child welfare practice' inherently carries 'moral, social and emotional concerns' (Broadhurst *et al.*, 2010, p. 1047), but that these are driven out by '[i]nstrumental risk assessment tools' which 'seek to render either coherent or extrinsic the moral aspects of child welfare practice' (Broadhurst *et al.*, 2010, p. 1050).

Within the family, Clarke claims that the emphasis on targets and outcomes reconstructs parents as 'simply another environmental influence', meaning that '[g]ood parenting then comes to be regarded as a question of technique instead of being fundamentally about quality of relationships' (Clarke, 2006, p. 708). It is not that these authors are opposed to any kind of intervention to assist parents in raising children or to the necessity of systems of child protection for particularly vulnerable children. Rather, they are concerned that the drive towards broader and deeper interventions threatens to undermine the very thing which policy seeks to preserve: the strength of the family. In the final chapter of Part I, we now turn to discuss how this unintended consequence of the ever-widening scope of intervention has worked to undermine not only relationships between parents and children, but also those in communities more generally. As we indicate, the pressing question this poses for all of us is, 'Who cares for children?'

Chapter summary

- The 'politics of parenting' is the latest form taken by a much longer tendency to identify childhood as a site through which problems of social order can be addressed. Political divisions over family form have given way to political consensus around the need to address the quality of family relationships.
- Recent family policy in the UK can be characterized as moving from being 'implicit' to being 'explicit'. Intimate relationships are more overtly targeted for behaviour change and a growing population is identified as requiring state support or intervention, in particular, parent training.
- 'Cyclical' explanations for the intergenerational transfer of poverty have developed into an even more reductionist 'parental determinism'. The infant brain has most recently become a focal point for early intervention policies, providing a 'now or never' imperative to train parents in evidence-based parenting.
- Concerns have been raised about whether these attempts to strengthen families may in fact serve to undermine the intimate bonds underpinning family life.

Further reading

Arai, L. (2009) *Teenage Pregnancy: The making and unmaking of a problem* (Bristol: The Policy Press).
Arai's analysis of the priority given to tackling teenage pregnancy during the New Labour years is exceptionally comprehensive. It deals not only with the policy claims and the political rhetoric which constructed the 'teenage mum' as a significant and growing social problem, but also contextualizes a truer picture of contemporary young motherhood within an understanding of longer-term fertility patterns, tied to geography and social class. It is an invaluable tool for the teaching and study of both the policy and politics of the family and fertility, and the construction of social problems. It also provides the most authoritative account so far of the UK experience, for scholars with a special interest in teenage pregnancy and motherhood.

Furedi, F. (2004) *Therapy Culture: Cultivating vulnerability in an uncertain age* (London: Routledge).
This influential book explores the opening up of the intimate sphere of life to public scrutiny and the dominance of cultural, political, and social life by a therapeutic culture. Furedi argues that a new idea of personhood founded on a presumption of vulnerability has come to the fore with profoundly troubling consequences for the individual and for society. Importantly, it sets out the historical and conceptual underpinnings of the ideas of infant and parental determinism that are so central to our understanding of contemporary parenting culture.

Parton, N. (2006) *Safeguarding Childhood: Early intervention and surveillance in a late modern society* (Basingstoke: Palgrave Macmillan).
Parton's analysis of recent changes in thinking about child abuse contains numerous insights into the changing relationship between parents, children, professionals, and the state. Focused on the UK, the book takes a long view of child welfare before dealing with the particular ideas and trends shaping the systematization of child welfare measures around the need to identify and pre-emptively rescue the vulnerable child. Although concentrating on child protection and social work, this study is pertinent to any scholarly attempt to understand contemporary conceptualizations of childhood.

Gillies, V. (2011) 'From function to competence: engaging with the new politics of family', *Sociological Research Online*, 16(4), 11, http://www.socresonline.org.uk/16/4/11.html.
This paper is just one of very many produced by Gillies in recent years, all of which provide significant insights into, and important analyses of, the new ways in which family life has been conceptualized by policymakers and academics. In 'From Function to Competence', Gillies is particularly sensitive to the influence of therapeutic thinking in social policy, offering a critique of the increasingly internal, individualized, and instrumental ways in which the moral significance of the family relationships are understood.

Ramaekers, S. and Suissa, J. (2012) *The Claims of Parenting: Reasons, responsibility and society* (London and New York: Springer).
This book offers a philosophical exploration of the nature of the parent–child relationship, but its probing of, and reflection upon, the intricacies of the parental experience will be of value to any scholar interested in contemporary parenting culture. The authors are very much concerned with the present, and in particular with the impact of instrumentalism on the meanings imbued in family life. The work is accessible to non-philosophers, adding an enriching dimension to the historical and sociological study of family life.

4
Who Cares for Children? The Problem of Intergenerational Contact

Jennie Bristow

Our analysis of parenting culture leads us to reject the claim that expert-driven parent training improves life for parents. This does not mean, however, that 'parenting' should be viewed as a task that should simply be left to parents in nucleated families. 'Parents do need support', argues Furedi, and this includes access to childcare and child-friendly communities – but '[m]ost important of all, they need to know that the decisions they make about the future of their children will be supported and not undermined by the rest of society' (Furedi, 2008a, p. 171). We suggest that a more progressive parenting culture than the one we have presently would make two matters central. The first is active support for parental authority and judgement. The second is community 'friendliness' towards children, acknowledging general adult responsibility in everyday life for the care and socialization of children.

This chapter reviews the way that cultural and regulatory developments undermine informal mechanisms of adult solidarity and support. Our book so far has described and discussed the emergence of a culture of 'intensive parenting', which emphasizes the role ascribed to parents in managing the myriad risks that are seen to beset children in the twenty-first century. This culture contains an isolating dynamic, where the individual parent's personal 'parenting strategies' are seen to determine directly the health, safety, and well-being of his or her child. In this way, intensive parenting culture works against the idea that childrearing should be conceptualized as a generational responsibility, whereby all adults can and should play a positive role in shaping the next generation.

Historically, it has been understood that children are introduced into the rules of the adult world by a combination of social institutions and informal practices. The imperative of expert-driven parent training, which casts 'parenting' as a set of distinct skills that parents practice upon their own children, weakens the tacit understanding that informal interaction between children and adults within their communities is beneficial. Furthermore, the contemporary preoccupation with risk encourages parents to view other adults, less as a source of protection for their children, than as a source of potential danger.

This is exemplified by the rise in awareness of 'stranger danger', where parents and children alike have become sensitized to the notion that all adults unknown to them may pose a threat. Writing in *The Times* (London), the journalist Helen Rumbelow (2008) encapsulates the effect of 'stranger danger' sensibility, in her report on a television documentary that featured an 'educational chat' between a mother and her nine-year-old daughter during a visit to the supermarket:

> Where others might have pointed out the nice clouds, this woman pointed out an innocent pedestrian. 'See that man?' she said to her daughter, barely suppressing the terror in her voice. 'He's a stranger isn't he?'
>
> Yes, her daughter dutifully replied, he was a stranger. That meant, her mother continued, her voice rising to screeching pitch, that there was a good chance he was a killer, paedophile or kidnapper. (Rumbelow, 2008)

This chapter explores the problem of 'intergenerational contact' exemplified by the preoccupation with 'stranger danger', and the fear that all 'other adults' pose a potential danger to children. First, we focus on two recently introduced and far-reaching regulatory schemes – Megan's Law in the US and the Vetting and Barring Scheme (VBS) in the UK. Both these schemes intend to prevent children from having unsupervised contact with 'convicted sex offenders': that is, adults within their local communities who have in the past been convicted of committing sexual offences and have now served the terms of their sentence.

Megan's Law and the VBS could be viewed as attempts to both improve children's safety and ameliorate adults' anxiety about children's safety, through weeding out 'dangerous' adults and thus demarcating a group of adults whom parents can trust. However, as Liberman (1999) notes, 'in trying to solve one problem' such regulatory projects 'can create others'. The suggestion in this chapter is that such projects institutionalize a parental fear that other adults are potential paedophiles who may harm their children.

Further examples of the way that mistrust between the generations is becoming formalized are provided by the proliferation of 'no-touch' policies in childcare settings, again on both sides of the Atlantic. After briefly reviewing such policies and their impact, the chapter draws together the isolating features of the expert-led parenting culture discussed in Chapters 1 and 2, with what Furedi has described as 'the breakdown of adult collaboration'. 'Parental cooperation helps to minimize the effects of isolation', he writes. 'But it is also the most effective alternative to the disempowerment brought about by professionalized parenting' (Furedi, 2008a, p. 196). The rapid development and acceptance of official projects that regulate relations between the generations within local communities is, our book suggests, testament to the extent of parents' disempowerment within a risk-averse, isolated, and expert-led parenting culture.

Megan's Law

> Rhode Island's first foray into community notification is a textbook case of everything Megan's Law is not supposed to do: it is not meant to provoke public hysteria; it is not meant to encourage vigilantism; it is not supposed to drive the sex offender underground ... Yet, Rhode Island's bumpy inaugural run illustrates how Megan's Law, in trying to solve one problem, can create others. (Liberman, 1999)

Accounts of the development of Megan's Law generally begin with the story of the legislation's namesake, Megan Kanka, situating this as a legislative response to a personal tragedy. On 29 July 1994, seven-year-old Megan Kanka was raped and strangled by her neighbour, Jesse Timmendequas, who had two prior sexual convictions for sex offences against children. The outcry provoked by this case led to the establishment of 'community notification' laws, whereby the public is informed when a convicted sex offender is living within their community. Daniel Filler's study of the 'legislative rhetoric' used in making the case for Megan's Law provides a succinct account of the way in which the tragic murder of this young girl led to the establishment of new laws across the US:

> The story of this crime, which occurred in a small central New Jersey community, received national attention. Within days of Megan's death, Megan's parents, Richard and Maureen Kanka, began a campaign to pressure the New Jersey legislature to adopt a sex-offender community-notification law in her memory ... The state legislature

responded quickly and on October 31, 1994, New Jersey Governor Christine Todd Whitman signed Megan's Law. The call for new sex-offender registration and community-notification laws spread across the nation, motivated by the constant recitation of Megan's tragic demise. Although many states adopted these provisions of their own accord, in 1994 the U.S. Congress passed legislation effectively requiring every state to establish a system for registering certain offenders. In 1996 Congress raised its demands, requiring every state to provide for community notification as well. Under pressure from both Congress and public opinion, every state has now adopted some version of Megan's Law. (Filler, 2001, pp. 315–16)

On one level, Megan's Law could be viewed as a practical response to a real and established danger. The force of the argument posed by Megan's parents lies in the idea that if only they had known that their neighbour was a convicted paedophile, they could have taken precautionary measures to protect their daughter; thus, the impassioned campaign for a law that would notify other parents about dangerous neighbours was premised on the idea that future tragedies could be prevented. Maureen Kanka's proclamation that '[t]his was God's way of using Megan as a tool to make sure this never happens again' reveals the conviction that precautionary legislation of this kind can prevent future abhorrences (cited in Filler, 2001, p. 315). The emotive character of the crime itself, combined with the moral weight carried by Megan's bereaved parents as advocates for a new law, gave the arguments in favour of Megan's Law a common-sense character, and it received 'overwhelming' support within both Congress and the state legislatures (Filler, 2001, p. 316).

However, Megan's Law has had a number of destabilizing consequences for communities, which challenge the claim that community-notification laws should be considered as merely practical, common-sense responses that will increase public safety. Filler summarizes some of the reasons why Megan's Law has attracted some disquiet:

Megan's Law is controversial legislation because it targets a narrow segment of the criminal-offender population, sex offenders, subjecting them to public shame and, potentially, vigilante violence. Offenders' names and faces are distributed throughout the community. Schools send notices home with the children, police mail grainy pictures to anxious neighbors, and an entire nation peruses sex offender photos on state-operated Web sites. Legislators openly acknowledged that the provisions' benefits came at significant cost to offenders' privacy and security. (Filler, 2001, p. 318)

Questions have been raised about whether such laws will work as intended. Liberman (1999) notes that 'for all of its emotional and political appeal, there is little proof that community notification reduces the chances that a sex offender will commit future crimes', and indeed 'some experts who have studied or worked closely with those men and women argue that Megan's Law makes it more likely that sex offenders will victimize others again'. Another noted area of concern has been the way that notification laws can provoke vigilante attacks. Liberman (1999) reviews the 'explosions' of vigilantism that have taken place within communities as a result of notification laws, including arson and gun attacks on offenders; although the most common consequence has been 'the sting of community disapproval in verbal harassment and threats'.

A further 'unintended consequence' of community-notification laws is that rather than making communities feel safer against the threat of child molesters, such policies appear to increase presentiments of danger. They do so through the mobilization of rhetoric, imagery, and regulation that continually promotes the message that children are at risk. Best's (1993a) analysis of the rhetorical claims made about 'threatened children' over the 1980s reveals how the campaign to draw attention to, and implement policies around, the problems of child abduction and abuse continually inflated the scale of the threat. A later contribution, by Jenkins (1998), situates the development and implementation of Megan's Law within a wider context of a politically endorsed 'moral panic' about paedophiles, an 'eruption of fear' that gathered momentum over the late 1980s and early 1990s (Jenkins, 1998, pp. 189–210). He contends that the environment in which Megan's Law developed contained both themes familiar from previous 'panics', and features novel to the present era:

> This eruption of fear, which led to new federal legislation in 1995–96, is notable testimony to the protean quality of the child abuse idea and its ability to adapt to changing political and technological environments. Today's sex crime panic is as fierce as that of the late 1940s, and it has given the predator a role in the national demonology that is quite as pronounced as that of his psychopathic predecessor. (Jenkins, 1998, pp. 189–190)

Best and Jenkins thus make a similar, and crucial, point. Regulatory schemes that are justified on the grounds of keeping children safe rely, in the first place, on wider cultural fears and inflated claims about the extent to which children are in danger, rather than on the *actual* prevalence of tragedies such as that of Megan Kanka, which have such an impact precisely because they are comparatively rare. New policies that are conceived as a result of these fears tend, in turn, to contribute to the notion that children are at risk.

Thus, with regard to Megan's Law, 'one of the most ambitious and perhaps alarming aspects of the get-tough attitude' is, according to Jenkins, that it 'involved public participation in the supervision of sex offenders' (Jenkins, 1998, p. 199). Such 'public participation' – where people are incited, effectively, to police their neighbours – necessarily involves a shift in the dynamic of community life. Community notification laws, and the processes by which they operate, involve a process of active re-education of the public, away from the assumption that neighbours can be trusted and towards an acceptance of suspicion and surveillance as the norm.

This point is well illustrated by Seattle police detective Robert Shilling, who 'has trained numerous departments in the United States and Canada on how to introduce a neighborhood to a sex offender' (Liberman, 1999). Shilling suggested that the problem of public vigilantism provoked by community notification laws can be contained by educating the public in the idea that sexual crimes are in fact a feature of everyday life:

> Key to community notification is dispelling the common myths surrounding sexual crimes. The stranger in the bushes everyone fears is a rare creature, he said. Kids are far more likely to be assaulted by someone they know and trust. Once people understand the dynamics of sexual crimes and how common they are, 'they realize as a community that they have a vested interest in having this person succeed,' Shilling said. 'In cases where you are just handing out fliers and not following up, you might as well be smoking a cigarette in a pool of gasoline'. (Liberman, 1999)

In summary, since the introduction of Megan's Law there has been some sensitivity at a policy level to the 'hysteria' (Liberman, 1999) that can follow a local community's knowledge that a convicted sex offender lives within their midst, and that an unintended consequence of this can be actions that destabilize communities and make them feel less safe – for example, by provoking vigilante attacks on offenders. However, the response to this problem is to attempt to normalize the idea that other adults may be sexual criminals – that, as Shilling would have it, '[k]ids are far more likely to be assaulted by someone they know and trust' than by a stranger.

This speaks to a wider trend in child protection, where the desire to ensure that children are protected from any possibility of contact with a paedophile has led to an *a priori* assumption that all adults should be 'vetted' in advance. We explore this point further, through the example of the UK's VBS.

The Vetting and Barring Scheme

In Chapter 3, we noted that policies developed in the US often shape, via the process of 'diffusion' (Best, 2001), subsequent policy developments in the UK. This is the case with community notification laws. The Child Sex Offender Disclosure Scheme, under which parents can ask the police if someone with access to their son or daughter has been convicted or suspected of child abuse, is commonly called 'Sarah's Law', in reference to the murder of eight-year-old Sarah Payne in West Sussex in 2000, by a convicted sex offender. Sarah's mother, Sara Payne, has been a prominent advocate of this new law, and many of the features of the law's rhetoric and practice bear striking similarities to Megan's Law.

In contrast to the US situation, however, Sarah's Law has attracted relatively little controversy. This may be because it has been introduced in a piecemeal fashion: first as a pilot scheme in 2008, involving just four police forces, and then gradually being extended to the rest of the country. The relative lack of controversy may also be explained because notification is provided in a more limited and discreet way than in some US states. As Filler (2001) explains, in the US some states only notify 'citizens with an interest in a particular person', while '[i]n more aggressive jurisdictions, the identity of offenders is widely publicized, often via the internet' (Filler, 2001, p. 316, footnote). Partly due to fears that Sarah's Law could result in the displays of public vigilantism seen in the US, the British law follows an even more limited notification model, where parents receive information about particular individuals only when they ask for it, and they are not (legally) permitted to pass it on to others (BBC News Online, 2010).

A related scheme, which has proved far more controversial in the UK, is the VBS. The VBS was introduced following the Soham murders of 2002, in which two 10-year-old girls, Jessica Chapman and Holly Wells, were abducted and murdered by Ian Huntley, a school caretaker who knew the girls through his partner, a teaching assistant in the girls' school. Before the murders, Huntley had been suspected of offences in other areas of the country, but never convicted; thus, the system that existed to prevent previously convicted sex offenders from working in schools was seen to be inadequate.

These horrific murders resulted in the Labour government commissioning an official inquiry, chaired by Sir Michael Bichard, that went far beyond the case itself, to examine the broader issue of how individuals who had previously been suspected of misdemeanours in relation to children could be prevented from having unsupervised access to children in the future. One of the Bichard Inquiry's recommendations 'proposed requiring the registration of those who wish to work with children or vulnerable adults', and the 2006 Safeguarding Vulnerable Groups Act was introduced 'specifically' in response to this recommendation (DCSF, HO, DH, 2007, p. 1).

The VBS, which was introduced under the Safeguarding Vulnerable Groups Act, brought about extensive surveillance arrangements of any adults who wanted to work or volunteer with children or other designated 'vulnerable groups'. These new arrangements meant that any adult who wished to have frequent contact with children, through their job or their involvement in community voluntary groups such as the Scouts or youth football, was required to undergo a check of their police records before they were permitted to take up their position. For many positions, 'enhanced' disclosures were required, which revealed not only convictions for offences against children, but also allegations, cautions, and what was termed 'soft' information held by the police (Manifesto Club, 2006; see also DfE, DH, HO, 2011).

While the VBS received few objections at the time of the Safeguarding Vulnerable Groups Act becoming law, controversy subsequently emerged in relation to both the principle and the practicalities of this scheme. As with Megan's Law, some objections rested on a concern with civil liberties: amplified, in the case of the VBS, because it was seen to threaten the civil liberties not only of convicted sex offenders, but also of anyone who wanted to work or volunteer with children, and who would be required under this scheme to have information about them disclosed. This was seen to be particularly problematic in regard to information being provided that was factually wrong; the persistence of 'false' allegations on individuals' police records; information being lost or disseminated more widely than to its intended target; and the phasing in of the requirement that those who wished to work or volunteer with children would have to register on 'an intrusive database containing the details of 9.3m people' (DfE, DH, HO, 2011, p. 2; see also Furedi and Bristow, 2010; McAlindon, 2010).

The larger problem with the VBS was perceived as its impact upon community life: in particular, the extent to which it was seen to discourage people from engaging in voluntary work, and indeed interacting with other people's children. In 2008, Frank Furedi and I published *Licensed to Hug*, a critique of the impact of the VBS upon local communities (a second edition was published in 2010). We found that the requirement to subject volunteers to criminal records checks had a rapid and significant effect at the practical level of placing formal 'barriers to involvement' in the way of people who wished to engage in *ad hoc* help with children's voluntary groups. More significantly, the institutionalization of vetting had the effect of casting doubt upon the traditional assumption that adults could be trusted to care for children:

> The implementation of a national vetting scheme directly challenges positive assumptions about the relationship between adults and children that until recently were taken for granted. The demand that adults be licensed before they can engage with children signals the sentiment that it should no longer presumed that adults will have a positive, protective influence upon children. The very act of vetting makes the prior negative assumption that an adult's motivation for helping children could be malign, which further weakens the necessary bonds between generations in our communities. (Furedi and Bristow, 2010, p. 26)

Many of the problems noted above were addressed by an official review of the VBS that began in 2010, by the newly elected Conservative–Liberal Democrat Coalition government. Noting that '[m]any thought the VBS, while well intentioned, was a disproportionate response to the risk posed by a small minority of people who wished to commit harm to vulnerable people', the government halted the planned implementation of the VBS while its review was conducted (DfE, DH, HO, 2011, p. 2). Upon publication, the review proposed a more 'convenient and proportionate' system, encompassing a smaller range of people; discarded the idea of a database; and reiterated some of the wider problems that had been raised about the impact of the VBS on civil liberties, professional practice, and community life. This included the statement: 'People should not be viewed as suspect simply because they wish to work with children or vulnerable adults' (DfE, DH, HO, 2011, p. 3).

However, despite the Coalition government's recognition of the negative consequences provoked by the VBS, it did not propose abolishing the scheme. Rather, it affirmed its intention to 'retain the best features of the VBS' and to 'scale it back to common sense levels' (DfE, DH,

HO, 2011, p. 2). The VBS was subsequently renamed the Disclosure and Barring Service (DBS). These developments indicate two important aspects of the dynamic behind the VBS specifically and the regulation of intergenerational contact in general.

First, such policies do not set out to damage relations of trust between adults and children: indeed, policymakers often appear to be horrified when this is their effect. Second, even when confronted with the destructive impact of such policies, there seems to be little appetite – either on an official or public level – to discard them completely. The assumption is that regulation is necessary, and that policymakers merely need to find more effective (and less destructive) ways of doing it. We dwell on these points a little more, below.

Like the episodes of violent vigilantism provoked in some US communities by Megan's Law, the fragmentation of communities provoked by the VBS should be seen primarily as an *unintended consequence* of this policy. Indeed, the VBS had been in operation for only three years before Sir Roger Singleton, chair of the Independent Safeguarding Authority, was forced to review the scope of the scheme in the light of the problems caused by its implementation. In a speech, he stated:

> We need to calm down and consider carefully and rationally what this scheme is and is not about. It is not about interfering with the sensible arrangements which parents make with each other to take their children to schools and clubs. It is not about subjecting a quarter of the population to intensive scrutiny of their personal lives. And it is not about creating mistrust between adults and children or discouraging volunteering. (Cited in *Daily Telegraph*, 2009)

This quote indicates that the VBS was not intended to fragment communities or to set parents against other adults. The dynamic behind policy that promotes expert-led parenting is, as we described in Chapter 2, implicitly destructive of informal relations, spontaneous actions, and lay knowledge. However, such policy is generally developed as a *response* to the perceived instability of traditional community and family bonds. The policy's intention is not to weaken these bonds further – yet this is its inexorable effect.

Both the original rationale behind the VBS and the official review of the scheme in 2011 provide a good example of how this process works. The Bichard Inquiry, and the statutory measures that followed, assumed that effective methods of child protection needed to come from a more systematic form of state regulation. No longer could workplaces and voluntary organizations be relied upon to use their judgement about which adults might be unsuitable to work with children. The 2011 review of the VBS accepted that this approach had proved problematic and counterproductive, stating that:

> 'Blanket' approaches such as the VBS have the potential to place the emphasis for safeguarding in the wrong place – on the State rather than on employers and individuals. (DfE, DH, HO, 2011, p. 2)

However, while this statement speaks to a desire for a less bureaucratic approach to regulation, it formulates a call for every individual to take on board a policing role, based on a heightened awareness of risk. 'It is the effective management of risk rather than aversion of risk which is most likely to protect vulnerable people', claims the review, concluding its Executive Summary with the statement:

> [E]veryone needs to be vigilant in order to keep children and vulnerable adults safe. (DfE, DH, HO, 2011, p. 2)

Here, the language of the British VBS comes to echo that of the American 'community-notification' laws, by emphasizing that adults who pose a danger to children are a feature of everyday life, and that it is every individual's responsibility to be 'vigilant' and to manage this risk. This imperative has far-reaching consequences for intergenerational contact. As Furedi and I noted in *Licensed to Hug*, the impact of normalizing the assumption that those who participate in voluntary activities with children may have ulterior motives for doing so would, necessarily, be to encourage a sentiment of mistrust between parents and other adults in the community:

> Although proponents of the scheme contend that it is designed to prevent 'worst case scenarios', the very institutionalisation of the scheme encourages 'worst case scenario' assumptions to become the norm. (Furedi and Bristow, 2010, p. 26)

Furthermore, this sentiment of distrust does not apply only to adults who engage in voluntary activities, but fuels a wider sense of 'intergenerational unease', in which 'adults feel increasingly nervous around children, unwilling and unable to exercise their authority and play a positive role in children's lives' (Furedi and Bristow, 2010, p. 27). It is to this problem that we now turn.

Risk, regulation, and 'no-touch' policies

As we discussed in the Introduction to this book, a key feature of today's parenting culture is its orientation towards the management of risk, and in particular the risks posed by 'unknown unknowns': the dangers that have not yet manifested themselves. We can see both Megan's Law and the VBS as models of the kind of social regulation that arises from such a conceptualization of risk. Hunt's (2003) analysis of 'risk and moralization in everyday life' indicates that the moralization of risk does not merely affect the personal strategies adopted by individuals, but also the strategies employed by society at large in its attempt to manage danger. Thus, an overbearing preoccupation with risk 'gives rise not only to a specific conduct (driving children to all their activities), but also leads to the launching of regulatory projects (imposing post detention restrictions on sex offenders)' (Hunt, 2003, p. 174).

Like the individualized responses that parents adopt to the fear of danger – driving their children to activities because they worry about their children being hit by a car or abducted, or hovering over their toddlers at the playground because they fear the child will fall and break a bone – Megan's Law and the VBS respond to an uncertainty about the motivations and behaviours of other adults within the community by attempting to pre-empt a problem from arising. These schemes tap into the parental 'worst nightmare' that his or her child will fall prey to a paedophile by attempting to ensure that paedophiles and children are kept physically separate, wherever possible.

As with the attempts to pre-empt dangers to a child's safety arising from accidents (falling out of a tree, or being hit by a car), it is never possible entirely to eliminate the risk that a child will, like Megan Kanka, Sarah Payne, or Jessica Chapman and Holly Wells, become the victim of a sex offender (Guldberg, 2009; Skenazy, 2009). In this context, a society preoccupied with managing risk has two options: either to accept that child sex offences will occasionally happen or to extend the practice of surveillance and regulation to 'make sure this never happens again'. This latter perspective informs Megan's Law and the VBS, and it is this that accounts for the 'expansionary logic' of the schemes, whereby adults are presumed to pose a risk to children unless it can be proven otherwise.

McAlindon's critique of the statutory regulations that have been introduced in the UK to prevent 'unsuitable individuals' from working with children draws out this point. Citing Zedner (2009, p. 47), she notes that 'the category of "unknown unknowns"' – 'those sex offenders "we don't know we don't know about"' – forms a significant problem for regulatory schemes such as the VBS to deal with, and leads the state to dispense with measures designed to assess the risk posed by particular individuals in favour of 'undifferentiated strategies' that treat everyone as a potential suspect (McAlindon, 2010, p. 41). This undifferentiated strategy has significant consequences at a community level:

> This blanket approach to risk, instilled in the recent expansive measures on vetting, merely perpetuates public fears and anxieties concerning the pervasiveness of sexual offending against children in particular. The resulting feelings of insecurity, suspicion and mistrust which attach to all who come into contact with our children undermines our ability to make discerning judgements about the likelihood of harm. This may ultimately help to further mask 'unknown risks' until they manifest themselves in the form of actual harm to children or the vulnerable. (McAlindon, 2010, p. 41)

Here, McAlindon draws attention to two distinct, but related, outcomes of regulatory projects that attempt to manage a community's fear of child sex offenders by treating all members of the community as potential suspects. Firstly, such schemes have the consequence of actively increasing a sentiment of insecurity: they become 'exceptionally uncertain and unsafe policies', where members of the community are incited to scepticism about the ability of the state 'to deliver on its self-imposed regulatory mandate to effectively manage risk' (McAlindon, 2010, p. 25). Second, by encouraging adults to distance themselves from children within their communities for fear that they might be suspected of having improper motives, such policies undermine adults' ability to act as adults, in the sense of making judgements for themselves about the actions they need to take to protect and nurture the children around them.

In this regard, McAlindon develops the point emphasized by *Licensed to Hug* that '[t]he formalisation of intergenerational contact contributes to the deskilling of adulthood' (Furedi and Bristow, 2010, p. xxxii). Furedi and I explained that the VBS 'has crystallised the assumption that adults who take responsibility for children should be somehow qualified to do so: that holding the status of an adult is not enough'; and that clearance by the VBS has 'come to be seen in similar terms to having a First Aid certificate or teaching qualification – as though being officially cleared of child abuse gives these adults some particular knowledge of, and skill with, children, whilst the rest of the adult population is effectively blacklisted and cautioned to keep its distance' (Furedi and Bristow, 2010, p. xxiii).

The 'deskilling' of adulthood is a phenomenon that has been widely researched in the context of 'no-touch' policies and child protection regulations in daycare centres and schools. Such policies do not seek to keep adults and children physically separate, as with the laws examined above; rather they regulate the kind of contact between adults and the children in their care. Like Megan's Law and the VBS, policies that explicitly regulate interaction between adults and children in early years settings have their roots in the 1980s and 1990s, when concern about 'extra-familial' abuse, in the form of the paedophile, gathered momentum (Jenkins, 1998; Parton, 2006, p. 117). Formal child protection regulations have become ubiquitous in Anglo-American societies, attracting some critical attention from scholars. It has been argued, first, that their primary aim is to provide the *impression* that risk is being managed, rather than protecting children from concrete and evident dangers; and second, that such policies have had harmful consequences, in that they actively fuel insecurity amongst parents and other adults about intergenerational interaction. We briefly review some of this literature below.

For example, Jones's (2004) study uses 'a series of booklets written during the 1990s as a case study of the entry of official anxiety about sexual abuse in early childhood centres in New Zealand'. Her research found that the consequent policy development 'reflects risk anxiety rather than a proper, informed appraisal of any real dangers to children' in these settings. The consequence of this development has been to 'legitimate unprecedented ongoing (self)regulation of teachers' practices, regulation about which critical questions cannot be asked without being understood as a "denial" of abuse', leading to a context in which '"risk of abuse"' has been produced as 'a normal aspect of contemporary childhood education' (Jones, 2004, p. 321).

In the US, Murray (2001) writes that, over the four years she spent conducting participant-observation research at two childcare centers, 'I found child care workers "doing child caregiving" within a climate of suspicion. This climate, moreover, was punctuated by periodic accusations lodged against workers suspected of some kind of "inappropriate" behaviour with a child' (Murray, 2001, p. 513). Murray goes on to observe that many of the childcare workers whom she talked to 'spoke about experiences where, in the course of doing their jobs, they or someone they knew, had been falsely accused of some form of child abuse'; and that this sensitivity to the possibility of 'accusations of abuse and the "panics" that followed, shifted the way they thought about their jobs, the parents of the children they cared for, and in some cases, the children themselves' (Murray, 2001, p. 513).

In the UK, Piper *et al.* (2006) reviewed some of the literature and current practice related to 'the touching of children by professionals in social and educational settings' (Piper *et al.* (2006, p. 152). They begin by noting the paradox, that '[m]any child-related settings are becoming "no touch zones" as adults become increasingly fearful of accusations that may ensue if any touch is misunderstood or misinterpreted', yet that 'touching is nevertheless still regarded as vital to children's emotional and physical development' (Piper *et al.*, 2006, p. 152). In reviewing how this paradox worked its way out in practice, these authors claim that '[c]urrent practice is more dependent on fears of accusation and litigation than any concern for the child' – and that 'most child care workers "know" this on the one hand, but nevertheless still attempt to justify their actions as sensible decision making' (Piper *et al.*, 2006, p. 151).

Piper and Stronach's (2008) book, *Don't Touch! The educational story of a panic*, is based on the results of a qualitative and case-based research project into 'the problematics of touching between professionals and children in their care', which addressed children and young people 'of all ages and across a range of educational settings' in Britain (Piper and Stronach's, 2008, p. viii). Here, the authors examine the ways that those working with children are trained to conduct themselves in particular, and peculiar, ways in order to avoid allegations of misconduct. From the practice of wearing gloves to change a baby's nappy in a nursery to teachers in secondary schools taking care not to be alone with a pupil at any time, their research indicates that everyday interaction between children and their carers or teachers is now conducted with a high level of deliberation. The starting point for their investigation of this topic was:

> [T]he impression that the touching of children in professional settings had increasingly stopped being relaxed, or instinctive, or primarily concerned with responding to the needs of the child. It was becoming a self-conscious negative act, requiring a mind-body split for both children and adults, the latter being controlled more by fear than a commitment to caring. (Piper and Stronach, 2008, p. viii)

All of the above studies speak to a situation in which the view that childcare workers are potential abusers of children has become institutionalized. Policies that regulate interactions between adults and the children for whom they are caring assume that, if such interactions are left unregulated, adults might either behave inappropriately or *be seen to behave appropriately*. As the studies above suggest, in practice it seems to be the latter problem – how behaviour might be perceived – that forms the main justification for 'no-touch' policies, and the odd, self-conscious behaviours adopted by childcare workers as a result, such as the 'sideways hug', leaving classroom doors open, and refusing to help apply sun cream.

The paradox of no-touch policies

For the scholars cited above, the extent to which the daily practices of teachers and childcare workers now appear to be dictated less by the needs of the child than by the imperative of avoiding allegations of inappropriate behaviour has had a negative effect on professional practice. The problem that they identify is that the state of 'risk anxiety' (Jones, 2004) that currently frames adult–child interactions, and the resulting 'climate of suspicion' or 'culture of fear' (Murray, 2001; Piper et al., 2006), makes early years education or daycare a difficult or unpleasant working environment, although this criticism is implicit. Rather, the central criticism is the way that risk-averse childcare practices actively undermine adults' ability to provide children with the right kind of care.

Two key ways in which this argument is articulated is through the need for touch and the particular problems facing male teachers and childcare workers. As we noted above, the observations of Piper *et al.* (2006) on the contradiction between the transformation of child-related settings into '"no touch" zones' on one hand, and the continued insistence on the importance of touching to children's emotional and physical development on the other (Piper *et al.*, 2006, p. 152). Indeed, the basic practicalities of caring for young children mean that it would be impossible, in practice, to have a 'no-touch' environment. For babies, diapers and clothes need to be changed on a frequent basis, and they need to be held to be fed and winded. Toddlers and young children need to be picked up when they fall down, physically separated when they fight with one another, and helped to go to the toilet. Beyond these practical matters, babies and young children look to adults to provide them with physical comfort when they are hurt, unhappy, or otherwise distressed. This fusion of physical and emotional care is summed up in the standard treatment for minor injuries at British nurseries: 'cold compress and cuddle'.

One aspect of the paradox of no-touch policies is, therefore, that parents, childcare workers, and official bodies alike recognize that any humane form of childcare involves adults touching children, and that if 'risk anxiety' were to be taken to its logical consequence, there would be no possibility of providing professional childcare. Another aspect of this paradox, however, is that modern parenting culture arguably *over-emphasises* the importance of touch.

In Part II of this book, Charlotte Faircloth's essay on 'The Problem of "Attachment"' discusses how the imperative of 'attachment' has become a significant feature of 'good' parenting in the twenty-first century. This orthodoxy emphasises the need for both physical prox-imity and emotional sensitivity on the part of the parent toward the (presumed) needs of the infant or young child, even where this conflicts with other practical pressures upon parents: such as having more than one child, or returning to work and needing to use paid-for daycare. As Faircloth notes, there are a number of problems with the discourse of attachment, and this should be understood as a socially constructed model of a particular kind of parenting rather than a statement about what parenting is. Nonetheless, the influence of this discourse in Anglo-American society should be considered in terms of how it conflicts with 'no-touch' policies and risk-averse, defensive forms of childcare practice.

When the concept of attachment was first developed in the 1950s by the psychiatrist John Bowlby, it was widely interpreted as an argument as to why mothers should remain at home with their infant children. The phrase 'Bowlbyism' came into existence to denote pseudo-scientific arguments as to why maternal employment should be considered prob-lematic (Riley, 1983). In the twenty-first century, maternal employment has become normalized; daycare is far more widely available, and its use is far less stigmatized than in the immediate post-war period. One con-sequence of this has been that the concept of attachment has evolved to frame, not only the activities of the primary caregiver (mother), but also the activities of childcare workers. Thus, in Britain, children are assigned 'key workers' to facilitate continuity of caregiving, and the number of children whom childcare workers are allowed to care for at any time is strictly controlled on the assumption that care will be 'hands on'.

The orientation of professional daycare around the need for prox-imity and touch between adults and children indicates the extent to which no-touch policies and similar regulations are designed not to *prevent* intergenerational interaction, but to regulate it. This is consist-ent with the contemporary 'cult of expertise' discussed in Chapter 2 of this book. Today's parenting culture recognizes the need for adults to raise children – indeed, the imperative of 'intensive parenting' over-states as deterministic the importance of the adult's influence over the developing child. But spontaneous, instinctual contact is highlighted as problematic: the adult's influence has to be continually monitored and upgraded to meet the standards set by the 'evidence' of the present time. This leads to a situation where aspects of childrearing that were once taken for granted – such as the need for touch – become reframed as instrumental techniques, to be employed consciously and with care.

A similar paradox is apparent in relation to the question of male childcare workers. On one hand, it is noted that in early childhood settings 'particularly men … are at risk of being accused of abusing children in their care' (Jones, 2004, p. 321); indeed, 'certainly in the Anglo-American literature, a recurring theme is the representation of men early childhood workers as a source of suspicion' (Cameron, 2001, p. 430). This focus on men as a source of suspicion, it is suggested, has less to do with the *actual* threat that male childcare workers pose to children, than with the association of childcare as 'women's work'. As Murray explains, this creates a loop of suspicion, whereby the peculiarity of men choosing to work as carers of young children leads to an assumption that all men who do this work must have peculiar motives for doing so:

> When men choose to do childcare work, they become suspect. This suspicion manifests in restriction of men's access to children in child care centres. Restricted access of men workers to children (compared with the access of women workers to children) implies men's desire for access to children is pathological. In these and other ways, the organization of child care and the accountability of persons to sex category systematically push men away from nurturing responsibilities and bind these responsibilities to women workers. (Murray, 1996, p. 368)

Yet while early years childcare remains female-dominated and culturally hostile to male workers, there is also a turn towards seeing male involvement in childcare as something to be positively encouraged. Cameron's (2001) review of the literature noted that three main arguments are put forward to encourage men to work in early childhood services. The first such argument relates to a concern about 'disappearing fathers' and the rise of lone parenthood, and suggests that 'the presence of male teachers and childcare workers could go some way towards providing stable, positive male role models for what is missed at home' (Cameron, 2001, p. 435). The second is that 'men can provide role models for the children, particularly boys': showing all children that caring is something that men do too, and giving boys 'someone to identify with and to help them develop their interests' (Cameron, 2001, p. 436). The third argument is a broader one, which revolves around 'social policy moves to achieve greater equality or "balance" between the sexes, both in workforces and for children attending services' (Cameron, 2001, pp. 436–437).

As Cameron's review suggests, these three arguments contain contradictions and flaws. However, the fact that they are posed in this way indicates the extent to which cultural expectations about men's *attitudes* to childcare have changed. Charlotte Faircloth's essay in Part II of this book explores the way that, in policy discourse about fatherhood, it is assumed that men should become more directly 'involved' in the day-to-daycare of their children (Collier and Sheldon, 2008); and at a wider cultural level, the father who refuses to change diapers or push a push-chair is very much perceived as a relic of past eras. Yet when it comes to working with children who are not their own, men are perceived as '"either homosexuals, pedophiles, or principals in training"' (King, 1998, p. 3, cited in Sumsion, 2000, p. 130); and they are 'subject to different unwritten rules regarding their physical access to children. Specifically, in many centers, men are more restricted in their freedom to touch, cuddle, nap, and change diapers for children' (Murray, 1996, p. 378).

Murray suggests that women childcare workers are perceived as mothers and men as fathers, thereby reifying traditional gender roles. However, she implicitly recognises that the degree of suspicion surrounding male childcare workers actually differs significantly from the tactile behaviour that would be expected of a modern father towards his own children: male childcare workers are 'fathers who cannot cuddle, kiss or comfort' (Murray, 1996, p. 383).

Indeed, even for fathers, the climate of suspicion surrounding men who have physical contact with children extends to fathers who, in other respects, appear to be exhibiting model 'involved fathering' behaviour. In *Licensed to Hug*, Furedi and I cited a series of anecdotes posted to a discussion thread on the British social networking site Netmums, from mothers recounting their partners' experiences. In one, 'Karina M' wrote:

> He's taking our 2 year old son out swimming at the moment and called me whilst waiting for the pool to open. It seems that the mothers if the cafe he was waiting in were giving him filthy looks (apparently when he walked in it was like a scene from a Western when the room goes silent and tumbleweed blows across the fore-ground). This happens whenever he goes out with our son on his

own, especially if he takes him into a joint changing/feeding room. Now, there is nothing strange looking about him, he's a perfectly normal guy, so I was just wondering if any other dads out there have the same experience? He's considering stapling his police check to his forehead every time he goes out! (Furedi and Bristow, 2010, p. 55)

The ingrained suspicion that today's society seems to exhibit towards fathers of young children, particularly in situations involving nudity, like public swimming pools or even bathtime, formed the backdrop to Gabb's (2012) study 'Embodying risk: managing father–child intimacy and display of nudity in families'. Here, Gabb presented to parents a series of six photographs, three of which 'depicted scenarios that would be ordinarily experienced in family life', and three of which were 'designed to be more provocative'. In the latter set, one picture showed a man sharing a bath with a young child, and another showed 'a "family group" in which a man and a woman (who appear to be naked) are playing with a child on a double bed' (Gabb, 2012, p. 3). (See also the discussion of Gabb's study in Charlotte Faircloth's essay on 'The (Un) involved Dad', in Part II of this book.)

Gabb's study yielded a number of interesting findings about the role played by new technology in shifting boundaries between the public and private, and also revealed a particular sensibility of risk with regard to '[i]mages depicting child nudity or father–child intimacy' (Gabb, 2012, p. 13). However 'innocently conceived' these images were, writes Gabb, they 'were identified by parents as potentially risky':

They could be appropriated and consumed in unforeseen ways by others (anonymous male adults) and their content was at risk of being misunderstood and therein lay bare the family and the father in particular. (Gabb, 2012, p. 13)

Here again, we see how a heightened suspicion of adult males as potential abusers coexists with a heightened sensibility of the dangers that practices will be 'misinterpreted' as abuse: both of which lead to an impulse for self-regulation.

That all men who have close contact with children are now automatically a potential target for suspicion indicates that the impetus for 'no-touch' policies in early years settings does not arise from a specific problem of male nursery workers abusing children, but from a more generalized climate of anxiety surrounding adult–child relations (See discussion in Furedi, 2013b). The extension of regulatory schemes, such as Megan's Law and the VBS, to entire communities – rather than specific institutions such as schools and nurseries – confirms this point. In this book, we contend that this climate of anxiety is driven primarily by a cultural unease about interaction between adults and children, rather than actual incidences of harm: but it is no less powerful for that. As Best explained, in relation to the rhetoric of 'threatened children':

> [T]he portrait of the adult who constantly runs the risk of doing more harm than good has implications of its own. Deviants who menace children merely extend the role of harmful adult to its logical conclusion. In short, the notion that children are precious, that they need protection from a harmful adult world, is basic to contemporary understandings of childhood. (Best, 1993a, pp. 181–182)

What gives rise to the suspicious surveillance and regulation of adult–child relations in the present day can best be understood as a wider cultural process of fragmentation and fear, which takes its most tangible form in formal no-touch policies, but is expressed in less tangible ways as well. In the final sections of this chapter, we look further at the implications of a sensibility that the danger facing children is, in fact, 'a harmful adult world' (Best, 1993a, p. 182).

Defensive parenting and the erosion of adult solidarity

> The erosion of adult solidarity transforms parenting into an intensely lonely affair. A climate of suspicion serves to distance mothers and fathers from the world of adults. In turn, this predicament invites parents to be anxious and over-react – not just to the danger they see posed by strangers, but to every problem to do with their youngsters' development. (Furedi, 2001, p. 23)

The literature reviewed above indicates that when adults are neither expected nor permitted to interact with children within their local communities in accordance with their own judgement, care for children comes to be conceptualized as a particular skill exercised by a distinct set of 'suitable' adults, rather than an assumed aspect of adult identity and social life. This divisive regulation formalizes the pre-existing sense of isolation and anxiety that parents already experience in a risk-averse parenting culture. It leads to the practice of 'defensive parenting', where 'good' childrearing becomes less about responding to the child's needs according to the adult's own priorities and more about self-consciously performing responsible behaviour by seeking to be aware of potential hazards and dangers.

Defensive parenting takes a number of related forms. In relation to the policies discussed above, the predominant form is one of normalized suspicion of other adults, whereby the imperative to conduct police checks on all adults who wish to spend time working or volunteering with children incites parents to seek reassurance that adults have been thus checked.

As an example of how far the imperative of formal reassurance that other adults are not paedophiles was provided by the British Labour government in 2010, when it was compelled to respond to the confusion and problems caused by the VBS. The Department for Children, Schools and Families (DCSF) produced a 'myth-buster' about the scope of the vetting scheme, which clarified that 'personal and family' arrangements were exempt from the VBS: so, for example, 'a parent who takes part in a rota with other parents to take each others' children to school once a week', or 'a parent arranging, with the parents of her child's friends, for the friends to stay at her home for a sleepover', did not need to be formally vetted (DCSF, 2010). The fact that a national government should need to reassure parents that they are permitted to organise lift-shares and sleepovers with other people's children is indicative of the level of insecurity about informal intergenerational contact that now prevails in communities.

As Furedi's quote, above, suggests, another form of defensive parenting is the competitive way in which relations between parents are often conceptualized and experienced. Parents anxious about their children's happiness, health, achievements, or personal development are encouraged by today's risk-averse parenting culture to see other parents (and their children) as a threat as well as a potential source of solidarity. The defensive competitiveness exhibited by mothers in relation to such everyday matters as the kind of food they feed their children or the type of activities they encourage them to do has become a familiar feature in the popular news media, along with novels, TV shows, and films. The academic literature, as we note in Chapter 1, has discussed this phenomenon in relation to the 'Mommy Wars' and the 'new momism', the 'tribalism' of parental behaviour, and the divisive strategies involved with projects of 'concerted cultivation' (Bristow, 2009; Douglas and Michaels, 2004; Hays, 1996; Lareau, 2003; Warner, 2006).

The existence of this critical literature indicates that while intensive parenting has become the dominant cultural script according to which 'good' childrearing is defined, responses to this script are far from stable.

The imperatives inherent in a risk-averse, highly individuated parenting strategy are continually contradicted both in principle (the lives that people want for themselves and their children) and in practice (the impossibility of keeping a child, or children, safe from every possible danger and at the same time engaging in activities and experiences that will help them get ahead in life).

Thus, parents are torn between the desire that their children should engage in soccer practice or music tuition ('concerted cultivation'); the anxiety that these activities will pose the risk of injury, or abuse at the hands of other adults; and the practical impossibility of being able to take two or three children to two or three different 'improving' activities at the same time. In addition, as we discuss in Part II of this book, parents are very aware that risk-averse parenting strategies can also be conceptualized as harmful to their children, and that a 'good' parent ought to be instilling in their child the qualities of independence and resilience. The essay on the phenomenon of 'helicopter parenting' in Part II examines the way in which critiques of risk-averse parenting are now becoming reframed as a new form of parent-blaming, leading to an impossibly contradictory demand: that parents actively seek to protect their children from being over-protected.

The contradictions of intensive parenting culture lead to a situation in which parental anxiety is both moderated and exacerbated by 'real-world' experience. For example, on one hand, children's continual engagement with other adults means that anxiety about potential paedophiles is ever present; on the other, it provides reassurance that most other adults are not paedophiles. Nonetheless, this experience is underwritten by a sentiment of deep uncertainty. What has been lost is the cultural sentiment that engaging with, and relying upon, other adults should be taken for granted as a good and necessary part of everyday life.

As noted above, the dynamic behind an expert-led parenting culture and regulatory projects such as the VBS is to transform the presumed role of adults, in socializing and protecting children, into a defined skill-set that can only be exercised by a particular group of checked or qualified adults. Waiton and Knight (2007) make this observation in a paper describing the phenomenon of 'paedophobia', or 'fear of children', whereby adults appear to be increasingly wary of engaging with children in their local communities, either to help them or to confront bad behaviour. They cite as an example the way that adults are encouraged to telephone the authorities with reports of low-level bad behaviour, rather than talking to the young people themselves: 'Adults intervening when young people behave is, quite frankly, no longer "the done thing" – a message promoted by politicians, housing officers, ASBOs [Antisocial Behaviour Orders], and implied by the "pick up the phone" advice from Strathclyde Police' (Waiton and Knight, 2007, p. 92).

Part of this is to do with adults' fear that they may be accused of inappropriate behaviour: Waiton and Knight quote a male academic saying that 'he wouldn't go near a young child today because of "what people might think". Nor will he meet with a female student at his university unless his office door is open'. But it speaks primarily to the 'disconnection between adults and children' that informs the current expert-led parenting culture; the idea that 'relating to other people's children is not the business of other adults but of experts' (Waiton and Knight, 2007, p. 93).

The trend towards the deskilling of adulthood has a practical impact on the experience of community life, parents' engagement with childcare professionals, and families' engagement with their neighbours and other families. While this impact is limited to some extent, by the combination of practical pressures and pragmatic common sense, the cumulative effect of the hyper-regulation of intergenerational contact should not be underestimated.

The existing literature on this topic goes a long way in highlighting the problems and contradictions within strategies of defensive parenting. Future critical scholarship in this area would do well to build on this critique and to develop a confident counter-narrative about why adult solidarity and informal intergenerational relations are not merely 'nice ideas', but fundamental to the project of raising children.

Chapter summary

- The increase in formal, hyper-regulation of adult–child contact can be understood as a response to a wider uncertainty about whether adults can be relied upon to protect children, rather than abuse them.
- The impact of such regulation is to exacerbate the fearful and privatized character of modern parenting culture, where it is assumed that neither 'strangers' nor childcare professionals can be assumed to have positive intentions towards children.
- This isolating dynamic not only comes from a defensive and competitive parenting culture, but also helps to codify it in regulation.
- Another consequence of the hyper-regulation of adult–child contact is the 'deskilling' of adulthood, where adults are dissuaded from acting upon their instincts to protect children and encouraged rather to hand over that responsibility to a 'qualified' person.

- This trend has important consequences for the way that adults and children in general come to view each other, where the element of threat weighs more heavily than the assumption of protection. It also contributes to the breakdown of adult solidarity within communities.

Further reading

Furedi, F. (2013b) *Moral Crusades in an Age of Mistrust: The Jimmy Savile scandal* (Basingstoke and New York: Palgrave Macmillan).
Through his analysis of a recent British historical child abuse scandal, Furedi explains how the concept of 'moral panic' does not encapsulate the workings of 'paedophile panics' in contemporary Britain, where the impetus arises not from the public but from the political elite. The confusion over fundamental moral values, Furedi argues, gives rise to 'moral crusades', which promote 'an ideology of evil' in an attempt to clarify values and to change public behaviour. Furedi's analysis draws out the destructive consequences of such crusades, both for the individuals embroiled in them and wider society.

Piper, H. and Stronach, I. (2008) *Don't Touch! The educational story of a panic* (London and New York: Routledge).
In this book, Piper and Stronach situate the findings of their research into 'no-touch' policies in daycare and early years settings within a powerful narrative about the way in which risk discourse has made it problematic for professionals to interact spontaneously – and often in ways that they believe to be right – with the young children in their care.

Jenkins, P. (1998) *Moral Panic: Changing concepts of the child molester in modern America* (New Haven and London: Yale University Press).
This is a solid and revealing account of the historical development of 'paedophile panics' and their roots in wider cultural anxieties about threats to the family, moving towards a growing sensibility about the problem of abuse *within* the family. Jenkins usefully explores the ways in which radical feminist agendas came to intersect with campaigns to preserve traditional morality.

Best, J. (1993a) *Threatened Children: Rhetoric and concern about child-victims* (Chicago: The University of Chicago Press).
This is a model study of the social construction of a social problem. Best's study of the rhetorical tools used by campaigners in making the case for why policymakers should respond more vigorously to the problem of children being abducted and abused reveals how the use of claims and statistics fuels an inflated sense of the problem.

Part II
Essays on Parental Determinism

Essay 1

Policing Pregnancy: The Pregnant Woman Who Drinks

Ellie Lee

This essay ...

- Draws attention to the further development of parental determinism through the insistence by medical/moral entrepreneurs and policy-makers that what happens when a woman is pregnant determines the health and development of the child-yet-to-be-born.
- Develops points made previously about risk consciousness in relation to the specific example of drinking alcohol in pregnancy.
- Explores the way that the perception that there is a conflict of interests between the mother and 'child to be' is expressed through claims about problem of drinking when pregnant.
- Reviews what research suggests about the effects of the demand that women do not drink when pregnant for parental experience and identity.

Introduction

Arguments about what influences a child's development are far from resolved ... Serious research, unlike the plethora of parenting advice available through child-rearing manuals and parenting magazines, is very hesitant on this question ... Inflating the public's perception of parental impact promises influence and power but inevitably delivers disappointing results. Unfortunately when this happens we don't discard the doctrine of parental determinism; we insist that mothers and fathers need to learn new parenting skills. (Furedi, 2008a, p. 68)

One observation to emerge from Furedi's work concerns the relationship between the outcomes of practices based on the idea of parental

129

determinism and the development of parenting culture. His argument, above, is that 'serious research' calls into question the notion that 'parental impact' has unparalleled 'influence and power'. Yet the failure of efforts to improve the lives of children through changing parental behaviour has not, unfortunately, led to a questioning of whether the emphasis on 'parenting' made sense in the first place. On the contrary: it appears to generate yet further efforts to improve 'parenting skills'.

The extract above is taken from a chapter in *Paranoid Parenting* that is partly concerned with pregnancy, where it is argued that one version of the development of 'the doctrine of parental determinism' (Furedi, 2008a, p. 64) is a marked tendency expand 'parenting' backwards, to the point *before* a child is born. 'The idea that experiences of early life are decisive in influencing what happens in later years is increasingly interpreted to include the experience of pregnancy', Furedi explains (2008a, p. 65). Pregnancy has become, he suggests, understood as the time when 'parenting' needs to begin, leading to the phenomenon of 'parenting before children' (Furedi, 2008a, p. 69). If this was true when *Paranoid Parenting* was published, it is even more the case today.[1] In Britain the formalization of pregnancy as the first stage of 'parenting' is expressed in the idea of the 'Foundation Years', the name given by the (Conservative-Liberal Democrat Coalition) government to the phase of life '[f]rom *pregnancy* to children age 5' (our emphasis). The government tells us 'early intervention' by professionals with parents during this time is 'crucial', as families are the 'key influence' in a child's development (4Children, 2013).

Claims of this kind, which justify early intervention, rework concepts conventionally applied to the period following birth, and recast them as relevant for pregnancy. Post-natal depression, for example (termed post-partum depression in the US), became a growing focus for policy-makers through the 1990s. They encouraged the expansion of efforts to assess maternal mood following birth on the basis that the mood of the mother has direct and profound effects for the development of the child (Lee, 2004; Godderis, 2010). Some have recently gone so far as to argue that how the mother feels is directly linked to her children's later 'antisocial behaviour' and even criminality. Claims of this kind were even made to explain the riots that scarred British cities in August 2011. 'What we are seeing in our society is the result of a few generations of people who didn't bond with their parents and went on to have babies and didn't bond with them', claimed the politician Andrea Leadsom (Bingham, 2012).

The view that the damage created by 'impaired bonding' can occur *even earlier* than has been previously envisaged is now also frequently expressed. A perspective has developed that contends that the mental state of mother should be monitored (and self-monitored) through pregnancy 'because it is claimed that the hormones associated with stress may affect their preborn child adversely. Psychologists have even developed psychometric scales such as the Maternal–Fetal Attachment Scale to measure maternal fetal bonding' (Lupton, 2012a, pp. 3–4).

Partly on this basis, some now express the view that the age of two is already *too late* for effective early intervention. The time from *conception* to *two years of age* has been described as the 'Age of Opportunity' for a child, with pregnancy represented as a critical time when the mother's state of mind needs to be assessed and improved through professional 'support' (Wave Trust, 2013).

Gatrell has coined the term 'maternal body work' to capture the way it is thus now insisted that women must relate to their bodies in a very different way once pregnant and perform new sorts of work. '[It is anticipated that mothers should prioritize maternal body work from the moment of conception, for life', she explains (2013, p. 627). A powerful system is in place that demands women change how they live in an array of ways, on the grounds that everything the pregnant woman does and feels (or does not do and does not feel) will impact on the foetus, for better or worse. An important observation made in literature critiquing such definitions of 'parenting', however, is how this process is developing further still. The expansion of parenting backwards does not stop at the conception, it is observed; the time *preconception* has also emerged as a focus of claimsmaking and policy development, with women's behaviours, habits, and feelings when they are *not even yet pregnant* construed an important matter if child health and well-being is to be improved (Karpin, 2010; Kukla, 2010). '[P]rospective parents, including men but particularly women, are exhorted to ensure their lifestyles are appropriately healthy enough both to conceive a child and then to ensure the optimal health and development of the preborn child', notes Lupton (2012a, p. 3).

Aspects of these developments in parental determinism are explored further in the essays that follow, where we look at claims about attachment and the foetal/infant brain. Here, we focus on one of the most developed examples of parental determinism: the social construction of the problem of drinking alcohol when pregnant (and before becoming pregnant). In this instance the message is now unequivocal; the claim that 'positive development during pregnancy' requires women 'not consuming alcohol' (Wave Trust, 2013, p. 10) is ubiquitous. The British National Health Service tells women:

When you drink, your baby drinks – avoid drinking alcohol while you're pregnant
What you drink, your baby drinks too. Swap booze for juice or tea.

We all like to relax and unwind at the end of a long hard day – and that doesn't change when you are pregnant. The thing is that what you drink, your baby drinks too. But as your baby's liver isn't even developed until the last month of pregnancy, even a little bit of alcohol can be damaging. It can cause birth defects like facial deformities, and can cause learning difficulties and problems with emotional development. It can stunt your baby's ability to grow, even after it is born, and increases the risk of having a miscarriage or a stillborn baby. (NHS, 2012)

Terrible damage to 'your baby' is here presented as directly attributable to 'even a little bit of alcohol'. There is, women are told, no mistaking the power and import of drinking alcohol for the health of their child. The message communicated in this way to all women is that there is a direct, causal relation between alcohol consumption (at any level) and impaired foetal development.

This proposition, that, 'birth defects like facial deformities ... learning difficulties, and problems with emotional development', as well as impaired growth, miscarriage, and stillbirth, can be traced back to any drinking in pregnancy has been formalized through the idea that all of these problems can be thought of as symptoms of a multifaceted spectrum of disorders and difficulties called Fetal Alcohol Spectrum Disorder (FASD). At one end of this spectrum is the rarely occurring condition Fetal Alcohol Syndrome (discussed further, below). Beyond this, FASD is described as a set of further terms that include 'Partial Fetal Alcohol Syndrome' (PFAS), 'Fetal Alcohol Effects' (FAE), 'Alcohol Related Neurodevelopmental Disorder' (ARND), and 'Alcohol Related Birth Defects' (ARBD) (Armstrong, 2003).

Taken together, this set of terms grouped as FASD have as symptoms almost any problems one can think of that may be detected in a child from birth onwards. According to those seeking to 'raise awareness' of FASD, these problems thus include intellectual disability, lowered IQ, memory disorders, learning disorders, attention disorders, sensory disorders, speech and language disorders, mood disorders, behavioural disorders, autistic-like behaviours, and sleep disorders. It is also argued that often FASD goes 'undiagnosed', or is misdiagnosed, 'for example as Autism or Attention Deficit Hyperactivity Disorder (ADHD)', or that autism and ADHD are in fact symptoms of FASD. Further, we are told that FASD, when undiagnosed, can lead to 'secondary disabilities' which can include loneliness, school expulsions, addictions, chronic unemployment, promiscuity, unplanned pregnancies, poverty, criminality, prison, homelessness, depression, and suicide (Egerton, n/d).

The birth defects and disabilities that appear this way in lists of symptoms of FASD have been hitherto considered complex (i.e. difficult or impossible to explain by reference to a single cause and likely involve the interaction of genetics, environment, socio-economic factors, and cultural perceptions of what is 'normal development'). Part of the case pressed by those who advocate 'no drinking' is, by contrast, that there is one, simple explanation, if a woman drank alcohol during pregnancy. Thus, claims one alcohol abstinence advocate, all of us (but pregnant women especially) need to face 'the truth' and 'stop hurting our children with alcohol'. In thinking otherwise, she argues, 'We are shutting our eyes to the damage we have already caused our children. Denying the consequences of our actions whilst pregnant' (Armstrong, 2013).

From this perspective, alcohol consumed in pregnancy is responsible for a vast range of problems. Indeed, those advocating that pregnant women (and also women looking to become pregnant) abstain from alcohol claim that 'FASD is more prevalent than Down syndrome, cerebral palsy, SIDS, cystic fibrosis, and spina bifida combined. Alcohol use during pregnancy is the leading preventable cause of birth defects, developmental disabilities, and learning disabilities' (NoFAS, n/d). In this chapter we look further at how this construction of pregnant women's behaviour and its alleged profound, causal link to the health of her child developed from the early 1970s to the present, with a focus on the interaction between science and medicine, medical entrepreneurs, and the wider culture.

Pregnancy, alcohol, and the expansion of risk

> Advice to pregnant and pre-pregnant women stretches far beyond the boundaries of what has been proven. (Furedi, 2008a, p. 72)

The contemporary social problem of drinking in pregnancy begins in the US; the story starts in the early 1970s, when it was first proposed that there is an association between a woman drinking a great deal of alcohol when pregnant and a specific set of health problems in babies, termed Fetal Alcohol Syndrome (FAS). FAS was (and remains) described as a condition identifiable by retarded growth pre- and/or post-natally; abnormalities of the face including a flattened nose, very rounded eyes, and heavy, drooping eyelids; and intellectual impairment and developmental delay, observed in babies born to alcoholic women (Golden, 2005).

It is emphasized in the literature that these health problems in the child are *associated* with very heavy drinking by the pregnant woman, but notably do not occur in the children of all pregnant women who drink heavily, suggesting that the detrimental effects of alcohol for foetal development *work in concert with other factors* (those emphasized in the literature, such as very poor diet, are mainly by-products of the socio-economic situation of populations in which FAS is more prevalent, for example Native Americans in the US) (Armstrong, 2003). That is, correlation or association does not equal causation. Secondly, there is the question of the size of the problem. FAS was initially described as a rare condition: 'The first prospective study [published in 1980] showed that FAS was a rare outcome of maternal alcoholism during pregnancy, an observation subsequently confirmed by numerous investigators', note Armstrong and Abel (2000, p. 278). Yet, as indicated above, the problem is now widely presented in terms that construe it neither complex nor rare. Women are told that *any* drinking in pregnancy is the cause of *most* health and developmental problems in children.

Armstrong and Abel (2000) explore the origins of this redefinition of the risk a woman's behaviour is said to present for foetal development through their discussion of 'exaggeration' and 'democratization'. Armstrong points to the import of what she calls 'medical entrepreneurs', whom she defines as individuals with a powerful sense of mission regarding their assessment of 'the evidence' who seek to 'impress their ... vision on the rest of society' (Armstrong, 1998, p. 2027). Their claims, she suggests, redefined risk from the mid-1970s onwards in two main ways.

First, exaggerated claims about the incidence of FAS were reported, based in part on broadening FAS as a category. As interest in the syndrome grew, an ever-widening range of anomalies were mooted as symptoms of FAS, 'more often than not based on single isolated incidences' (Armstrong and Abel, 2000, p. 278). Expansion of what 'counts' as FAS, and so exaggeration of the incidence of the condition, was also reflected in the use of terms listed above from this point onwards, leading eventually to the concept FASD (Armstrong, 1998, 2003). 'Democratization', secondly, also changed how risk was defined, through shifting claims about foetuses that should be considered to be at risk. This happened as FAS was less and less described as a condition associated with a very specific subgroup of the population – alcoholic women, usually also in poverty – to an 'equal opportunity disorder' (Abel and Armstrong, 2000, p. 279). In particular, those who organized to advocate for alcohol abstention, such as the National Organisation for Fetal Alcohol Syndrome (NoFAS), founded in the US in 1990, sought to emphasize how reported cases occurred in a wide variety of ethnic groups and social strata with just one, common causal factor: alcohol consumption. Through their work, the claim that every woman was equally at risk gained increasing visibility, although it contradicted research findings that showed not even every chronic alcoholic gave birth to an affected child, and that other factors, most notably poverty leading to poor diet, were significant (Armstrong, 1998, p. 2028).

Golden (1999, 2005) summarizes this shift in definition of the cause of FAS as a movement from *alcoholism* (defined as a complex, multi-causal medical condition, suggesting the need for focused, specialist assistance to a subgroup of women) to *alcohol* (the substance itself, consumed in any quantity, by any woman, leading to the claim that all women need to be warned against drinking when pregnant). These 'exaggerated' and 'democratized' claims have been joined by what has, perhaps, proved to be most significant aspect of the construction of this social problem: claims about *theoretical* risk.

Armstrong and Abel note how those who coined the term FAS later engaged in 'subtle broadening of the problem'. This happened as the case was pressed that no case of FAS had ever 'been reported in a human being with a negative maternal history of ethanol use' (2000, p. 278). In this approach, the absence of health or developmental problems in children of mothers who did not drink in pregnancy is construed as evidence of a possible (if unproven) relation between consuming alcohol at any level and these problems. From this perspective, in lieu of positive evidence that 'just one drop' of alcohol is undoubtedly harmful, it is 'better to be safe than sorry' and act as though that evidence exists.

The outcome in the US from this starting point was a shift in representations of risk. One form this took was the growth of portrayals of the detrimental effects of alcohol as a sort of sliding scale. 'In the public imagination and in much of the medical literature, it is assumed that if heavy alcohol exposure causes severe birth defects, then lesser levels of exposure must cause more moderate effects', explains Armstrong (2003, p. 6). The other is direct advocacy of thinking of risk in a possibilistic, theoretical way. As Ruhl notes, from her examination of Canadian advice manuals directed at the pregnant woman, by the 1990s Canadian women were 'informed that in the absence of thorough studies it is safer (less risky) for her to abstain from alcohol entirely' (1999, p. 104).

The policy response as it has developed internationally has reflected these risk-conscious constructions of the problem of drinking in pregnancy. In 1981 – just eight years after FAS was first named – the US was the first country to issue advice to women about the dangers of drinking when pregnant. The first Surgeon General's Advisory of Alcohol Use in Pregnancy cautioned women, however, to 'limit' alcohol consumption. By 2005, the advice was that *both* pregnant women and women who might become pregnant should *abstain completely* (Copelton, 2008). In 2007 the official advice from the British Department of Health changed similarly, with health officials making it clear that this was despite there being no evidence linking 'low to moderate' alcohol consumption with health problems, but rather because there are no studies proving what is 'safe' (Lowe and Lee, 2010a).

The evidence summarized above indicates that in a remarkably short space of time, the meaning of risk was redefined. FAS moved in the course of three decades from being 'a medical condition diagnosed by doctors and dealt with through effective management of pregnant women into a public health problem that required educating women not to drink during pregnancy' (Golden, 1999, p. 275). The need was thus established for what is considered in the sociological literature as a moral crusade – framed in the language of risk – to warn pregnant (and subsequently all fertile women) of the dangers of alcohol.

Those advocating for this approach have come to enjoy a high degree of success in gaining support for their perspective, notably among policymakers. Indeed, it is notable presently just how immune this commitment to abstinence advocacy is, in the face of competing evidence. Over the past few years, a series of studies have been published in which no relation was found between drinking occasionally or even quite frequently at low levels, and health and developmental problems in children. Indeed, a relation (not considered causal) has been found between drinking at low or moderate levels and *better* outcomes for children (Gavaghan, 2009). As I was writing this essay, a further such study was reported. Using 'childhood balance' as the measure (a proxy for motor development and coordination), the authors reported 'no evidence ... of an adverse effect of maternal-alcohol consumption on childhood balance', and that, 'Higher maternal-alcohol use during pregnancy was generally associated with better offspring outcomes' (Humphriss *et al.*, 2013).

The response from the UK Royal College of Midwives, however, was that, 'Our advice continues to be that for women who are trying to conceive or those that are pregnant it is best to avoid alcohol' (Press Association, 2013).

The sociological task, in this light, is not to debunk the existence of FAS; as Armstrong puts it: 'There is good evidence for a recognizable syndrome of severe birth defects associated with high levels of alcohol exposure *in utero*' (2003, p. 4). Rather, it is to understand the interaction between developments in science and medicine, claims made by medical and moral entrepreneurs about these developments, and the wider cultural and political context, that makes it possible for any drinking in pregnancy to be constructed as a social problem in the way it has come to be.

Science, culture, and the separation of the woman from her pregnancy

> Since the sixties, much attention has been devoted to what can and cannot harm a developing pregnancy. Medical science has demonstrated that the health of the baby is affected by the actions of the mother ... Parental determinism has attached itself to this discovery leading to a reorientation of the focus on modern antenatal and preconception care. (Furedi, 2008a, p. 70)

The prenatal period has been a focus of scientific attention in modern sense for over a century, and sociocultural research suggests that the motives, rationales, and effects of what is frequently termed the 'medicalization' of pregnancy over this time have been ambiguous (Fox *et al.*, 2009). The notion that this attention developed out of simple concern for improving the health of women and children does not adequately explain these developments. This ambiguity is clear, for example, in the history of campaigns for the development of contraception and 'family planning'. Recognition of the detrimental health effects of repeated pregnancy and childbirth, and the wish on part of women to be able to control their fertility, was synthesized through the twentieth century with eugenic and Malthusian preoccupations with the numbers of children born to families from poorer sections of society, taking a markedly racialized form in the US (Kline, 2005; Marks, 2001). In general, accounts of childbirth and the development of the medical care of pregnant women emphasize a combination of improvements in health but as part of a wider picture of what can be broadly termed 'population control'.

As Furedi notes, above, matters took a particular turn from the 1960s. These included scientific innovations Ann Oakley describes as 'Getting to Know the Fetus'. Oakley comments that until this time, by and large, 'knowledge of the foetus could only be acquired through knowledge of the mother – by asking her questions, by clinically examining her abdomen and by laboratory examination of her metabolic products'. However, through the 1960s and 1970s, what she describes as a 'revolution' in antenatal care took place. For Oakley, developments in medicine at this time were revolutionary because:

> [F]or the first time, they enable obstetricians to dispense with mothers as intermediaries ... It is now possible to make direct contact with the fetus, and to acquire a quite detailed knowledge of his or her physiology and personality before the moment of official transition to parenthood – the time of birth. (Oakley, 1986, p. 155)

Ultrasound imaging of the foetus is the most obvious and widely discussed example of this 'direct contact', but it has come to take other forms (Lupton, 2013b; and see Casper, 1998, on fetal surgery).

There is a rich and extensive literature on the interaction between these scientific developments and the wider culture, demonstrating how these developments in science and medicine are recycled, giving rise to new cultural tropes and constructions of the foetus and the pregnant woman (Lupton, 2012a, 2013b). While the foetus today is no more a fully developed person and is no less part of the pregnant woman that it was before ultrasonography, it has come to be perceived as if it is. The foetus exists in culture (and in at least parts of the world of medicine) as an independent entity, imagined to be really identical to an already-born baby; the foetus has become simply the baby 'unborn'.

The dimensions and ramifications of this cultural shift are numerous, but for parenting culture, central among them is the emergence of a more or less explicit conceptualization of the mother and foetus as separate but also *in competition*, with their interests pitted against each other. This development is neatly summarized by Armstrong this way:

> [T]he crucial movement ... is from thinking of the woman and the fetus as a single entity to thinking of the woman and the fetus as two separate individuals. From thinking of pregnant as something a woman *is* to regarding pregnancy as something she *carries*. Once we conceive of the pregnant woman and the fetus as two separate individuals rather than as one, it becomes possible to think of the woman and her fetus as potential antagonists. (Armstrong, 2003, p. 9)

The 'abortion problem' has been viewed as the archetype of this idea of 'maternal foetal conflict', with literature on the development of the so-called abortion war indicating how medical and scientific developments are utilized and drawn upon by, in particular, those opposed to abortion, to press their case about the vulnerability of the foetus in the womb. The modern abortion debate – featuring the free-floating foetus with its own needs and interests, set against the woman who exists as a person somehow separately (although the foetus is within her) – develops as claimsmakers opposed to abortion draw on the language and imagery of science and medicine.

This same conceptualization is, however, very apparent in the instance of drinking and pregnancy. A video produced by the UK-based alcohol abstinence advocacy organization FAS Aware, for example, promotes an image of a 'talking' foetus imperilled by its mother. In this video the foetus 'comments' on what it feels at the point of the first ultrasound scan (performed at around 12 weeks in Britain). The words spoken by the foetus, pictured as a shadowy ultrasound figure, go as follows:

> It's my first scan today. They'll check for Down's Syndrome. They'll check for abnormalities. But I wish they'd check for how much alcohol my mum drinks. (FAS Aware UK, 2010)

The unborn has, in this video, literally come to life as an already-existing person (who can, for example, speak), but one who is also entirely vulnerable in the face of her mother's actions. Indeed, given her total dependency on the mother – and the mother alone – by merit of location in the womb, the construction of the mother as manager and minimiser of risk is absolute, even compared to that of the mother following birth. Following Armstrong (2003), the mother literally and individually, in this portrayal of matters, 'conceives risk' and 'bears responsibility' for any problems that emerge once the child is born.

Lupton discusses this way of thinking about the foetus as follows, highlighting how the assumption of potential antagonism is framed in conditions of risk consciousness. The separated foetus, she indicates, comes to be considered 'in danger, not least from the mother':

> Preborn organisms are considered as particularly fragile, open to harm. The womb that is in some ways viewed as a warm, nurturing, safe protective place for the preborn, where the outside world cannot enter, has in recent times been conceptualised as opened to danger, not least from the mother who is supposed to protect her child. (Lupton, 2012a, p. 3)

This separation of the woman and foetus now finds its reflection in the stream of warnings issued and advice given about the detrimental effects of the actions (or inactions) of the pregnant woman for the future child, about everything from hair dye to tuna fish (Fox *et al.*, 2009). Yet while a precondition for this separation may be technological developments, in that they make it possible to see the foetus (through ultrasound) and understand more about its development (through medical research about, for example, FAS), it is by merit of developments *in culture* that this comes to reflect itself in the barrage of warnings and rules that now surround pregnancy. While FASD takes the form of a medical diagnosis and is at some level dependent on new scientific knowledge about the foetus, this social problem is the product of wider and definitively *sociocultural* concerns.

For this reason, Armstrong's major work on the subject is titled 'Fetal Alcohol Syndrome and the *Diagnosis of Moral Disorder*' (our emphasis) to capture her notion that medical knowledge, in the late twentieth century, became the key way in which society struggled to manage uncertainty. In a context where society lacked clarity about its future, that is, experienced moral disorder, 'what science tells us' came to attain particular significance (2003, p. 9). As she explains, 'Medicine provides an arena in which society can sift through and express moral ambiguities' (2003, p. 12). It was, this suggests, certain cultural and social conditions that developed from the 1970s onwards (not science or medicine in the abstract) that made it possible for an expanded and all-encompassing definition of the problem of drinking in pregnancy to become dominant so fast.

A central issue identified of the social and historical context of this time is the changing social role of women, which is discussed in the literature in two ways. The growth of concern about female consumption of alcohol, and recognition of alcoholism as a female as well as male disorder, is highlighted. 'The discovery of FAS in the 1970s, notes Golden, 'coincided with the growing visibility of female alcoholism with evidence of its increasing relevance, especially among younger women, and with expanding government concern' (1999, p. 272). That women seemed more and more to be 'behaving like men', in particular in their adoption of the 'risky' practice of drinking alcohol, is an important part of the story of this social problem. The changing social role and position of women is also discussed as important in a second way, as more and more women came to be involved in the world of employment and other public arenas. This shift in the social role of women, away from motherhood first and foremost, is viewed by both Armstrong and

Golden as important to perceptions of 'moral disorder', which come to take a 'medicalized' form.

These American analyses suggest a linkage between drinking in pregnancy as a social problem and a cultural context of what could be termed a conservative response to changes in gender roles and cultural norms in post-1960s America. More recently, however, other countries have followed suit. This century has seen changes to advice and to the messages communicated to pregnant women in countries with contrasting wider and social contexts including Britain (Lowe and Lee, 2010a) and notably Finland, which, as Leppo notes, has been, 'characterised as women-friendly', scoring high when it comes to gender equality and women's reproductive rights (2012, p. 180), but where abstinence has been officially recommended since 2006 to pregnant women and women planning pregnancy. Media analysis has shown, similarly, that warning women about drinking is not distinct to more conservative sections of the press (Lowe and Lee, 2010b).

Important insights are also offered by studies that have looked at a variety of sorts of pregnancy advice. One finding is that there is very little difference in what is said by Armstrong's 'medical entrepreneurs', and those who self-define as advocates for, representatives of, or a friendly support to, pregnant women. As Copelton notes, 'Most popular pregnancy books warn that there is no safe level of alcohol consumption on pregnancy and often conflate any amount of drinking during pregnancy with Fetal Alcohol Syndrome (FAS)' (2008, p. 13). Marshall and Wollett (2000) analysed information about pregnancy from the British National Childbirth Trust (NCT) alongside that from other sources. Although the NCT defines itself as the feminist, consumer voice of the pregnant women and mother, opposed to the disempowerment of women by the medicalization of pregnancy and childbirth, its message was that drinking in pregnancy can lead to serious health problems in the baby. They argue that the NCT's account, in line with others, characterizes the 'risks and dangers facing women ... as numerous' (2000, p. 360).

Overall, evidence thus suggests that the precept of parental determinism has come to find political and cultural support far beyond that arising out of 'traditional' ideas about women and motherhood – parental determinism crosses the old boundaries of 'feminist', 'liberal', and 'conservative'. Indeed, research indicates this precept now informs a thoroughgoing acceptance of maternal–foetal separation on the part of diverse social actors. We conclude this essay with brief comments about two areas. First, we consider the relation between this cultural context and law and policy, and second, what evidence suggests about its effects for the experience of pregnant women themselves.

Policing (and self-policing) pregnancy

[T]he construal of pregnant women as actively engaged in warding off risk contrasts with that of the 'passive' pregnant woman ... The maintenance of the safety of the body is cast in terms of an individual locus of responsibility. (Marshall and Wollett, 2000, p. 360)

This important insight from Marshall and Wollett indicates that the present way the pregnant woman is thought of is not as a passive patient, who should simply take orders from medical professionals. The contemporary form of her medicalization, instead, construes her as 'actively engaged in warding off risks'. Ideally, she should be fully engaged in working out how best she can manage and minimize risk, and she should conduct her pregnancy accordingly. As Armstrong (2003) notes, a consensus about the power of the pregnant women as this manager of risk spans the worlds of medicine, abstinence advocacy campaigns, health care provision, and advice books and contemporary culture. As risk management requires the woman to seek out and absorb all the information about risk she can and take advice from those who seek to support her as she manages risk, this also means a new intensity is given to the 'public' pregnancy. The management of pregnancy becomes everyone's business.

The ways in which laws and policies define what this project of risk management requires, it has been argued, comprise both 'occasionally draconian state interventions' but more commonly policies and programmes that 'depend on the entrenchment on a sense of personal responsibility' (Ruhl, 1999, p. 96). The former, most apparent in the US, have drawn on a definition of maternal alcohol consumption as 'nothing less than child abuse through the umbilical cord' (Golden, 1999, p. 270). This linking of the behaviour of the pregnant woman to child abuse has been most apparent in the US. Examples emerge from the 1990s onwards of the incarceration of women once their child was born on the grounds they had abused their offspring, drawing clear attention to the link noted in the introduction between risk consciousness and (literal) pregnancy policing. Golden (1999) explains further that by the early 1990s, this claim came to feature in explanations for violent crime, with one convicted murderer presented as damaged by FASD and child abuse. It was thus claimed that violent crime 'goes back to the womb', in a clear instance of extreme infant (and parental) determinism.

Yet evidence suggests the dominant *modus operandi* through which women are made accountable for their child's health relies on 'the interiorization of social constraints' and a 'process of psychological assimilation' (Queniert, 1992, p. 167 [in Ruhl, 1999, p. 96]). In other words, the main effect of the cultural dominance of risk consciousness is to modify and change the nature of the inner world and identity of women, who come to participate in, and adopt, 'the "risk model" of pregnancy' (Ruhl, 1999, p. 96). What does evidence suggest about how this process of 'psychological assimilation' is working itself out? There is a relatively small empirical literature that has addressed this area, through qualitative studies of the experience of pregnant women and drinking. I conclude this essay with a brief summary of what emerged from research that has been conducted on this area, by Copelton in the US (2008) and Fox and colleagues in England (2009; see also Nicolson *et al.*, 2010, and Heffernan *et al.*, 2011). Copelton's study was part of a larger project about the experience of pregnancy, based in part on interviews with 55 pregnant women living in the US. The study by Fox *et al.* took the innovative approach of conducting in-depth interviews with recent mothers, and their own mothers, to explore changing perceptions and experiences of pregnancy in the late twentieth and early twenty-first centuries.

A finding to emerge from both studies was the now pervasive influence of the 'no drinking' message. This aspect of pregnancy was an inescapable part of women's experience, with respondents in both the US and UK keenly aware that whether and how much they drank was considered a matter of great import. In line with the constructions of risk outline above, *any* drinking at all, including very small amounts on one or two 'special occasions', was at issue. What both studies detected, further, was that in instances where women did drink, it has become an everyday matter of comment from strangers. The policing of pregnancy went far beyond advice giving or questioning by health professionals, as these comments from women in the English study indicate:

> I think people frown upon certain things and are certainly not slow in telling you. I found a lot of people (particularly men!!) had something to say about me having one glass of wine, which I found quite offensive and insulting. Often from people who hardly knew me and had little or no experience of pregnancy. (Anna, 28) (Fox *et al.*, 2009, p. 558).

> I once went into a restaurant when I was about five months pregnant and was about to order a glass of wine with my meal, but the waiter

said 'a soft drink for you madam?' and I know he was only trying to be nice, but then I felt I couldn't order one because he'd said that. (Lola, 37) (Fox *et al.*, 2009, p. 559).

Copelton describes one of her respondent's experiences this way:

> For Eleanor, drinking during pregnancy was not something she could do just anywhere with anyone ... [She] was worried about her server's reaction [in a restaurant], which was pleasant and nonconfrontational, she believed, only because he had not noticed that she was pregnant. On a different occasion, Eleanor's sever responded to her request for a margarita by questioning, 'With alcohol?' Eleanor explained, 'They look at you, like, "But you're pregnant!"' Though the waitress did serve her, Eleanor swore 'they didn't put any alcohol in!' (Copelton, 2008, p. 21)

This evidence suggests that pregnant women are now treated as a 'class apart' for whom different rules are applied in the informal world of everyday life. That parenting culture now sustains this degree of discrimination attests to the power of the regulatory effects of risk consciousness outlined previously.

Copelton draws attention to another important aspect of the present situation, namely the divisive consequences of 'no drinking' rules. Women who abstained from alcohol that she interviewed often went far beyond considering this simply their personal decision based on how they wanted to manage risk. Rather, they were 'especially likely to judge negatively other pregnant drinkers' (2008, p. 15) and indicated they found hard to see what they could have in common with these other pregnant women. 'I felt a certain disconnect', commented one of her respondents (2008, p. 16). The 'psychological assimilation' of the idea that to abstain is to be a good mother (and to drink is to be a bad one) in this way strongly influences maternal identity. Similarly, Copelton documents the identity work engaged in by those of her respondents who *did* drink. As they felt the need to justify their actions, one strategy they adopted was to draw distinctions between themselves and other sorts of pregnant drinkers, whom they positioned as being not like them.

Fox *et al.* draw this conclusion from their work, regarding the overall position of women in a context of risk consciousness. They argue:

> Whilst today's women experience increased freedoms to work or dress attractively during pregnancy in comparison with their own

mothers, they also experience new pressures in the form of restrictions on diet, alcohol, smoking and unrealistic expectations regarding body size and shape. (Fox *et al.*, 2009, p. 564)

This identification of the way society limits the freedoms of women in an ostensibly far more liberated world that that of 30 years ago, through the growing insistence that they restrict and modify their behaviours is an important observation.

In relation to this area of parental experience, the aspect that remains manifestly under-researched is the experience of parents whose children do have 'something wrong'. Furedi has argued the following, of the general effect for such parents of 'parenting before children':

> When a child arrives less than perfect – and around 2 per cent of newborns are affected with an abnormality – most parents scrutinize their lives to discover if they could have 'done anything' to cause the problem. (Furedi, 2008a, p. 74).

Given the scope of the problems, alcohol abstinence advocates attribute to drinking in pregnancy, the proportion of mothers who may be now expected to 'scrutinize their lives' and conclude that they caused their child's problems could be predicted to be considerably larger. A task for the study of parenting culture is to research the ways and (and variations in them) that parents of 'less than perfect' children experience the messages and activities of those who seek to suggest they are to blame because the woman 'touched a drop'.

Note

1. In 2010, the Centre for Parenting Culture Studies held a two-day event to explore this development. Abstracts and slides from papers and a summary of the discussion are here: http://blogs.kent.ac.uk/parentingculturestudies/ pcs-events/previous-events/changing-parenting-culture/seminar-5/.

Further reading

Armstrong, E. M. (2003) *Conceiving Risk, Bearing Responsibility: Fetal Alcohol Syndrome and the Diagnosis of Moral Disorder* (Baltimore and London: John Hopkins University Press).
This (together with the text by Golden) remains the seminal work on drinking and pregnancy from a sociological/historical perspective. The text uses a range of sources to provide a groundbreaking reading of how the definition and meaning of risk, and so morality, has changed over time. Important

distinctions are drawn between perceptions of alcohol in the past and in the late twentieth century onwards, generating important insights about the relation between medicine, culture, and the meaning of risk in the present. This work includes discussion based on interviews with doctors in the US working in obstetrics and gynaecology, paediatrics, and family practice.

Golden, J. (2005) *Message in a Bottle: The making of Fetal Alcohol Syndrome* (Cambridge MA and London: Harvard University Press).

Like Armstrong's book, this work is about the US and offers a reading of the relation between medical knowledge and the wider culture. Golden is an historian and first offers a clear and really informative account of both the story of FAS and what she calls 'historical sightings of alcohol and pregnancy'. Her focus through the rest of the book is then on how FAS has played out in culture and politics. Golden shows us how representations of drinking in pregnancy have taken us further and further away from what the original diagnosis suggested to, instead, a repressive system of public health warnings, pregnancy policing by media, and legal sanctions.

Lupton, D. (2013b) *The Social Worlds of the Unborn* (Basingstoke: Palgrave Macmillan).

This is a recently published book by Deborah Lupton, whose body of work as a whole has made a major contribution to sociological analysis of the concept 'risk', the development of public health programmes in the twentieth and twenty-first centuries, and pregnancy and parenthood. This book appears in the 'Palgrave Pivot' series of short books offering a responsive commentary on issues of our time. Beginning with a discussion of what is meant by the term 'unborn', the text covers ultrasound and imaging, maternal–foetal separation, death and disposal of the unborn, and pregnancy in risk culture. This text can be read alongside other commentaries on 'the unborn' by the same author, which are referred to in this chapter.

Essay 2

The Problem of 'Attachment': The 'Detached' Parent

Charlotte Faircloth

This essay …

- Explores how, and why, the detachment (and attachment) of parents and children has become a social problem.
- Looks at the claimsmaking undertaken by a particular group of advocates (attachment parents) to explore how this has been formulated as a problem in political, medical, and lay terms.
- Draws on earlier chapters, to look at the intersections between 'attachment' and 'intensive' parenting, looking at the ways in which various forms of care are naturalized (and gendered).
- Looks at how parenting styles have become increasingly 'tribalized', with negative social implications.

Introduction: the emergence of problematic attachment

It hardly seems controversial to say that, today, we have a cultural concern with how 'attached' parents are to their children. Midwives encourage mothers to try 'skin-to-skin' contact with their babies to improve 'bonding' after childbirth (UNICEF, 2013), a wealth of experts advocate 'natural' parenting styles which encourage 'attachment' with infants (for example, Sears and Sears, 2001), and politicians regularly talk about 'Broken Britain' being the fault of 'absent' parents, whether physically or emotionally (for example, Jones, 2007).

Kanieski (2009) sees the concern with detachment as part of a broader trend in the twentieth century towards the medicalization of parenthood: in particular, the medicalization of maternal emotion and mother love itself. Where, for example, mothers' love was promoted and idealized in the late eighteenth and nineteenth centuries as an extension of women's inherent virtue (Badinter, 1980), during the late nineteenth and early twentieth centuries, maternal emotion came under much greater scrutiny with the rise of what Apple has termed 'scientific motherhood' (Apple, 1995).

Mothers' own 'instincts' were increasingly considered inferior to the findings of experts, who based their guidance to mothers on a more rational account as to what promoted the emotional well-being of children (see Chapter 2). This turn towards an interest in children's emotional well-being was due, in part, to the emergence of the psychoanalytic framework, described in Chapter 1, where early infant experience was understood to be responsible for later mental health in children and adults. The 'mother–infant dyad' became an object of the scientific gaze, with the interactions of this dyad held to have important social ramifications:

> The belief that what mothers did would have such permanent consequences for both the individual and the society legitimized the medicalization of mothers. Social problems became viewed as problems with mothers. (Kanieski, 2009, p. 7)

Fairly rapidly, the idea that children's health and emotional well-being were at risk from maternal disorders took purchase. Where failing mothers in the eighteenth century were perceived as immoral or sinful, they were now understood as ill. Consequently, says Kanieski, 'maternal emotion became worthy of medical scrutiny because it was viewed as the foundation for successful mothering and healthy children' (Kanieski, 2009, p. 8). Initially psychologists' concern, as expressed in Watson's *Psychological Care of Infant and Child* (1928), was about the purported dangers of *too much* mother love and the risk of spoiling children. By the 1930s and 1940s, however, concern had turned towards the emotional rejection of children by mothers (Figge, 1932; Levy, 1943).

Attachment theory

As Kanieski observes, early medicalizers of maternal emotion saw maternal love as something which began in a woman's own childhood – that is, if she had not been loved by her mother as a baby herself, this 'damage' risked being passed on to her own children in due course. By contrast, later medicalizers tended to view the development of maternal love as 'a nearly instantaneous process, related to pregnancy, birth, and the postpartum period' (Kanieski, 2009, p. 11). Whilst one might expect this to reduce anxiety about the correct development of maternal love, in fact, the shorter time frame meant that the risks of failure were considered to be greater.

In this latter ilk, the work of Bowlby and Ainsworth in the 1950s and 1960s formed the basis of what is now known as 'attachment theory' (Bowlby, 1969). The central tenet was that infants must form an emotional attachment with their caregiver as the foundation for future emotional health. Based on observations of institutionalized children, Bowlby (1969, 2005 [1988]) coined the term 'maternal deprivation' to argue that if the mother was absent (either physically or mentally) during the formative period of attachment, the child could suffer personality disorders such as anxiety or depression. He suggested that a (biological) mother was predisposed to respond to her child, particularly due to the hormones related to birth, and attachment was framed in an evolutionarily logic as beneficial for both parties.

Bowlby realized, however, that not all mothers would relate to their children like this. Indeed, Ainsworth's research showed that many mothers responded to their children in ways that did not promote 'attachment'. As a means of gauging attachment, Ainsworth developed what is called the 'Strange Situation' test. The infant, who was left alone in a room with a stranger, was categorized based on their behaviour on being reunited with their parent. The clinical definition of a securely attached infant is one who is distressed when the parent leaves but easily comforted on their return. Ainsworth showed that sensitive mothers who were aware and responsive had the most 'attached' children. Thus for these researchers, attachment was synonymous with love.

The bonding mystique

Building on the interest in maternal attachment, animal studies became the basis for arguments about the importance of 'bonding', a specialized form of attachment. Some of the first work in this area was done by Lorenz (1937, 1950) who introduced the term *imprinting* to refer to a phenomenon of an 'attachment window'. The basic principle was demonstrated by studies conducted by Hess (1966), whereby ducklings were shown to form an attachment to whichever caretaker they first came into contact with (Gardner, 1997).

Initially, the focus was on the critical period immediately after birth, though this later expanded to the period around birth as a whole. The argument was that a child's first hours, weeks, and months of life had a lasting impact on the entire course of the child's development (see, for example, Klaus and Kennell, 1976). Birth, in particular, was singled out as one of the 'critical moments' for bonding to take place. After birth, new mothers were told to look into the eyes of their infant, hold their naked child, preferably with skin-to-skin contact, and breastfeed for optimal bonding (Klaus *et al.*, 1995). Mothers should be sheltered from society for a period of three to four weeks so that they could devote themselves to becoming acquainted with their babies, and learn the 'primary maternal preoccupation' of putting themselves in the place of their infants' (Klaus *et al.*, 1995, paraphrased from Kanieski, 2009).

From the outset, successful bonding thus required both a set of behaviours that maintained proximity with one's child *and* an emotional bond (Kanieski, 2009, p. 14). Thus behaviours such as 'fondling, kissing, cuddling, and prolonged gazing' (Klaus and Kennel, 1976, p. 2) could not just be performed, but must be matched by an emotional commitment to the child.

Attachment today

Recently, attachment researchers have found new instruments for identifying the attachment status of adults (whether through self-reporting or analysis of narratives, Kanieski, 2010, p. 341). As a result, they claim to be able to link adult attachment status to 'parenting style, success in romantic relationships, psychopathology', and even, 'a tool for determining child custody' (Kanieski, 2010, p. 341).

There has also been, as Kanieski (2010) observes, a shift from focusing on attachment *disorders* to seeing normal attachment as something to be 'achieved'. In this way, (poor) attachment has become a *risk* factor, whilst (good) attachment has become a *protective* one. 'Achieving' normal attachment in children is therefore both a means of ensuring the benefits of secure attachment and a way of avoiding the risks of less secure attachment. This intersects with contemporary parenting culture, in encouraging mothers to engage in intensive parenting, with clear implications for parents' (and particularly mothers') subjectivity:

> To be a responsible mother meant that one needed to be a sensitive, responsive mother. Mothers were taught to monitor themselves in relation to their behaviour towards their children as advice regarding attachment and bonding that appeared in parenting magazines and books in the 1970s and 1980s. (Kanieski, 2010, p. 341)

Similarly, where Bowlby recognized that mothers' social environments had an impact on women's attachment disorders, today, even children in stable, middle-class homes are seen as at risk from insecure attachment (see discussion in Chapter 1). The social context is thus eclipsed:

> As with other individualizing projects, the emphasis on attachment as a risk factor linked to the quality of mothering took attention away from external factors such as the social and economic structure that might also impact a family's ability to create a sense of security for their children. (Kanieski, 2010, p. 342).

As we explore here, much of the evidence in support of this theory of 'attachment' has been called into question by critics. Diane Eyer's (1992) book *Mother–Infant Bonding: A scientific fiction* notes, for example, that rather than being tied to a consistent primary attachment figure, or restricted to a specific sensitive period, 'attachment' should be considered a highly plastic phenomenon amongst human beings (Eyer, 1992, p. 69; see also Bruer, 1999; Burman, 2008; Kagan, 1998, and discussion in Chapter 3). But despite the critiques, the ideas of Bowlby and Ainsworth remain extremely influential in discourses around contemporary parenting – partly, we suggest, because they latch on to a wider cultural anxiety around childhood, and a view of society in breakdown.

This cultural concern with 'detachment' is not a new one, of course (Kukla, 2005). There has long been a wish to protect the family (and the domestic sphere in general) from a harsh outside world, which is seen as corrosive to bonds of intimacy (Lasch, 1977; Schneider, 1969). But today, this anxiety around protecting childhood (and motherhood) seems particularly pronounced – chiming with Hays' comments about the contemporary cultural ambivalence we have around mothering in general. 'In pursuing a moral concern to establish lasting human connection grounded in unremunerated obligations and commitments, modern-day mothers, to varying degrees, participate in the implicit rejection of rationalized market society', Hays writes. The tension between the 'contemporary ideal of intensive mothering' and the norms and demands of the market is, she argues, 'indicative of a fundamental and irreducible ambivalence about a society based solely on the competitive pursuit of self-interest', and motherhood 'is one of the central terrains on which this ambivalence is played out' (Hays, 1996, p. 18; see also discussion in Chapter 1).

For the purposes of this essay, we look at how these anxieties and ambivalences have been mobilized by a group of advocates – 'attachment parents' – who understand their parenting style to be a means (perhaps the primary means) of bringing about wider social harmony, through the production of emotionally aware, 'attached' children. As we explore, however, their vociferous claimsmaking about the benefits of attachment parenting are an expression of a parenting culture that exacerbates a corrosion of adult solidarity (Faircloth, 2013).

Advocating for attachment

In the mid-1970s, the author Jean Liedloff aimed to reintroduce a style of 'traditional' parenting to the 'modern' world (see Bobel, 2002, p. 61, for an account of this). Based on the time Liedloff spent with the Yequana of Venezuela, *The Continuum Concept* method of childcare expounds a 'chain of experience of our species which is suited to the tendencies and expectations which we have evolved' (Liedloff, 1985, pp. 22–23). Babies parented according to the continuum concept mimic those whom Liedloff witnessed in South America – they are held constantly by the mother or another close relative, nursed on demand, and sleep with the parents.

It was not until the 1980s, however, that William and Martha Sears coined the term 'Attachment Parenting' (AP) in *The Baby Book*. Like Leidloff, they argue that 'AP' is:

> [A]n approach to raising children rather than a strict set of rules. Certain practices are common to AP parents; they tend to breastfeed, hold their babies in their arms a lot, and practice positive discipline, but these are just tools for attachment, not criteria for being certified as an attachment parent ... Above all, attachment parenting means opening your mind and heart to the individual needs of your baby and letting your knowledge of your child be your guide to making on-the-spot decisions about what works best for both of you. In a nutshell, AP is learning to read the cues of your baby and responding appropriately to those cues. (Sears and Sears, 2001, p. 2)

Sears and Sears argue that the optimum way of caring for a baby is to keep the mother and child in extended physical contact ('attached'). Drawing on historical arguments they say that this is really just 'common sense' parenting that 'we all would do if left to out own healthy resources' (Sears and Sears, 1993, p. 2). They provide the following 'tools' of attachment parenting (Table E2.1).

In line with the 'attachment' philosophy, which values long-term proximity between caretaker and infant as a means of optimizising

Table E2.1 The tools of AP (Sears and Sears, 2001, p. 4)

The ABC'S of attachment parenting		
When you practice the Baby B's of AP, your child has a greater chance of growing up with the qualities of the A's and C's:		
A's	B's	C's
Accomplished	Birth bonding	Caring
Adaptable	Breastfeeding	Communicative
Adept	Baby-wearing	Compassionate
Admirable	Bedding close to baby	Confident
Affectionate	Belief in baby's cry	Connected
Anchored	Balance and boundaries	Cuddly
Assured	Beware of baby trainers	Curious

child development, typical practices amongst attachment parents include breastfeeding until the child 'outgrows the need' (often for a period of several years); breastfeeding 'on cue' (whenever the child shows an interest); 'bed-sharing' (until the child decides to move to their own bed); and 'baby-wearing' (with the use of a sling or similar).

Today, Attachment Parenting International (API), a non-profit organization founded in the US in 1994, is a global movement, existing to support parents who practice 'AP', with over 19,000 members in 70 cities worldwide (API, 2012). Drawing heavily on the work of Sears and Sears, API's website states:

> API provides parents with research-based information, tools and support that affirms positive, healthy parenting, and helps parents create the kind of legacy that they can be proud to bequeath to their children: family strength, reduced conflict, feelings of love and being loved, trust and confidence. A legacy of love. (API, 2009)

The API's eight principles read:

(1) Prepare for Pregnancy, Birth, and Parenting;
(2) Feed with Love and Respect;
(3) Respond with Sensitivity;
(4) Use Nurturing Touch;
(5) Ensure Safe Sleep, Physically, and Emotionally;
(6) Provide Consistent and Loving Care;
(7) Practice Positive Discipline;
(8) Strive for Balance in Your Personal and Family Life (API, 2009).

Accounting for attachment

Whilst attachment parenting cannot be described as a majority pattern of childcare (in terms of the number of people who practice it), it is clear that this style of parenting is gradually becoming more popular in Anglophone countries around the world (Faircloth *et al.*, 2013), as well becoming ideologically more prominent in the expert literature available to contemporary parents (Gross-Loh, 2007; Jackson, 2003; Sears and Sears, 2001).

It is interesting to consider why this might be Certainly, fashions in parenting are best understood as barometers of wider cultural trends, which, recently, have seen a growing validation of the 'natural' way of doing things in issues as diverse as what we eat, how we learn, and how we treat illness. There is an enduring conviction in this position that 'nature' is a force to be trusted and respected, and with respect to parenting, deference to the 'natural' bond between mother and child (paraphrased from Bobel, 2002, p. 11).

In recent years, this philosophical belief has intersected with the growth of a wider environmentalist consciousness – 'natural' food, 'green' solutions to modern life, and so forth. Moscucci (2003) notes that 'natural' childbirth and parenting as a philosophy has long served as a political and cultural critique aimed at the various crises of modern society – be they industrialization, capitalism, materialism, or urbanization. Klaus and Kennel certainly saw their work as a critique of the contemporary management of the perinatal period (the period around birth) (Kanieski, 2009). The solution to these problems is seen to lie in a return to nature, variously understood as the rural, the primitive, the spiritual, or the instinctive (Moscucci, 2003).

In my own research with attachment parents in the UK and France (Faircloth, 2013), I identified three 'accountability strategies' that mothers would use in rationalizing their choice to be attachment parents. Typically, they would talk about their decision as the 'natural' one: 'evolutionarily appropriate', 'scientifically best', and 'what feels right in their hearts'. (The first two are discussed here; see Faircloth, 2013, for a discussion on the role of instinct and 'affect' and parenting.) As above, each of these was narrated as part of an argument about the importance of mother–child attachment in guarding against the breakdown of wider communal bonds, endemic to 'modern' society.

Evolutionary evidence

In lay terms, the logic behind AP is that women should 'parent' in the way primates and primitive humans did (or do), because our bodies adapted to a specific form of lactation which was evolutionarily advantageous. The biological anthropologist Katherine Dettwyler (a prominent advocate of AP) uses cross-cultural, cross-species, and cross-temporal examples of a range of factors including age of eruption of first molar and length of gestation to come to a blueprint for human weaning, free of 'culture':

> [I]f humans weaned their offspring according to the primate pattern without regard to beliefs and customs, most children would be weaned somewhere between 2.5 and 7 years of age. (Dettwyler, 1995, p. 66)

Certainly the idea that humans have the same body as humans 400,000 years ago is, for many, a way to rationalize 'attachment' parenting, and specifically, 'full-term' breastfeeding. They reason that our physical make-up is primarily the same as those early humans who hunted and gathered for millions of years, because the time that has passed since their emergence is 'only a blip in an evolutionary sense' (Hausman, 2003, p. 128). The environmental conditions under which the early humans lived shaped their physiology and their biosocial practices: danger from predators (meaning a need to have infants close at hand so as to stifle any loud cry, usually by nursing); a lack of appropriate weaning foods (meaning prolonged breastfeeding); and a continuous cycle of pregnancy and lactation for fertile females (during which prolonged lactation, inducing amenorrhoea, helped to space childbirth at optimal intervals for infant survival) (paraphrased from Hausman, 2003, p. 128). As an aside, it is interesting to note that recent research into the age of weaning in prehistoric communities tends to put it at between two and four years old, as opposed to six or seven (Clayton *et al.*, 2006).

The evolutionary perspective presents norms of modern infant care, such as scheduled sleeping and feeding routines, as being out of sync with the biological requirements of human beings. Part of the appeal of attachment mothering is that the model is imitative of infant care practices that follow an ancestral pattern, biologically appropriate to the human species; that is, not only traditional, but *adaptive* in a biological sense. This is a very powerful idea. To quote Hausman:

> The idea that specific, supposedly traditional, mothering practices are really evolutionary adaptations – rather than cultural constructions that emerge at specific historical juncture – is a persuasive rhetoric, delineating natural and unnatural maternal practices within a speculative evolutionary paradigm (Hausman, 2003, p. 125).

Extended breastfeeding, for example, is therefore part of attentive mothering and appropriate to a child's need for emotional and physical support. Child-led weaning is 'natural', whereas mother-led weaning is 'cultural' and therefore not appropriately biological (Hausman, 2003, p. 125).

Scientific evidence

Increasingly, attachment parenting advocates also refer to neuroscientific work to bolster their claims about providing the optimal form of care for children. This is a 'breakthrough', as an article in the AP advocacy publication *Mothering Magazine* puts it, since proponents of attachment theory have, until recently, had little 'unbiased and testable information' with which to back up their claims (Porter, 2003). In the UK, writers such as Gerhardt (*Why Love Matters: How Affection Shapes a Baby's Brain*, 2004) and Sunderland (*The Science of Parenting*, 2006) have drawn on work looking at the interactions between parents and children and how these affect the structure of the infant brain. The argument is that from late pregnancy through the second year of life, the human brain undergoes a critical period of accelerated growth. With the use of MRI scans and other technologies, interaction between the development of the brain and the social environment (nature and nurture) can (arguably) be observed.

Thus, the *Mothering Magazine* article states, citing Schore (2001): 'What has emerged is mounting evidence that stress and trauma impair optimal brain development while healthy attachment promotes it'. It continues, further citing Bowlby (1969) and Spangler *et al.* (1994):

> Babies, we know, cannot survive on their own. All basic needs must be met through a relationship with a caregiver ... In order to maintain emotional equilibrium, babies require a consistent and committed relationship with one caring person. As you might expect, the research indicates that the person best suited for this relationship is the mother. (Porter, 2003)

The claim made is that during the early stages of distress – perhaps at the absence of the mother, as in the Strange Situation test – a baby's heart rate, blood pressure, and respiration will be heightened, to which the brain responds by releasing stress hormones, elevating the brain's levels of adrenalin, noradrenaline, and dopamine (Brown, 1982). Should the distress continue, the infant may go into 'shut-down mode' – a 'survival strategy' allowing the infant to restore homeostasis.

Prolonged periods in this state have damaging effects on the development on the infant brain.

The focus on restoring equilibrium can, according to this argument, permanently alter the chemistry of the brain, to the extent that 'states becomes traits' and the child's personality shaped accordingly; so children who experience stress in early life, it is argued, are more susceptible to mental health disorders in later life. This claim appears to be gathering momentum and influence in recent years. As Jan Macvarish's essay in this book explores, a move towards early intervention based on the same logic is now a key target for policymakers with an interest in social mobility.

Attachment policy

In the UK, this advocacy of attachment is not confined to individual mothers, parenting experts, or even lay support groups, but is increasingly evident in policy, which relies on evolutionary narratives in recommendations of appropriate infant care. Infant sleep is one good example (Ball, 2007). Ball, who advises the English government's Department of Health, advocates the practice of bed-sharing, saying at a conference, for example, that the practice of putting infants to sleep in a separate bed was 'historically novel, culturally circumscribed, developmentally inappropriate, and evolutionarily bizarre' (Ball, 2005). Her argument is that in comparison to other primates, human infants are drastically more neurologically immature at birth due to the play-off between being big-brained and bipedal (which requires birthing through a narrow pelvis). This means that human infants therefore require more intensive care than other primate infants (constant bodily contact to regulate heat, for example). More recently, the Department of Health has endorsed the importance of on-demand breastfeeding and skin-to-skin contact with a similar logic (UNICEF, 2013).

What is also interesting is that many members of groups such as La Leche League (or the National Childbirth Trust, or Attachment Parenting International) now serve in an advisory role to policymakers and government. (An example of this is the *Breastfeeding Manifesto Coalition*, a grouping of diverse organizations who came together in 2006 to counter health inequalities across the UK through the promotion of breastfeeding.[1] So whilst many advocates of attachment claim to be 'marginal' with respect to their parenting philosophies, many of the 'attachment' ideas have quite considerable airtime in mainstream discourse.

Tribalization

In my research, I noted that one of the reasons mothers felt so compelled to 'account' for their decision to 'attachment parent' with reference to nature and science (particularly robust sources of authority in contemporary culture, unlike affect, or 'what feels right') was because of the moralized atmosphere that currently engulfs contemporary parenting culture. Because of the vital importance for the survival and healthy development of infants, feeding is arguably the most conspicuously moralized element of mothering – a highly scrutinized domain in which mothers must counter any charges of practicing unusual, harmful, or morally suspect feeding techniques (Murphy, 2003). In breastfeeding their infants into childhood, these mothers are in a minority (we do not have statistics for those who feed beyond a year, though by six months, over 75 per cent of infants in the UK are weaned from breastmilk entirely, and the number of women who breastfeed beyond toddlerhood is marginal). Thus many of my informants were aware that they were often viewed as 'unusual', even 'sick', or 'abusive' (showing that, for all the cultural concern with detachment, one can be considered 'too attached', albeit in extreme cases). Not surprisingly then, 'judgement' was a commonly cited challenge women mentioned to their full-term breastfeeding.

Logically, then, this culture around feeding (and parenting) leads women to seek out 'evidence' to support their decisions. Yet as we saw in Chapter 1, these mothers are in a bind: they are affirmed because they claim that what they are doing is 'healthiest' (in the nutritional, physiological, or even psychological sense endorsed by the 'breast is best' message), yet they are open to the charge that they are doing something 'risky' with respect to the social and emotional development of their children. The constant bolstering and defence against these charges has the effect of accentuating the differences between different parenting 'camps'.

Sociologists have noted that one of the enduring features of social groups is their 'commitment mechanisms'. To some extent, the women in this sample are already success stories; they are those who have 'persevered' through the often-difficult early stages of breastfeeding. At the same time, they need validation of their continuation of breastfeeding and attachment parenting. A person's commitment to their choice rests, say Kanter, on their knowledge of excluded choices, and a validation of the one they have made. This is a process which intensifies over time:

> A person becomes increasingly committed both as more of his own internal satisfaction becomes dependent on the group, and his chance

to make other choices or pursue other options declines. (Kanter, 1972, p. 70)

Echoing this, these mothers said, in a joint interview:

Lila [37, breastfeeding her four-year-old son]:	And people make out [breastfeeding] is such a long time, and so tedious, and you think … it really is not that long a period, it's just a few years.
Rachel [41, breastfeeding her three-year-old son]:	Their IQ and things, it really makes a difference, and I don't think people are aware of those facts … I think if people knew about it, they would change their attitudes.
Lila:	People are more selfish today. People still have this idea of self-sacrifice with breast-feeding … So they have to promote it in terms of losing weight … this 'me' thing comes through, they have to watch what they eat, can't drink. People have such a drive towards selfishness.
Rachel:	My sister-in-law wanted to go out drink-ing! So she stopped [breastfeeding] at six months!
Lila:	People have such a drive for individuality. They see it as a sacrifice. People don't see that investing now will save time later. It is a fraction of their lives … Other people are too selfish to mother like we do – we are all too much part of the 'me' generation. (Faircloth, 2013, pp. 218–219)

These mothers see attachment parenting as a social movement which can make the world a more harmonious place, with little sympathy for those who have yet to 'see the light'. This, in turn, had the effect of making 'other mothers' feel uncomfortable. One particular woman says, for example, that although she was 'very pro all the natural stuff', and breastfed her children for a year each, she found some members of her local La Leche League (breastfeeding support group, with a significant proportion of AP members) to be 'spoiling for a fight' or 'militant lactivists' (Faircloth, 2013). Yet again, this brings us back to questions around 'identity work' and working patterns: for women who have given up careers to fulfil the attachment parenting philosophy fully might be said to have a greater investment in motherhood as a source of identity work than those who had not.

Assessing the advocacy

It is worth reiterating here that there is no evidence that attachment parenting is harmful, either psychologically or physiologically. Nor, however, is there evidence that parenting in 'normal' (i.e. non-attachment ways) is damaging. What follows is a contextualization of the claims that attachment parenting is positively beneficial. It is also important to note a nominative slippage here: 'attachment' parenting, as a specific way of raising children, has little correlation with the 'attachment' theory of Bowlby: practices such as co-sleeping, breastfeeding, and baby-wearing are not necessarily tied to the development of greater 'attachment' in mother–infant pairs.

First, there are some problems with the secure attachment, or 'Strange Situation' test, when used to defend attachment parenting methods. According to a meta-analysis of studies using the test (van Ijzendoorn and Kroonberg, 1988), 75 per cent of British babies tested in 1988 were securely attached – at a time in Britain when bottle-feeding and separate sleeping were at even higher rates than today. In the 'primitive societies' considered to exhibit ideal parenting by attachment parenting advocates – such as the Gusili mothers in Kenya who wear their babies, breastfeed into toddlerhood, and respond quickly to their babies' crying – only 61 per cent of babies were shown to be securely attached.

This might, of course, say something about the cross-cultural applicability of such a test – though in that case, there is no way of comparing psychological well-being cross-culturally, and little argument that replicating 'primitive' parenting in contemporary Britain is superior to other forms of care. If the test *is* applicable cross-culturally, then there is clearly little correlation between attachment parenting and the rate of securely attached babies. (For critiques of the 'Strange Situation' test, see Burman, 2008; Eyer, 1992; Mainstream Parenting Resources, 2008.)

Furthermore, even though some research has shown that mothers who are sensitive and responsive to their infants' needs are more likely to have 'securely attached' children, the mother–infant dyads studied have not included mothers who show atypically high levels of involvement with their children. It has even been claimed that maternal overprotectiveness shows an association with raised levels of anxiety in children, suggesting that high intensity 'attachment' parenting leads to insecure rather than secure attachment relationships between children and their mothers (McNamara, 2006): however, there is little research on this topic.

Problematizing 'evolutionary' parenting

Typically, in advocacy literature (such as that by Leidloff, or Sears and Sears), contemporary foraging societies are used to represent 'natural' patterns of lactation and care. As stand-ins for earlier hominid hunter-gatherers, statistics concerning length and frequency of lactation are used to demonstrate the ancestral pattern. Local cultural traditions are largely ignored and the !Kung, for example, are treated as passively representative of human biological patterns, existing outside of wider cultural trends and with no culture of their own. The primitive is thus constructed as a site for fantasies of the natural to be played out. That the !Kung wean their children by pasting bitter herbs on to their breasts (Small, 1998, p. 82), or that they use enemas with their infants, both of which would be considered dangerous by attachment parents is overlooked.

Similarly, the popular cross-species blueprint for the time of weaning assumes no interaction between animal and environment. As many primatologists will argue, this is a misrepresentation. Whilst some primates *might* wean their offspring at a very late age where suitable weaning foods do not exist, it is not necessarily the case where resources are more bountiful. Indeed, where weaning foods are readily available, primate behaviour is characterized by decreased length of lactation and active weaning behaviour, to enable the mother to invest her labours in gestating and nurturing other offspring (Wells, 2006).

There exist a set of cultural blinkers, then, in mothers' attempts to emulate natural patterns of lactation. Few women actually want the 'primate' or 'hunter-gatherer' lifestyle of course, where health and mortality are concerns of a different order to contemporary British mothers (Hausman, 2003, p. 147). Rather, they wish to cherry-pick those elements that fit with our sensibilities. To assume that, given the real possibility, !Kung mothers would not use painkillers in childbirth or formula milk for weaning, is to ignore the evidence of numerous other societies. As soon as agriculture made soft weaning foods more available, weaning occurred earlier and babies were spaced more closely together (Blaffer Hrdy, 2000, pp. 201–202; Palmer, 1993). Human adaptation to local environments moves in a steady direction away from !Kung patterns of infant feeding, child care, and fertility, which are extreme because of the harsh conditions they live under. Thus:

> It is one thing, then, for a !Kung mother living where suitable weaning foods do not exist to breastfeed her 4-year-old, and quite a different thing for a woman living in London – and neither of them is more 'natural' than the other. A view of culture as something external to nature presents a dichotomy in which human interaction with, and manipulation of, the environment is considered artificial. Arguably, this adaptation – finding the best fit – is what evolution has always been about. (Faircloth, 2013, p. 130)

Problematizing 'Science'

Furedi (2008b) has remarked that the use of 'Science' as an arbiter of good policymaking is a trend on the increase. This is pertinent to family life, because parenting is not only an exercise in creating scientifically optimal children:

> [T]urning science into an arbiter of policy and behaviour only serves to confuse matters ...Yes, the search for truth requires scientific experimentation and the discovery of new facts; but it also demands answers about the *meaning* of those facts, and those answers can only be clarified through moral, philosophical investigation and debate. (Furedi, 2008b)

This reliance on science is problematic when 'science' becomes a yardstick by which we outline appropriate human interactions. 'Science' has the capacity to flatten out the affective, joyous qualities of the parenting relationship. Maternal love, according to the title of Gerhardt's book, is not only an enjoyable part of the parenting experience, but *also* a tool for optimizing brain development.

Apple (1995) describes the ideology of scientific motherhood as one that designates good mothers as those who are guided by scientific information, subjugating their own perspectives to authoritative experts (Hausman, 2003, p. 3). Similarly, the ideology of intensive motherhood celebrates scientifically informed care (Hays, 1996). Although Apple talks specifically about the almost wholesale shift from breastfeeding to bottle-feeding in twentieth-century America, based on offering a 'scientific, modern' form of feeding, her insights might just as well be applied to this new generation of 'neuroscientific motherhood'. Today, this kind of science – seen as a battle against the 'scientization' of the formula manufacturers Apple describes – has been given the extra twist of 'returning to nature', rather than moving away from it.

Unrealistic attachments

The articulation of 'natural truths' which stress the availability of mothers to children is often in contrast to the actual experiences, and indeed, identities of many mothers today (Buskens, 2001). After Hays, following 'natural' patterns of lactation in the social and economic context of post-industrialized societies creates a 'cultural contradiction' for the women who practice it (Hays, 1996).

Numerous anthropologists and historians have shown how intensive, romanticized caregiving carried out by biological mothers in the private sphere is a result of modern economic and political arrangements (Ariès, 1962; Badinter, 1981; Blaffer Hrdy, 2000; Engels, 1884; Maher, 1992). Yet proponents of 'natural' or 'attachment' parenting seem 'blissfully unaware' (to quote Buskens, 2001, p. 79) of the social differences between a hunter-gatherer society and those of mothers in the contemporary UK or US. The approach eclipses the social surroundings of women – and the presence or otherwise of alloparents, who share the job of parenting.

A gendered split in capitalist society has rendered parenthood an isolated business for many mothers. Early childhood *is* a period of high emotional and physical dependency: this is not just an invention of an 'intensive parenting' culture. As Buskens argues,

> infants do require a long period of intensive, embodied nurture. *The problem is not the fact of this requirement but rather that meeting this need has come to rest exclusively, and in isolation, on the shoulders of biological mothers.* This historically novel situation is precisely what is left unsaid and therefore unproblematized in popular accounts of 'natural' parenting. (Buskens, 2001, p. 81, emphasis in original)

Conclusion

The growing popularity (and cultural presence) of attachment parenting is but one manifestation of a wider cultural concern with parent–child 'detachment'. The central idea – that parenting not only has important implications for a child's development, but also the fabric of society more broadly – clearly resonates with the wider culture of intensive parenting, and specifically, intensive mothering. Yet again, we see how risk consciousness and individualization operate to intersect with contemporary trends in the making of parenting policy.

Yet this project, which portrays motherhood as a means of countering social breakdown, is a deeply ironic one. Ironic, because can pit groups of women *against* each other (those who do it 'right', those who do it 'wrong'). The climate of intensive parenting (of which AP is one particularly voluble permutation) has created a situation where mothers feel less certain of their ability to turn to each other for support in the general business of raising children (Lee and Bristow, 2009). Instead, the 'tribe' that does it 'right' is pushed further inward, away from society, identifying others 'out there' not as partners in a shared endeavour of community building, but as 'feckless', or victims in need of education.

Note

1. The Breastfeeding Manifesto Coalition counts among its members pro-breastfeeding advocacy groups, environmentalist groups, health profession-als' organisations and other NGOs. At the time of writing the membership was listed as Amicus the Union, Association of Breastfeeding Mothers, Baby Feeding Law Group, Baby Milk Action, Best Beginnings, Biological Nurturing, Birthlight, BLISS, Bosom Buddies, Breastfeeding Network, Childfriendly Places, The Community Practitioners' and Health Visitors' Association, Friends of the Earth, Independent Midwives Association, La Leche League Great Britain, Little Angels, The Midwife Information and Resource Service, National Childbirth Trust, National Obesity Forum, Royal College of General Practitioners, Royal College of Midwives, Royal College of Nursing, Save the Children, The Baby Café Charitable Trust, The British Dietetic Association, The Food Commission, The Mother and Infant Research Unit, The Royal College of General Practitioners, The Royal College of Paediatrics and Child Health, The United Kingdom Association for Milk Banking, UNICEF UK, UNISON, WOMB, Women's Environmental Network.

Further reading

Bobel, C. (2002) *The Paradox of Natural Mothering* (Philadelphia: Temple University Press).
This is a useful study, based on research with 'natural mothers' in the US, look-ing at how their style of motherhood intersects with a trend towards 'ecologi-cal living' and 'voluntary simplicity'.

Burman, E. (2008) *Deconstructing Developmental Psychology* (London and New York: Routledge).
Especially Chapter 7, 'Bonds of Love – dilemmas of attachment'. This book is an excellent critique of the psychological literature around attachment, along similar lines to both Bruer and Kagan.

Faircloth, C. (2013) *Militant Lactivism? Attachment Parenting and Intensive Motherhood in the UK and France* (Oxford and New York: Berghahn Books).
Especially Chapters 6–8, on 'Accounting for full-term breastfeeding'. This book profiles my research with attachment mothers in the UK and France, looking at how they 'account' for their choice to be attachment parents as a 'natural' one. This choice might be framed as evolutionarily 'appropriate', scientifically 'optimal', or emotionally 'instinctive'.

Essay 3

Babies' Brains and Parenting Policy: The Insensitive Mother

Jan Macvarish

This essay ...

- Explores how, since the late 1990s, 'brain claims' have entered parenting discourse in the US, Canada, Australia, New Zealand, and the UK.
- Describes how 'brain claims' tend to emphasize the extreme vulnerability of the infant brain to the influence of parents, thereby raising the stakes of parenting and concretizing ideas of parental determinism.
- Discusses how neuroscience has been appropriated by policy advocates to argue for early intervention into parent–child relationships in the name of preventing social problems.

Introduction

The rise of 'brain claims' relating to parenting can be located within a broader culture of 'neuromania' in which the study of the brain is held to offer insights into the meaning of almost all aspects of human behaviour (Legrenzi and Umilta, 2011; Tallis, 2011). Many scholars have drawn attention to the significance of the idea that 'new brain research' provides us with a new way of understanding how to raise children (Furedi, 2001; Hulbert, 2004; Romagnoli and Wall, 2012; Rose, 2010; Rose and Abi-Rached, 2013; Thornton, 2011; Wall, 2004, 2010; Wilson, 2002). As the Canadian academic Glenda Wall argues:

> Throughout the 1990s, claims about the potential of early education and appropriate stimulation to enhance brain capacity in children have gained a new and prominent place in child rearing advice literature and discourse. These changes in the social understandings

of infant and child development have significant implications for mothers, with whom the majority of responsibility for child outcomes is placed. (Wall, 2004, p. 41)

One of the most forthright critics of 'neuromania', Raymond Tallis, stresses the importance of distinguishing between *neuroscience*, which has brought significant insights to our understanding of brain function and dysfunction, and *neuroscientism*, which is an ideological attempt to discover the essence of humanity in the brain (Tallis, 2011, p. 28). This distinction is useful because it allows us to separate the work of scientists within the scientific domain from the activities of those who appropriate the authority of scientific objectivity to pursue moral, political, or commercial agendas in the public sphere. Most of the time, neuroscientists themselves have been notably absent from, and even critical of, brain-based advocacy; however, there is a tendency for some of those conducting research on brain function to speak beyond their scientific findings, to suggest that their research may allow lessons to be learnt for the proper conduct of human relationships (Bruer, 1999).

Optimizing and warning

In cultural and political discourse, the lessons drawn for child-rearing from apparently new neuroscientific discoveries tend to take one of two forms: 'optimizing' or 'warning'. The following article, promoting a public lecture by Canadian psychiatrist Dr Jean Clinton, demonstrates the brain 'optimization' approach, in which neuroscientific knowledge is claimed to underpin new insights into how we might enhance our child's brain capacity by loving and stimulating them in particular ways:

'I'm going to be talking about, it's not the terrible twos, it's the terrific twos, and talking about some of the behaviours that we see in the little ones, and ways of understanding where the behaviour comes from,' Clinton said. 'It's their brain developing and their curiosity and their need to learn.

'Sometimes parents can misinterpret the behaviour as either not doing what they are told or doing things over and over again like dropping keys from the high-chair, and we have to look at that and say "Wow! She's experimenting" rather than, "Oh! She's driving me crazy"'.

'We now know that babies are more like little scientists and are observing us all the time,' said Clinton. 'We now know that we are, quite literally, building the architecture of their brains, and quite literally sculpt what areas will be strong and what areas will be weak' ... 'I don't just talk about the science,' she said. 'I talk about how does this science apply to me as a mom, as a dad and what I can do.' (Roach, 2013)

As we can see from her description of the baby as a 'little scientist', Clinton sees the infant brain as a source of wonder, with babies naturally predisposed to forge connections with caregivers and to experiment with the world around them. This positive-sounding approach lends itself to the marketing of parent-training seminars and books, as well as products such as 'Baby Mozart', 'Baby Einstein', or 'Baby Newton' toys and DVDs, which have been advertised as tools to assist parents in maximizing their child's emotional and cognitive potential. Expert mediators, such as Dr Clinton, are positioned as necessary to educate parents in appropriate ways of interpreting and interacting with their child.

The 'warning' perspective has more pessimistic connotations, expressing anxieties about social disorder and alienated individuals but also constructing particular social groups (usually the poor) as neurologically disadvantaged and behaviourally problematic. The 'warning' outlook predominates in the arguments of those calling for greater policy intervention in the 'early years'. Here it is evident in an interview with Andrea Leadsom, a Conservative Member of the British Parliament, and an eager advocate of brain-based early intervention policies:

'The period from conception to two is about the development of a baby's emotional capacities,' she says. 'Mum saying: "Oh darling, I love you", and singing baby songs and pulling faces literally stimulates the synapses in the brain.'

Citing the example of neglected Romanian orphans whose brain growth was stunted, and research into the impact on babies of the stress hormone cortisol she argues that poor early parenting experiences and weak attachments make it far more likely that there will be a whole range of problems later on.

'If you're left to scream and scream day after day, your levels of cortisol remain high and you develop a slight immunity to your own stress, so what you find is babies who have been neglected tend to become risk-takers,' Leadsom says. 'The worst thing, however, is the parent who is inconsistent – you know: sometimes when I cry my mum hugs me and other times she hits me. That is where the baby develops an antisocial tendency. Kids who go and stab their best mate, or men who go out with a woman and rape and strangle her – these are the kinds of people who would have had very distorted early experiences.' (Rustin, 2012)

In this invocation of brain science, the effects of inappropriate parenting are inscribed in the infant brain, bearing consequences not just for the child and its parents but for society as a whole. Despite the apparently social orientation of the 'warning' perspective, it is ultimately what individual parents do with their children that are seen to create social disadvantage and social problems, with a clear imperative for the state to act to ensure that all parents follow a path proven to be correct by scientific evidence. Similarly, within the apparently more optimistic 'optimization' approach articulated by Clinton, which seems to see babies as possessing an in-built drive to develop, parents are still ultimately held responsible for the way their children mature, for good or bad.

According to Clinton, the brains of babies are 'literally sculpted' by their parents, and so the importance of getting it right could presumably never be underestimated. Importantly, although parents are said to be the most significant influence on their child's development, it is clear from the words of Clinton and Leadsom that they are also assumed to be out of step with their baby's true emotional and cognitive state until they familiarize themselves with the latest scientific explanations for their child's behaviour. In both the 'optimizing' and the 'warning' strands of neuroparenting discourse, then, the feature they hold in common is the dual presumption of parental determinism combined with parental incompetence.

This essay will begin by illustrating the prevalence of brain claims and the form they take in the media and in policy. We will then discuss some of the explanations given for the increasing centrality of neurothinking to parenting culture, before finally exploring some of the ways in which this development has been critiqued.

Brains at risk

As discussed in earlier chapters, a defining feature of contemporary parenting culture is the exponential expansion of apparent risks to the child that a parent is obliged to take account of and avoid. The body and mind of the child is constructed as vulnerable in multiple ways, but of all the infant organs, the brain is constructed as the most absorbent of maternal care and susceptible to maternal misdemeanours. This vulnerability is particularly pronounced in claims about the brains of babies yet to be born. One study of UK newspaper articles reporting on brains and child development found that prenatally, the foetal brain was constructed as vulnerable to a wide variety of risks, primarily through the ingestion of harmful food, drink, or other intoxicants by the mother. Besides the threats to intelligence, the researchers found that:

> Diverse phenomena, ranging from psychiatric disorders and obesity to alcoholism, romantic success and sexual orientation, were presented as direct consequences of prenatal events. Considerable coverage was given to research that suggested that intra-uterine conditions influenced 'naughtiness' in childhood and elevated risk of antisocial behavior in adulthood. (O'Connor and Joffe, 2013, p. 301)

It is not just inappropriate food, drink, and drugs that are said to harm the foetal brain. Maternal stress (often talked of in terms of the hormone cortisol) is also claimed to represent a determining factor in a baby's future. Thus one newspaper article asserted:

> Uptight mums can pass on stress to their unborn babies, experts claimed yesterday. And it could have a major impact on a child's behaviour and brain function in later life. (*Mirror*, 31 May 2007, cited in O'Connor and Joffe, 2013, p. 302)

These examples seem to fit the 'warning' model of brain claims; however, the 'optimization' model is also evident. Mothers in particular, but also fathers, are increasingly told of the benefits of 'bonding' with their baby while it is still *in utero* (see Charlotte Faircloth's previous essay, on 'The Problem of "Attachment"'). This is sometimes advocated in terms of creating a secure and comforting environment, with familiar voices and touch, which will ease the transition of the baby from womb to world; but parents are also encouraged to connect with the developing foetus in order to maximize the intellectual potential of the child in its future life. Pitts-Taylor explains how the foetal brain has even been targeted in order to 'stave off' dementia at the end of life, with mothers recommended to eat diets rich in folates, expose the foetus to classical music, and to devote maternal attention to the 'bump' to ensure optimal brain capacity throughout life (2010, p. 645). Parents are thus required to secure the emotional development of their baby and to optimize their cognitive capacity before it is even born: an example of the tendency to expand 'parenting' backwards, discussed in Ellie Lee's essay on 'Policing Pregnancy'.

Once the child is born, as discussed in earlier chapters, brain claims have also been mobilized to make the case for breastfeeding rather than formula feeding, with the breastfed baby claimed to be both emotionally and cognitively more advanced than the formula-fed baby. 'Attachment parenting', as described in the previous essay, is also increasingly argued for in terms of brain development, with the 'new brain research' promoted as confirmation that 'ancient' maternal practices of extended breastfeeding and continuous physical contact between mother and infant are necessary to safeguard the physical and emotional wellbeing of the infant now and in the future.

The idea that 'love' is a 'tangible resource that has a demonstrable effect on a child's neurobiology' (O'Connor and Joffe, 2013, p. 302) has been popularized in bestselling parenting guides, such as Sue Gerhardt's *Why Love Matters: How affection shapes a baby's brain* (2004). An example of how this claim is articulated is provided by an article from the British *Guardian* newspaper:

> Optimal brain development was promoted when love was demonstrated to the child through regular physical affection and attentiveness. Normal neurobiological development required caregivers who devoted considerable time to engaging the child in meaningful and reciprocal exchanges. Depriving young children of cuddles and attention subtly changes how their brains develop and in later life can leave them anxious and poor at forming relationships, according to a study published today. (*Guardian*, 22 November 2005, cited in O'Connor and Joffe, 2013, p. 302)

Besides the media appetite for exaggerated neuroscientific claims emanating from university laboratories, and the promotion of particular neuroparenting styles in books, on the internet, and through parent-training courses, manufacturers have also employed brain claims to sell products to parents. These include special 'belly' earphones to play stimulating or soothing music to the foetus, DVDs designed to stimulate babies with images and music, and toys developed with neuroknowledge in mind.

Interestingly, there has sometimes been a tension between the imperative to optimize intellectual capacity and the need to nurture a child's emotional resilience. The Baby Mozart range of DVDs and toys was part of the Disney Corporation's 'Baby Einstein' brand, and the company initially claimed that such items could produce smarter babies. However, in 2006, a US campaign forced the company to drop the word 'educational' from its Baby Einstein marketing and the company was made to refund parents who, it was decided, had been falsely led to believe that the products would enhance brain development (Pitts-Taylor, 2010, p. 649). Thornton (2011, p. 403) argues that this signified a backlash against the commercialization of brain science and a competitive parenting culture in which parents are persuaded to spend money on raising their child's IQ. However, the campaign against Baby Einstein made use of brain claims to argue that watching DVDs is actually harmful to babies, because 'research shows' that excessive 'screen-time' can inhibit linguistic development (Park, 2007).

Baby Einstein continues as a brand, but is now marketed as producing happier babies rather than smarter babies. Other products designed to enable foetuses to 'listen' to music tend to promote the 'bonding' effect of mother and baby listening to music together and only cautiously refer to making smarter babies. Thus we see the attempt to resolve the tension between emotions and intellect, with the idea that the emotions provide the foundation of cognitive development (Thornton, 2011).

Brain claims and policy

The increasingly central position of parenting in political discourse discussed in Chapter 3 has also been motivated using the language and legitimacy of neuroscience. Hulbert identifies 'the beginnings of a deferral by policy-makers to neuroscience' in a report by the US Carnegie Corporation in 1994. This report, titled *Starting Points: Meeting the Needs of Our Youngest Children*, began its discussion of a 'quiet crisis' caused by family change and persistent poverty in dramatic terms:

> Our nation's children under the age of three and their families are in trouble, and their plight worsens every day. (Carnegie Corporation, 1994, p. 1)

According to Hulbert (2004), although Americans had become 'habituated' to outcries about imperilled children, the attention-grabbing claim of *Starting Points* was not its doom-laden call to arms but its 'perfectly pitched' claims that a new neuroscientific evidence base existed, proving that the 'quiet crisis' was caused by the child's 'environment' in the earliest years of life (Hulbert, 2004, p. 311). Of course, when it comes to very young infants, and in particular to foetuses, 'the environment' is not communities or society, but their parents, or more particularly, their mothers. So while the focus appears to be on deprived areas and poor neighbourhoods, in fact, the object of attention is the womb and the home. *Starting Points* went on to set out the case for taking heed of the 'new brain research':

> With the help of powerful new research tools, including sophisticated brain scans, scientists have studied the developing brain in greater detail than ever before. This research points to five key findings that should inform our nation's efforts to provide our youngest children with a healthy start:
>
> - First, the brain development that takes place during the prenatal period and in the first year of life is more rapid and extensive than we previously realized.
> - Second, brain development is much more vulnerable to environmental influence than we ever suspected.
> - Third, the influence of early environment on brain development is long lasting.
> - Fourth, the environment affects not only the number of brain cells and number of connections among them, but also the way these connections are 'wired'.
> - And fifth, we have new scientific evidence for the negative impact of early stress on brain function. (Carnegie Corporation, 1994, p. 3)

The claims of *Starting Points* were popularized by the 'I am your child' campaign, set up in 1997 by American actor and film director Rob Reiner, with the aim of helping to:

> [R]aise public awareness about the critical importance the prenatal period through the first early years plays in a child's healthy brain development. (Parents' Action for Children, 2013)

The 'I am your child' campaign was incredibly influential. Its activities included producing and disseminating the video 'The First Years Last Forever', corralling celebrity support, and taking the argument for brain-based childcare approaches into policymaking at the highest level. Reiner's conviction that brain science created a new imperative for the provision of early years education and parenting support initiatives was shared by President Bill Clinton and First Lady Hillary Clinton, who in April 1997 hosted the conference 'Early childhood development and learning: What new research on the brain tells us about our youngest children' (Bruer, 1999).

Rob Reiner and the Clintons were not, of course, neuroscientists; and as Bruer points out, a significant feature of the 'brain message' is that it has not been disseminated by scientists but by child welfare advocates. In fact, both Hulbert and Bruer note that at the 1997 White House Conference, the experts present, Dr Carla Shatz, a neurobiologist, and Dr Patricia Kuhl, a psychologist, made far more modest claims than the campaigners organizing around the apparently new claims from brain science. Hulbert suggests that the enthusiasm for brain claims in policy circles and the media was out of step with the fact that neuroscientific claims were being 'stretched to the limit':

> Along with most of the media, Reiner failed to note the fact that no such radically new evidence of neural vulnerability actually existed. It was an admission that the Carnegie report made in passing: 'Researchers say that neurobiologists using brain scan technologies are on the verge of confirming these findings.' In truth, they were nowhere near demonstrating that the 'cognitive deficits' measured in toddlers growing up in poverty reflected irreversible neurological damage caused by under-stimulation and stress during the first three years. Nor had their studies proved that 'enriched' environments in babyhood are responsible for the long-term social, emotional, and cognitive success of many who have the luck to start out in them. (Hulbert, 2004, p. 311)

Despite this, the brain claims made in the US by *Starting Points* in 1994 are startlingly similar to those made by early intervention advocates in other countries and in subsequent decades. As Wall describes, the 'I am your child' campaign was heavily promoted by the Canadian Institute of Child Health (Wall, 2004, p. 42). Back in 2002, Wilson reported the incorporation of the same brain claims into family policy in New Zealand (Wilson, 2002). The persistence of such claims suggests that the idea that a neuroscientific revolution has brought about a new rationale for tackling social deprivation has served an important purpose in reinvigorating demands for resources but also in reconceptualizing the nature of social problems such as poverty and inequality.

In the UK, the argument that focusing on babies' brain development is the only way to prevent a multiplicity of social problems, from unemployment, lack of social mobility, and educational underachievement to crime, violence, and antisocial behavior, has strengthened since its emergence in the mid-2000s (Cabinet Office, 2006; DfES, 2007). Brain claims have become a notable feature of family policy since the election of the Conservative–Liberal Democrat Coalition government in 2010 (Wastell and White, 2012), and brain-based training programmes for professionals are now being rolled out nationally in health, social care, and education services. The repetition of claims echoing the Carnegie Report is evident in Labour MP Graham Allen's 2011 report, *Early Intervention: The Next Steps*:

> The early years are far and away the greatest period of growth in the human brain. It has been estimated that the connections or synapses in a baby's brain grow 20-fold, from having perhaps 10 trillion at birth to 200 trillion at age 3 ... The early years are a very sensitive period ... after which the basic architecture is formed for life ... it is not impossible for the brain to develop later, but it becomes significantly harder, particularly in terms of emotional capabilities, which are largely set in the first 18 months of life. (Allen, 2011a, p. 6)

Politicians who advocate brain-based strategies argue that if individuals with fully functioning brains are created from conception, state services will not have to cope with the consequences and costs of poverty 'upstream' in future years (Allen, 2011a, 2011b; Allen and Duncan Smith, 2008, 2009). This argument has been made with increasing intensity in government-commissioned reports, such as the one pictured below (Figure E3.1):

In reports such as these, poverty and social disorder are attributed to individual emotional and cognitive dysfunction, 'written into' the brain in the earliest years of life by inadequate parenting. This approach is prominent in the UK's Nurse Family Partnership programme (adapted from the US Family Nurse Partnership scheme) described in Chapter 3, which claims to 'break the cycle' of dysfunctional behaviour presumed to be evident in, and transmitted intergenerationally by, those who have babies in their teens.

Accounting for the appetite for brain claims

We will now turn our attention to some attempts to explain the appeal of brain claims to parents, policymakers, and practitioners, before moving on to discuss the critiques which have emerged in response to these

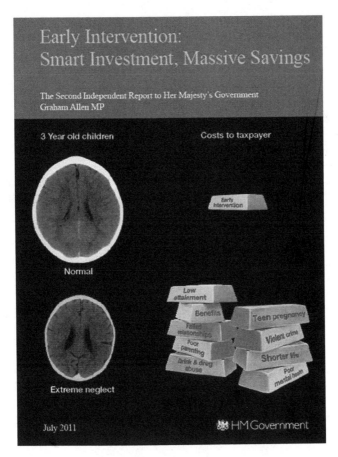

Figure E3.1 Front cover of the official report, Early Intervention: Smart investment, massive savings (Allen, 2011b)

developments. Kagan (1998) argues that the appeal of brain claims resides in the prior cultural tendency towards 'infant determinism' in which the early years are said to determine adult lives. Yaqub (2002) observes that the scientific vocabulary endows pre-existing common-sense ideas of infant determinism with renewed authority. Although Wall (2010) and O'Connor and Joffe (2012) trace societal concern about the impact of early experiences on later development to the popular-ization of psychoanalysis and attachment theory in the early and mid-twentieth century (see previous essay), they suggest that the expansion of the influence of brain research has become an 'important reference point in child-rearing decisions' used to 'indicate the "correctness" of parenting practices' (O'Connor and Joffe, 2012, p. 221). While the use of a neuroscientific vocabulary of synapses, neurons, and cortisol appears to bring scientific advancements to bear on parenting, the recommendations derived from it tend to chime with existing common-sense ideas about what constitutes good parenting, indicating that shifting cultural norms shape the kinds of scientific 'truths' on which claims about correct parenting are made (Thompson and Nelson, 2001, p. 5; Wilson, 2002, p. 96).

The dual construction of the brain as both wondrous and vulnerable, as susceptible to both optimization and damage, lends brain discourse a potentially universal appeal. While attending baby-signing classes, playing Mozart to a foetus via specially purchased 'belly' speakers, or committing to extended breastfeeding may appeal only to a particular kind of mother keen to optimize her child's life-chances, other parents may be subject to targeted attempts by state agencies to persuade (or compel) them to engage with professionals in parent-training programmes in the name of safeguarding their child's development.

'Five to Thrive' is an attempt by UK brain advocates to make attachment ideas accessible to all parents and to educate them in brain-based understandings of child development (Kate Cairns Associates, 2012). Based on the 'Five-A-Day' public health campaign to promote the consumption of fruit and vegetables, the recommended parental priorities promoted by the 'Five to Thrive' campaign are 'Talk, Play, Cuddle, Relax and Respond'. Those who designed the campaign for policymakers were particularly sensitive to the need to reinforce what parents already do, rather than to alienate them from state services by being seen to preach novel techniques from on high. We can see here that by rooting official parenting guidance in brain-based claims and delivering it through child health professionals, the advice gains the legitimacy of being objectively health based, rather being perceived as promoting a particular moral agenda.

The critique of brain claims

We have already established that brain claims have most often been promoted by individuals and organizations which are not themselves rooted in neuroscience (Bruer, 1999; Hulbert, 2004). A critique therefore emerged soon after the launch of 'I am your child' which explored the disjuncture between brain claims and actual brain science. Most influential have been John T. Bruer's book, *The Myth of the First Three Years* (1999), his other articles (1997, 1998a, 1998b), and Jerome Kagan's essay 'The Allure of Infant Determinism' (1998). Many scholars have since made use of these works to challenge the most prevalent brain claims underpinning the argument that new brain research provides proof that a child's experience in the early years is determinate of its future outcomes.

The fact that the growing critique has remained unacknowledged by those advocating brain-based early intervention indicates that such initiatives are motivated, not by the scientific pursuit of truth, but by non-scientific, ostensibly well-meaning, agendas of social reform of the kind discussed at length in Chapter 3 of this book. Here, we briefly review the specific ways in which brain claims have been challenged in their own terms and by those concerned about the consequences of such claims for ways of understanding social problems and for parent–child relationships.

1. *Scientism not science*

As we suggested at the beginning of this essay, a useful way of understanding the influence of claims about the infant brain, despite their contested scientific validity, is to draw a distinction between *science* and *scientism*. Here it is useful to outline Bruer's specific critique of the most influential brain claims, before we look at some other challenges to the apparently scientific claims of the early intervention advocates.

a. *'Developmental synaptogenesis' or a synaptic explosion in the early years.* This finding is often interpreted as meaning that the early years represent a 'use it or lose it' opportunity to shape infant brains. However, Bruer argues that more synapses do not equate to more brain power: in fact, increased dendritic density occurs at any age, and only certain areas of the brain show increased density in the early years.

b. *The years 0–3 represent a 'critical' or 'sensitive' period in brain development.* This claim tends to be based on experiments concerning the visual development of kittens and studies of severely deprived Romanian orphans. The conclusion is drawn that if the right kinds of conditions are not experienced at the right time, particular aspects of brain development will never be possible. Bruer argues that critical periods are the exception, not the norm, in human brain development. While there seems to be evidence that language acquisition is particularly rooted in the early years, this is atypical of other aspects of development.

c. *Enriched environments are necessary to stimulate infant brain development.* Bruer takes up this claim in a number of ways. He argues that invalid inferences are made from animal experiments (usually in rats), noting that, for ethical reasons, very little research is possible on children. Those children who have been studied tend to have existing brain disorders or have been raised in very extreme conditions. In the case of the latter, evidence from studies of severely deprived children shows that normal development can occur after deprivation ends.

A review, by psychologists Thompson and Nelson (2001), of media coverage of early brain development, concludes that the media tend to exaggerate the extent of knowledge about the developing brain, inflate the importance of the first three years by not acknowledging the life-long nature of brain development, and overemphasize the developmental significance of parental care relative to other influences. Besides the misuse of brain science to overstate infant and parental determinism, those who use brain claims to strengthen their arguments have also been criticized for taking a cavalier approach to the evidence they invoke, suggesting that the mantle of science is adopted to add neutral authority without a sincere engagement with scientific method (Maxwell and Racine, 2012; Wastell and White, 2012).

The disjuncture between neuroscience itself and the way in which neuroscience is appropriated by others to legitimize particular causes or ways of thinking can be seen in the way the brain is conceptualized. When scientists describe the brain as 'plastic' and 'resilient' they mean that it is not determined from conception or birth by genetics nor is it inevitably shaped down particular routes or particular experiences. Psychologist Professor Michael Rutter, who conducted some of the most famous studies of the impact of severe neglect on child development with Romanian orphans, argues that even in extreme cases of trauma or neglect:

> The ill effects of early traumata are by no means inevitable or irrevocable ... the evidence runs strongly counter to views that early experiences irrevocably change personal development. (Cited in Kagan, 1998, p. 112)

Even Professor Bruce Perry, whose image of two contrasting brains, one 'normal' and the other 'neglected', has become ubiquitous in brain-advocacy literature (to the point that it was used on the cover page of the UK government report shown in Figure E3.1, above), says that 'the majority of individuals who are emotionally neglected in childhood do not grow into violent individuals' (Perry, 1997, p. 133, cited in Wilson, 2002, p. 195). Indeed, products such as Baby Einstein DVDs coexist in a marketplace for 'brain-training' products selling the promise of enhanced cognition *throughout* the lifecourse, or the prevention or delaying of the onset of dementia by cognitive interventions. And yet, in much of the popular and policy extrapolation of brain science to childhood, 'plasticity' tends to be talked of as being limited to the very early years of a child's life and, even more importantly, tends to be equated not with resilience but with vulnerability: it is *because* the infant brain is extremely adaptable that it is inherently 'at risk' from its environment.

What we can see here is a wilful misinterpretation of scientific evidence by those seeking to don the garb of scientific authority to make their arguments, based on a prior disillusionment with the capacity of families to provide adequate love, care, and guidance to children. The persistence of deterministic ideas despite evidence to the contrary, indicates that the ideology of infant and parent determinism is prior to, and stronger, than, actual evidence emanating from the scientific domain. As Furedi puts it, this is 'prejudice masquerading as research' (Furedi, 2008a, p. 163).

2. *Individualizing social problems*

As we discussed in Chapter 3, a corollary to the politicization of parenting is the individualization of social problems. A strong theme in the critique of neuroparenting is the resonance between the belief in parental determinism and what is described as the ideology of neo-liberalism. Wall describes neo-liberalism as placing greater emphasis on 'the ability of individuals to adapt to change, to engage in self-enhancing behaviour, and to manage the risk they pose to themselves and thus reduce their potential burden on society' (Wall, 2004, p. 46). Others have also associated the arguments for brain-based early intervention with a desire to cut welfare spending and to 'responsibilize' the raising of children solely to parents, in particular mothers (Gillies, 2013). This concurs with Wall's assessment that:

> The focus on educating parents fits well with a model of individual responsibility and privatized parenting. It does not require

governments to re-invest in the welfare state and design policy to alleviate poverty, provide affordable housing and child care services, and improve employment practices. (Wall, 2004, p. 47)

However, it is clearly not the case that families are being 'responsibil-ized' to the extent that they are left to their own devices in the way they raise their children. Chapter 3 outlined how the state currently seeks to become more intimately involved in shaping parental behavior than ever. Wall acknowledges that 'while governments may not be prepared to invest socially in families with children, they are prepared to increase scrutiny and control in an effort to ensure that parents fulfill their individual responsibilities' (Wall, 2004, p. 47). More recently, Wastell and White conclude that neuromania is 'the latest of modernity's jug-gernauts reifying human relations into "technical objects" to be fixed by the State' (Wastell and White, 2012, p. 399).

Policies enacted by the state to ensure 'correct' child-rearing have clear moral and political underpinnings and ramifications, and yet recourse to the biological serves to obscure what should be a highly controversial agenda and shuts down debate with the claim that 'the evidence says' or 'research shows'. As Bruer writes: 'The findings of the new brain science have become accepted facts, no longer in need of explanation or justification' (Bruer, 1999, p. 61), but more than this, such claims 'float free' of particular experts, theories, or interest groups by gaining the authority of nature in the form of the biological organ of the brain.

In 'The Allure of Infant Determinism', Kagan argues that brain claims serve to avoid moralizing parental behaviour and therefore divert atten-tion from the absence of consensus about what is right and wrong in family life, or about the role of the state. The problem represented by dif-ferential child 'outcomes' is therefore redefined as one of knowledge and expertise, not right or wrong behaviour. The solution is for parents to commit to improving their knowledge and skills by engaging with expert knowledge to improve the outcomes for their children. Kagan character-izes this construct thus: '... poor mothers love their children, but do not know the basic facts of human development' (Kagan, 1998, p. 90).

3. *Writing children off*

An additional effect of brain claims on thinking about social inequal-ity and other social problems is to consolidate a profoundly pessimistic view of children's potential. If the years 0–3, or even 0–2, are indeed the most important in a person's life, then there is no scope for the older individual to transform themselves or for society to help in the later amelioration of disadvantages. As Hulbert draws out, despite the intentions of the US brain advocates such as Rob Reiner to make a case for public funding of programmes to help children, the consequences of the way brain science has been used has been a profound fatalism.

> If young brains subjected to deprived conditions, and to the inadequate parenting that often goes along with them, are irrevocably damaged – pickled in stress hormones, stripped of synapses – there is no time to waste, that is true. Yet such alarm, though it conveys urgency, can all too easily fuel defeatism. If children become neurologically unresilient at an early age, then only intrusive and intensive remedial efforts seem equal to the job. And if – or, let's face it, when – such intervention fails to materialize, the case for subsequent help is bound to seem weaker. (Hulbert, 2004, p. 316)

However, it is equally important that this fatalism is not absolute – it takes a negative form only if parents fail in their duties to nurture and stimulate the child. The idea of a critical period for development between conception and three years of age, while reducing any sense of a child's agency to a remarkably short time frame, actually creates an imperative for the parent to exercise a huge amount of agency in doing the right thing for their child. Despite this apparently de-moralized framework, brain claims not only shut down any discussion about different ways of raising children but they also promise to make parental love directly measurable in the behavior of their offspring.

In this way, parental love becomes literally embodied in the child's brain, evident in the child's happiness and achievements and theoretically 'readable' through the technology of the brain scan. Parents are held to account for an impossibly burdensome range of decisions by an apparently objective locus of authority – the brain – and their actions and feelings are opened up to public evaluation.

According to Nadesan, brain science, as popularized in the US, functions as a 'tool of social engineering for the poor' while it also 'exacerbates aspiring middle-class parents' anxiety by holding them accountable for each and every state of their infant's "development"' (Nadesan, 2002, p. 424). If nurturing their child's neural development is the most important job in the world, it must be too important to be trusted to parents themselves, who, after all, are not experts in neuroscience. At the most extreme end of 'early intervention' in the name of

protecting infant brains, scholars are raising concerns with the strengthening rationale for the state to remove children from their birth parents
on preventative grounds. In that case, the argument is made that we
can now identify which babies are at risk of neglect prior to any neglect
actually occurring, and that therefore such children should be removed
and adopted by other, more suitable parents at the earliest opportunity,
to prevent damage being inflicted on their brains by inadequate care in
the early months of life (Featherstone *et al.*, 2013).

Conclusion: reinforcing intensive parenting

The instructions issued to parents on the authority of neuroscience are
familiar to us from a broader understanding of the culture of intensive
parenting. According to this orthodoxy, parents must be attentive, available, responsive, cheerful, free of stress, sensitive, and warm. In the quest
to avoid below par neurological development (whether with cognitive or
emotional consequences), parents are exhorted to play with their children,
to limit time spent watching television, to read bedtime stories, to avoid
shouting, never to leave babies to cry or to let them sleep unattended.

Although we cannot yet be sure how individual parents interpret, act
on, or reject this way of thinking, Lupton's interviews with Australian
mothers indicate that the demand to be attentive to their child's brain
has permeated parental consciousness: amongst their descriptions of
what they see as their roles as mothers, they speak of the importance
of 'stimulation' to optimise intellectual and physical development
(Lupton, 2011, p. 646).

For parents, the primary imperative constructed from brain claims is
that they (mothers in particular) should pay extremely close attention
to potential risks to their baby's neurological development and do as
much as possible to stimulate the growth of the child's brain by their
interactions with the baby (Thornton, 2011). In this respect, the 'new
science' is likely to form an additional layer to the existing culture of
intensive parenting rather than independently revolutionise the way
parents think about their role. As Wall suggests:

> The focus in child rearing advice on brain development thus
> increases pressure to conform to a model of intensive parenting. It
> is now not only children's emotional and psychological well-being
> that are at stake if parents neglect to spend adequate time with their
> children, but also their full potential in terms of brain development.
> (Wall, 2004, p. 45)

Brain claims promise to concretize in the form of the brain, the idea that what parents do has lifelong consequences for their child, which can presumably only further add to the extent to which 'parenting [is] turned into an ordeal' (Furedi, 2008, pp. 89–99).

Looking at the implications of the expansion of brain claims for the meaning and experience of the parent–child relationship, we can see that Hays' components of intensive motherhood (Hays, 1996, p. 8) are each strengthened by the imperative to focus parental efforts on the appropriate development of their child's brain. The focus on nurturing the foetal brain and developing extremely 'attached' and 'attuned' parenting skills in the early months and years can only further intensify the responsibilization of mothers for the care of children. The demands on women's time, labour, and emotions by the need for constant love and nurture are rendered even less negotiable by the threat of long-term, biologically rooted damage to their children's brains.

Further reading

Bruer, J. T. (1999) *The Myth of the First Three Years: A new understanding of early brain development and lifelong learning* (New York: The Free Press).
This unique book was a passionate early response to brain-based advocacy in the US, and is cited in much of the literature critical of the appropriation of neuroscience by policymakers. It offers a convincing summary and critique of the most prevalent 'neuromyths' and provides an invaluable history of the entry of brain claims into US policymaking.

Kagan, J. (1998) Chapter 2 – 'The allure of infant determinism', in J. Kagan (ed.) *Three Seductive Ideas* (Cambridge, MA: Harvard University Press).
Kagan's influential essay draws out the connections between neuroparenting claims and the prior development of attachment theory. In a richly humanistic piece of work, brain claims are contextualized within a longer history of the appeal of deterministic ideas of infant development.

O' Connor, C. and Joffe, H. (2013) 'Media representations of early human development: protecting, feeding and loving the developing brain', *Social Science and Medicine*, 97, 297–306, http://dx.doi.org/10.1016/j.socscimed.2012.09.048.
This article reports on a remarkably comprehensive review of UK media coverage of brain-based explanations of child development between 2000 and 2010. Reflecting on the critical literature of neuroparenting, the authors identify the wide range of claims made about how parental behavior impacts on infant brains and discusses the normative implications of such arguments.

Essay 4

Intensive Fatherhood?
The (Un)involved Dad

Charlotte Faircloth

This essay ...

- Reviews the discussion about fathers in contemporary parenting culture, suggesting that the model of 'intensive mothering' is being extended to men.
- Argues that men provide a useful case study in the 'expertise' culture around parenting, because they are not considered to have a 'natural' foundation for parenting.
- Draws on earlier work around risk consciousness and authority, to look at how traditional ideas of paternity are being increasingly 'fragmented'.
- Explores the gap between model of the 'new father' promoted by experts and policymakers, and the experiences of fathers themselves.

Introduction: new fatherhood?

Children with positively involved dads tend to do better than those without: they make friends more easily, are better at understanding how other people feel, fit in better at school and have fewer behaviour problems ... The 'good father effect' can last right through to the teenage years (less risky use of drugs and alcohol, less likely to get pregnant young or get into trouble with the police) and even into middle-age (more contented love lives, better mental health). (Fatherhood Institute, 2010)

It's normal for you and your partner to have a lot of questions during pregnancy, especially if it's the first time. And it's natural for you to be worried about some things. There's a wide range of different information and advice to take in. A new baby can mean a lot of change, so talk through your concerns and make decisions together, if you can. You can get more information and advice at antenatal or parenthood classes, which are usually offered by hospitals. You could try joining a parenting or fathers' group or asking your partner's midwife. There are also many online forums and some are dad-specific. Or you could try joining or setting up a dads' group like the one in the film, *What To Expect When You're Expecting*. That way you'll get to benefit from others' experiences. (Start for Life, 2013)

Much of this book has centred on women's experiences of parenting culture, exploring, in particular, a trend towards the de-authorization of the mother. As chapters 1 and 2 showed, where motherhood has become 'intensive', it has also become expert-driven, having a profound effect on women's subjectivity (and confidence) as parents.

It is important to recognize that the process of de-authorizing the mother has not led to an endorsement of paternal authority in its place. Rather, we see that existing precepts about what is wrong with mothers – as critical yet incompetent, risky, and in need of support – are recycled and applied to fathers (however they might be defined[1]). In the extracts above, Start for Life, a UK government health promotion programme, and the Fatherhood Institute, an organization that works closely with government to generate resources for fathers, present the 'ideal father' as one who demonstrates the wider model of 'intensive' parenting: 'involved', properly schooled in the right 'parenting skills', and willing to 'seek support'. The Start for Life extract indicates the extent to which today's ideal father is not one who works things out for himself, in accordance with experience: he is one who absorbs official information and watches a film to learn how to interact with other dads.

This essay explores the extension of already established precepts of 'good parenting' to men, highlighting the 'gap' between the 'ideal' model and men's actual experiences of fathering. In doing so, it draws on and expands many of the points made in Chapter 2 around parental authority. Men provide a particularly useful case study in our exploration of these issues, because they are not thought to have the 'natural' foundation for fathering that women do for mothering. They are therefore considered in need of additional training to enable good parenting, for even the most everyday interactions. For example, one recent leaflet for dads provides guidance on the importance of 'warm-hugs' for children (GOSH, 2011).

In some ways, this process echoes the way that policymakers have approached the issue of 'teenage parenthood' in recent years (Macvarish, 2010a, 2010b). As Macvarish explains, policymakers hold up teenage parents as archetypes of the parenting problem, because they:

> [A]ffirm the idea that parenting is impossibly difficult for everybody, that it is to be expected that parents will sometimes act like children, and that raising children is a task that most ordinary adults require external support and expertise to perform adequately. (Macvarish, 2010a, para 5.1)

Both fathers and teenagers allegedly lack the natural instinct of (age-appropriate) mothers, and this is considered to justify an overt policy emphasis on the need for training. The teenage mother and the 'new father' therefore provide some of the clearest crystallizations of how norms around contemporary parenting culture displace the idea that parenting is instinctual or common sense.

Ambiguous authority

Whilst today's fathers are no doubt more monitored and scrutinized than generations past, it would be too simplistic to imply that that there was a golden age of paternalistic authority, where fathers were simply trusted to do the right thing with their children. History tells a different story. Whilst the emphasis of historical accounts of childrearing has largely been on mothers, what accounts we do have show that what fathers do with their children has continually been called into question.

Going back to early modern Europe, for example, we see that fathers were considered more important than mothers in the caring, raising, and education of children, including overseeing wet-nursing and feeding of infants, and taking primary responsibility for children's moral and religious instruction (Lupton and Barclay, 1997, p. 37). This was underpinned by

> [A]ssumptions about the rationality of men, their representing culture rather than nature and their ability to bestow order, whilst women were conceptualized as little more than the passive vessels in which children grew. Fathers were believed to be superior to mothers in providing such guidance because of their greater reason and their ability to control their emotions (Lupton and Barclay, 1997, p. 37).

Until the early decades of the eighteenth century, it was fathers who were considered the 'natural parent'. (Gillis, 1995, pp. 6–7)

However this did not exclude fathers from expert proscriptions. If anything, they were just as subject to guidance and expertise. The philosopher John Stuart Mill, for example, linked his call for the compulsory schooling of children to his distrust of parental (paternal) competence, believing that state-sponsored education would free children from the 'uncultivated' influences of their parents (Furedi, 2009a, p. 90). So as Lupton and Barclay make clear, the popular idea that fathers were either 'authoritarian' or 'absent' (either physically or emotionally) in the past is also something of a myth. For instance, whilst in Edwardian and Victorian Britain the upper-class father might have been regarded as 'remote', and may often have been absent on business, there is also evidence that such fathers were benevolent and affectionate toward their children (Lupton and Barclay, 1997, p. 15).

What is true, however, is that the model of fatherhood started to shift in the eighteenth century, when industrialization and urbanization created a watershed in gender relations. By the mid-nineteenth century, many fathers were away from the home for much of the day, undertaking paid work. As Lupton and Barclay explain, '[p]arenthood, including the close supervision and rearing of young children gradually became the province of mothers rather than fathers' (Lupton and Barclay, 1997, p. 38). And as we detail in Chapter 2 of this book, this was coupled with a growth in expert prescriptions around children's health and development, with mothers being encouraged to monitor their own activities in line with this advice.

The psychologization of motherhood and infant development, notably Bowlby's work on 'maternal deprivation' (discussed in Chapter 1 and in my essay on 'The Problem of "Attachment"') bolstered claims that men and women had different, but complementary, roles within the family, as well as society more broadly. The functionalist sociologist Talcott Parsons, for example, argued that whilst women performed the 'expressive or emotive function in caring for her children, the father performed a primarily instrumental function, in terms of engaging in paid work to support the family' (Lupton and Barclay, 1997, p. 53).

But whilst they were less intensively targeted than those which positioned women as mothers, men were not ignored by these expert discourses. Indeed, as Lupton and Barclay explain:

In the context of the spread of 'expert' knowledges on childrearing in western countries throughout the late nineteenth and twentieth centuries, both fathers and mothers have been portrayed as requiring professional assistance to carry out their parenting role, and as possibly neglectful if they fail to do so. (Lupton and Barclay, 1997, p. 41)

In more recent years, the psychoanalytic research into motherhood has been mirrored by a growing amount of research into the psychological dimensions of fatherhood. This has emphasized the psychological benefits for infants of a strong paternal attachment or 'bond' in particular. At some level 'new fatherhood' is modelled on the psychologized 'new motherhood', to the extent that there is presently a growing sensibility about the problem of male 'postnatal depression' (Lee, 2010; Burman, 2008).

Fragmenting fatherhood: breadwinning and the new dad

The relationship between fathers and their children has rarely (if ever) been considered a straightforward or common-sense one. What is clear in the accounts, however, is that insofar as there *was* a solidity around the role of fathers over the past few centuries, it was one concerned with breadwinning:

> Post-war debates about the level, structure and distribution of wages, taxes and welfare benefits reflected the idea that men and women had different primary commitments towards their families. Sociological research ... broadly reflected the extent to which these divisions had become embedded in household economies and prevailing cultural norms. (Collier and Sheldon, 2008, p. 109)

In this sense, long-standing concepts such as the 'family wage' or even more recently, 'child support', are manifestations of the idea that paid employment has 'a central part to play in the maintenance of a secure and stable masculine identity across many areas of law, with assumptions about a father's primary commitment to his work seen as largely, if not entirely, precluding his extensive participation within both childcare and domestic labour' (Collier and Sheldon, 2008, p. 110).

However, with women's wholesale entry into the workforce in the past 50 years, the traditional division of labour in the household has begun to alter – itself accompanied by debate over the 'crisis of masculinity' (see for a recent take, Roisin's *The End of Men*, 2013). By the 1990s, in line with a blossoming post-structuralist academic interest in masculinity, queer theory, and sexuality, discussion about fatherhood in academic, popular and policy spheres has largely been part of wider discussions around creating the 'new man' (see Connell,1995, for an overview).

Certainly, the model of the 'new father' today is one who has left the 'remote disciplinarian and breadwinner' model of the past behind to adopt a more 'emotionally involved' stance. This has been called the shift from 'cash to care' (Hobson and Morgan, 2002):

> [There has been a move] towards an increased expectation that men will be 'engaged', 'hands-on' fathers, parents who will 'be there' for their children ... Encapsulated in the idea of 'new fatherhood', contemporary fathers are now widely expected to have, and to desire, a closer, more emotionally involved and nurturing relationship to their children ... British fathers are now expected to be accessible and nurturing as well as economically supportive to their children. They are increasingly self-conscious about juggling conflicts between looking after children and having a job. (Collier, 2008, pp. 172–173)

For Dermott, the emergence of this 'new man' (and 'new father') can be seen as part of a wider trend towards the validation of 'intimacy' in personal relationships (Jamieson, 1998; Smart, 2007), whereby 'close association, privileged knowledge, deep knowing and understanding and some form of love' (Jamieson, 1998, p. 13) are valued as primary. What we suggest here is that this undermining of the breadwinning role has had some profound implications for the way men perceive and experience fatherhood.

Work-life balance: gender equality or intensive fathering?

The goal of having more mothers retained in, or returning to, work is often used as a rationale for measures to 'involve fathers', advocated as a means to ease the childcare burden that women generally shoulder for childcare (Hochschild, 2003). Indeed, policymakers' interest in improving the 'work-life balance' and 'shared parenting' practices of couples seems to be higher up the policy agenda than the provision of subsidised childcare facilities. From the early 2000s in particular there has been a strong emphasis on the importance of flexible working and longer parental leave to enable fathers to take a greater responsibility for the care of their children (Dermott, 2001, 2008; see also Marsiglio *et al.*, 2000, and Pleck, 1993).

For Asher, author of the provocatively titled *Shattered: Modern motherhood and the illusion of equality*, suggested changes to parental leave in the UK (whereby couples could split a year's leave between them) are a 'welcome step that enshrines in law the possibility of sharing care for very young children more equitably' (Asher, 2011, pp. 52–53). That said, Asher articulates some more widely held reservations about this new leave structure:

> Parents may worry about fathers taking the earnings hit involved ... Fathers may fear alienating bosses by going on extended paternity leave. Families in which mothers can afford not to return to work earlier than twelve months may be minded to stick with the status quo: habits within the household have already been formed at this stage in the leave period; and women may be reluctant to give up what has been established as 'their' leave. (Asher, 2011, pp. 52–53)

In her work with families, Gillies (2009) found that despite a policy discourse around 'gender equality', most fathers in her sample were in paid work, and most mothers were primary caregivers. Gillies' research, which looks at how working patterns and parenting strategies are correlated with social class, leads her to question the usefulness of measures to extend parental leave to men, when employment is often temporary or shift-based for men (and/or women) in lower socioeconomic groups. For many of her informants in these groups, taking unpaid leave is simply not an option. Further, even those in higher-paid professions, who *might* be able to afford a split leave system, do not appear to be taking it, partly because they are in jobs which demand long hours and have a 'presentee' culture (see also Dermott, 2008, and Doucet, 2006).

Things have, of course, changed in terms of men's actual experiences of looking after their children. Fathers are, on average, are spending more time with their children than 50 years ago. For example, British fathers' care of infants and children rose 800 per cent from 1975 to 1997, from 15 minutes to two hours on average for a working day (Fisher *et al.*, 1999). Between 2002 and 2005, the percentage of new fathers in the UK working flexitime to spend more time with their infants rose from 11 per cent to 31 per cent (Smeaton and Marsh, 2006), and since 1993 the number of 'home-dads' has doubled (Fatherhood Institute, 2011). These figures do, however, need to be put into the context of the wider parenting culture which has seen both men and women spend more time with children, a culture increasingly cemented in policymaking (see Chapter 1).

So as much as it is often framed as a means of promoting gender equality, one of the ways in which recent policymaking in the area of 'work-life balance' could be read is as fostering a shift from 'cash to care' (Daly, 2013; Hobson and Morgan, 2002). There has certainly been a change in how fatherhood is presented to fathers (and mothers) today when compared with the past. What comes out quite strongly in these arguments is that direct involvement with childcare is as, if not more, important to family life than is earning the main wage. As the Fatherhood Institute states:

> If you are the main breadwinner – that doesn't mean this has to be your role forever and this doesn't mean you can't be involved; do try to stay as involved as possible at home. (Fatherhood Institute, 2010)

In this light, current policy measures around work-life balance mentioned above could be said to be less about trying to effect gender equality than about a self-conscious policy goal to encourage both parents to spend more time with their children. One paradoxical outcome of this is that, rather than women being enabled to do more work outside the home because their partners are on hand to look after the children, such policies could simply extend the logic of 'intensive parenting' to men, thereby doubling the labour for both parents. This means that men become increasingly subject to the 'cultural contradiction' between work and home. This takes us back to our discussion in Chapter 1, where we discussed the cultural view of children as vulnerable and in need of intensive 'quality time' with parents.

Fostering the new father in policy

Opening her essay *Changing Fatherhood in the 21st Century: Incentives and Disincentives for Involved Parenting*, the sociologist Anastasia Prokos identifies a paradox at the heart of US discourses around fatherhood. On the one hand, there is a popular perception that fathers are more 'involved' with their children than ever before:

> This 'new father' spends quality time with his children, is nurturing and caring, and prioritizes family over all else. Popular media increasingly portrays fathers as actively involved in their children's lives, as creating organisations centred on fatherhood (including those geared towards helping fathers win custody cases), and employers as increasingly offering 'parental leave' rather than maternity leave. (Prokos, 2002, p. 1)

On the other, there is a considerable amount of public concern with what are called 'deadbeat dads' (in the US) or 'feckless fathers' (in the UK). These are fathers who fail to support or spend time with their children.

It is the latter group in particular that was the original target of policy and advocacy initiatives (in both the US and the UK) to 'engage' fathers. These are proposed largely with the aim of building stronger families (and communities) by providing 'positive male role-models' for children, particularly boys. This was encapsulated in the then Justice Secretary Jack Straw's 2007 campaign to tackle the problem of absent dads (notably in black communities). Straw told BBC Radio Four's *Today* programme:

> And as we know – lads need dads. Of course they need their mums as well, but there is a particular point in teenagers' development, of young men, where fathers are very important and they are more likely to be absent in the case of the Afro-Caribbean. (BBC News Online, 2007)

A similar rhetoric was apparent in politicians' response to the riots that swept through British cities in August 2011, where 'dadlessness' – and the consequent lack of male 'role models' – was seen as one factor contributing to what Prime Minister David Cameron described as a 'broken society' undergoing a 'slow motion moral collapse' (BBC News Online, 2011; Bristow, 2013).

The importance of fathers as 'role models' in general was highlighted in the New Labour government's 2007 policy document *Every Parent Matters*, which made explicit that a key policy goal is to 'involve fathers' in the project of intensive parenting. This document also noted some of the struggles that the policymakers experience in doing this, and the need, therefore, for a more aggressive programme of 'support' targeted at fathers specifically:

> Research shows that a father's early involvement in their child's life can lead to a positive educational achievement later on, and a good parent–child relationship in adolescence. It can, however, be a challenge to involve fathers and other males in services targeted at families with pre-school children ... Irrespective of the degree of involvement they have in the care of their children, fathers should be offered routinely the support they need to play their parental role effectively. (Every Parent Matters, 2007)

In more recent years, this talk of positive education outcomes has been biologized with the use of research around the importance of engaged fathering for enabling optimal brain development in children:

> Talking to and gazing at your baby, screwing up your face and waiting for a response (babies just a few days old can mimic you), mirroring his or her facial expressions ... all these things help develop the synaptic pathways in your baby's brain. Later on, this will affect their speaking/listening skills, their reading and writing, popularity and friendliness. (Fatherhood Institute, 2010)

As my essay on 'The Problem of "Attachment"' explores, under the rubric that reiterates the fragility of the infant brain, *both* a father's absence *and* his presence can be construed as a social problem. We therefore see again the way in which this neurological discourse precipitates a spread in the definition of neglect: where once 'deadbeat dads' were the original concern of policymakers, now 'engaging' *all* dads is seen to be important for ensuring normal brain development, down to the most intimate and specific of daily tasks.

Dad-proofing and avoiding exclusion

It is not the case, then, that the 'distant' breadwinning father has simply been called into question by policymakers. At the same time, there have been concerted efforts to construct an alternative model of what it means to be a good father today. Indeed, since fathers are not considered to have the same 'instincts' as mothers when it comes to parenting, it becomes possible for claims to be made in a much more direct way about the need for 'skilling up' dads.

Many scholars have noted that from the 1990s onwards, there was a deliberate effort to 'engage fathers' in services at the policy level. Concurring that there was an ideological background of the 'absent father' or the 'distant father', Featherstone traces the genealogy of British policy moves to 'engage fathers' to the election of the New Labour government in 1997 (2009, p. 2). The 1998 document *Supporting Families*, for example, which we discuss at length in Chapter 3, was the first government consultation on families that spoke explicitly about engaging dads, and this trope was continued in further policy statements and programmes. The 2007 document *Aiming High for Children: Supporting Families* expressed the government's trajectory thus:

> The government believes that much more can be done to release the potential improvements in outcomes for children through better

engagement between fathers and services for children and families. This requires a culture change – from maternity services to early years, and from health visitors to schools – changing the way that they work to ensure that services reach and support fathers as well as mothers. (HM Treasury/DfES, 2007, pp. 34–35, in Featherstone, 2009, p. 3)

Making sure that fathers were not 'excluded' from seeking this support became an underlying rationale for the policy approach. For example, the 2008 *Think Fathers* campaign contained an explicit aim to 'Dad-proof' public services (Featherstone, 2009). With the election, in 2010, of the Conservative–Liberal Democrat Coalition government, the dynamic around engaging fathers has continued apace, using very similar language. As the Department for Education's document *Supporting Families in the Foundation Years* puts it:

> From pregnancy onwards, all professionals should consider the needs and perspectives of *both parents*. Government and the sector have a role to play in setting the right tone and expectation, and helping professionals to think about how to engage fathers in all aspects of their child's development and decisions affecting the child. (DfE, 2012, our emphasis)

As Macvarish (2009) has noted, there is something of a paradox here, because the state appears to project its own relationship with fathers onto real relationships between fathers and children. If state services appear not to have any 'contact' with fathers, it is assumed that mothers and children also have little 'contact'. But this is not a necessary correlation. So when policymakers speak of the need to 'engage' fathers, do they mean that the state should engage with them, or that fathers should engage in their own families?

The new model father

Mirroring the expertise-led 'intensive' mothering, many of the interventions around fathering focus on enabling men to 'relate' to their children through listening and talking, as a means of fostering intimacy in the place of (assumed) distance that comes with more traditional breadwinning. In the US for example (as well as the UK), there have been numerous programmes which encourage fathers to read with their children, fostering the archetypal stereotype of the 'new model father':

> Dads have to make a special effort to read to their children ... It is important for dads to promote reading by reading to your children

when they are young. Encourage them to read on their own as they get older. Instill a love of reading in your children and you will help ensure that they have a lifetime of personal and career growth ... Take your kids to the library on a regular basis. Your community library offers your kids the chance to explore new interests and imaginary worlds through hundreds of books, 'every couple of weeks' make it a daddy–child 'date' to go to the library and pick out 5 or 10 new books to read together. Your library probably also offers reading programs or special events that will make reading fun and encourage your child to expand his or her literary horizons. (National Fatherhood Initiative, 2013)

This reiterates the point that men are considered to need to make a 'special effort' to relate to their children by demarcating particular activities at 'daddy–child dates'. (Featherstone notes that many of these schemes fail to recognize the importance of 'maternal gate-keeping', which often present the father's relationship as independent from the mother [Featherstone, 2009, pp. 155–175].)

As we explored in Chapter 1, it is not only 'extra-curricular' activities which have been subject to expert guidance. Other examples of this shift in expert discourse around fathering include schemes to encourage fathers to be present at the birth of babies (*Think Fathers*, 2009), and take an 'active' role in supporting perinatal health in women and breastfeeding in particular (see for example the Royal College of Midwives' report *Reaching out: Involving Fathers in Maternity Care*, 2013; Murphy, 2010). These schemes therefore mirror and reiterate the edicts of the 'intensive mothering' culture explored throughout this book so far.

On the one hand then, what we see in these moves to 'engage dads' is that there has been a shift in perceptions of the importance of fathering for children's development (something also picked up on by the range of fathers rights organizations who advocate for paternal custody, as discussed by Collier and Sheldon, 2008). On the other, fathers are a presented as a special case, who need particular help with enacting this 'new' parenting, even in the most basic of tasks, and that professionals must make special efforts to enable. There is therefore an implicit assumption that fathers need help to access the support they need in order to parent appropriately – and an overt need to develop 'dad-proof' services.

Men's experiences: does policy miss the point?

Exactly what the 'engaged' fatherhood policy makers and experts talk of actually translates to in practice remains a bit of a mystery. In general, in her study of 25 British fathers, Dermott found that notions of emotional openness, communication, and a close relationship with one's children were endorsed – although a wide variety of childcare and labour patterns were covered under this rubric (that is, variations in leave patterns and childcare arrangements between couples). As Dermott says, the discourse around good fathering (both at the level of policy and from her informants) stresses the development of an emotional and close relationship between father and child, rather than emphasizing childcare activities or economic provision (Dermott, 2008, pp. 39, 61). As noted above, many of the efforts to 'engage dads' seem to see men's role in the public sphere (that is, in employed labour) as less important than the 'emotional openness' associated with the private sphere. The broader discussion of adulthood in crisis, which we have discussed in Chapters 1 and 4, therefore shapes the context in which contemporary fathering takes place.

But as work by Dermott, Collier, and Sheldon has also shown, despite respondents' willingness to pay lip-service to the 'new fatherhood', being a breadwinner has remained an important part of the way in which men see themselves as involved fathers – both in theory and in practice. This is interesting, because it does not tally with the policy notion of 'involvement', which poses the two as mutually exclusive:

> [E]mployment and the 'breadwinner ethic' still remain of central significance in the formation of a distinctive masculine identity for many men, and ... not just fathers, but also other family members, perceive being a 'good father' as something bound up with the role of the breadwinner. (Collier and Sheldon, 2008, p. 130)

This is not only a question of 'choice', of course. Miller's work with heterosexual, middle-class, first-time fathers draws attention to the material constraints which families must negotiate as they go about enacting (and narrativising) their identities as mothers and fathers. Despite having an antenatal commitment to 'new fatherhood', for example for many fathers in her study, the exhaustion and financial implications of parenthood lead them to fall back into what she calls 'patriarchal habits' (see also Miller 2011a and Miller, 2011b, p. 1094).

Resisting intensive fathering: new directions in research

What emerges from these developments is that the 'new model father' is an externally generated idea of what a good father looks like – and it's not one that necessarily resonates with fathers themselves. With a focus on class, Gillies (2009) notes that whilst there is evidence of 'hands-on' fathering in very low-income families (because, for example, fathers might be unemployed), this seems not to be the 'engaged' caring or 'concerned cultivation' (Lareau, 2003) that policymakers desire. Rather, there is an inherent classed validation of activities like reading to children, which counted as 'involvement'. As Klett-Davis (2010) has observed, there is therefore a middle-class bias to what counts as good parenting. Not surprisingly, working-class fathers tend to be more hostile to, and more likely to reject, official initiatives to 'involve' them in the care of their children, which they felt were irrelevant to their lifestyles.

With a focus on gender, work by Shirani *et al.* (2012) has explored the ways in which expectations around what it means to be a 'good parent' have affected men differently to women. They showed that men, whilst very willing to be 'involved' in caring for their children, were less influenced by a culture of expertise around parenthood, and were more happy to rely on their 'common sense'. Mothers, by contrast, felt the weight of 'moral responsibility' more than fathers, and worried about doing the right thing to a greater extent. Instead, men in their study drew on a 'cultural resource of masculinity' and associations of independence and confidence. For many fathers (and indeed many mothers) in their study, being a breadwinner, and taking responsibility for financial planning, was their way of demonstrating their commitment as a father.

In a different era, fathers' articulation of self-confidence and focus on taking financial responsibility for their families would have been seen by policymakers as something to be encouraged. But in a recent government evaluation of British parenting classes, men's confidence and lack of interest in 'seeking support' is presented as a negative thing: a low uptake of the scheme apparently shows a 'lack of knowledge of the positive outcomes from parenting programmes' (DfE, 2013, p. 10). This is therefore used as justification to increase efforts to involve fathers (which, ironically, might well have the effect of undermining the confidence men had to begin with).

The policy drives to involve fathers in more and more aspects of perinatal care, particularly pregnancy care, might also be situated as a challenge to the intimacy of the couple. In a context where 'breast is best', Lee's research on feeding babies, for example, shows that mothers see the genuine and non-directive support their partners give them as very important. 'Many mothers value fathers doing night feeds with formula milk to relieve tiredness and share baby care', she says (cited in Murphy,

2010). Where fathers are increasingly the direct target of educational schemes around the benefits of breastfeeding (or the importance of a healthy diet or not smoking in pregnancy, for example), it is interesting to think about the implications of this 'opening up' of a couple's relationship. If women cannot trust their partners not to pressurize them into breastfeeding, or report them to the midwife for formula feeding (or smoking or drinking, for instance), this opens up a worrying space between the state, the couple, and individual mothers and fathers (see Ellie Lee's essay on 'Policing Pregnancy' for more on this theme). Indeed, a recent study by Ives (2013) has actually shown that many fathers feel it is appropriate that the focus of perinatal care be on women, and see little need for the services to be directed at them. Authentic 'involvement' was achieved by playing this supportive role, and many fathers felt that they would be 'transgressing a moral boundary' if they were to influence their partners by expressing their own ideas and preferences.

As a final point, the impact of the political and cultural developments reviewed here upon the subjectivities of parents and children also needs to be brought into these debates. Macvarish (2009) has noted an increasing association between parenting and panopticism: with fathers 'performing' their fathering for the social audience – for example reading to their children or being encouraged to be present for their children in the school environment. As we discuss in Chapter 4, men, in particular, are already tied to notions of risk because of their association with abuse in the private sphere and as a sexual or violent threat in public spaces. One question we might ask is how this impacts on men's experience of being parents. Gabb's (2013) work on responses to father–child intimacy, as expressed in family photographs, highlights how fraught this area has become.

Conclusion

This essay has mapped out some of the current trends in thinking around fatherhood, both in policy circles and in academic research. What it points to is an important gap in the way policy understands fathering, and the way fathers themselves experience it. Certainly, the emotionally involved 'new father' that current measures try to encourage acts as an important cultural model for the way in which many men shape their identities – but to say that this has come at the cost of the more traditional provider model would be a mistake. Instead, the new model father emerges as a *construct* of policymakers and researchers, and in so far as there is evidence to suggest that their ideas are connecting with fathers, it appears to be limited. However, this lack of connection has not deterred policymakers – indeed, in line with the wider dynamics of parenting culture, it has led to efforts to generate further initiatives. How this relationship between policymaking, intensive parenting, and the everyday experiences of fathers develops will be an interesting process to watch.

Note

1. We do not undertake a discussion of the changing definitions of fatherhood here, related to shifts in marriage and divorce, sexuality and reproductive technologies. See Featherstone (2009, pp. 19–39) for a good overview of 'who counts' as a father.

Further reading

Collier, R. and Sheldon, S. (2008) *Fragmenting Fatherhood, Socio-Legal Study* (Oxford: Hart).
This is a particularly useful overview of the changing discourses around fatherhood, with a focus on law. It makes the argument that fatherhood is increasingly 'fragmented' through the undermining of breadwinning.

Dermott, E. (2008) *Intimate Fatherhood: A Sociological Analysis* (London: Routledge).
This book is a helpful study exploring men's experiences of 'intimate' fatherhood, which Dermott positions in distinction to 'intensive' motherhood, with important implications for gender equality in parenting.

Lupton, D. and Barclay, L. (1997) *Constructing Fatherhood, Discourses and Experiences* (London: Sage).
This is an excellent overview of shifting discourses around fatherhood, with a particular focus on expertise. It shows how many of the psychological studies concerning motherhood were rolled out to fathers, despite important gender-based methodological limitations.

Essay 5

The Double Bind of Parenting Culture: Helicopter Parents and Cotton Wool Kids

Jennie Bristow

This essay ...

- Discusses the apparent reaction, in recent years, against the excesses of risk-averse, intensive parenting culture. This takes the form of highlighting the problem of stifling young children's ability to take the risks necessary to grow up ('cotton wool kids') and the problem of parents of teenage children hovering over them and not allowing them to achieve on their own ('helicopter parents').
- Argues that while these critiques raise some important points about the problem of risk-aversion in developing children's independence, their focus tends to be on the problem of parental anxiety. Thus, critiques of 'overprotection' tend merely to fuel the trend towards parent-blaming, rather than challenging the cultural source of the problem. This leads to the 'double bind' of parenting culture, where parents are criticized both for absorbing the imperatives of intensive parenting and rejecting them.
- One important theme to emerge is that of the 'diseasing of childhood', where wider anxieties about adulthood and modern life are projected onto children. This has important implications for the way that the task of socializing children into adult society comes to be conceptualized.

Introduction

Writing in *Time* magazine about 'the growing backlash against overparenting', Nancy Gibbs begins:

> The insanity crept up on us slowly; we just wanted what was best for our kids. We bought macrobiotic cupcakes and hypoallergenic socks,

hired tutors to correct a 5-year-old's 'pencil-holding deficiency', hooked up broadband connections in the treehouse but took down the swing set after the second skinned knee. We hovered over every school, playground and practice field – 'helicopter parents', teachers christened us, a phenomenon that spread to parents of all ages, races and regions. (Gibbs, 2009)

The 'widespread acceptance' that the culture of paranoid parenting has gone too far is noted by Furedi, introducing the second edition of his book (Furedi, 2008a, p. 2). For example, he writes, 'many parents ... recognise that the experience and that of their children bears no relation to their own childhoods and that childhood is in many respects less free than in the past'; '[s]ome experts now insist that our obsession with health and safety has gone too far and that childhood has become too risk averse'; and [e]ven politicians and policy makers now argue that children need more freedom and access to outdoor activities' (Furedi, 2008a, p. 2).

However, although the recognition that 'risk-aversion can have a harmful impact upon childhood' is a welcome development, it provides a limited counter to the dominant trend of intensive parenting culture. Furedi goes on to explain that, while it is increasingly common to hear concerns about children being 'wrapped in cotton wool', these tend to have 'a fatalistic and rhetorical character', where counter-panics about obesity or the threat of online bullying and paedophiles are mobilized to indicate that indoor play holds as many (if not more) dangers as outdoor activities (Furedi, 2008a, pp. 3–4). Furthermore, the 'normalisation of parent-bashing' has meant that concerns about the overprotection of children tend to be focused on the problem of the parent:

> We have a culture that not only continually promotes a hyper-alarmist orientation towards the well-being of children but also blames parents for internalising its message. Not infrequently parents are blamed for being anxious about their children. (Furedi, 2008a, p. 4)

This essay discusses this phenomenon through briefly reviewing the twin problems of the 'cotton wool kid' (the child who is over-protected) and the 'helicopter parent' (who hovers over the child, preventing him or her from taking the risks necessary to develop independence). We indicate that the 'backlash against overparenting' (Gibbs, 2009) that has taken place over the past decade is itself informed by central tenets of intensive parenting culture, which presume that what parents do (or don't do) is a central and determining importance, and that any problems with what parents do or do not do should be measured by their (presumed) impact upon the child.

To put this another way: 'overparenting' is considered to be problematic primarily insofar as it has a negative effect upon the child. The extent to which the orthodoxy of intensive parenting culture takes a toll on parents' time, emotional energy, and capacity to pursue their ambitions in the adult world is barely mentioned, and where these issues are raised, they tend to be couched in defensive terms. Thus, such erstwhile features of normal everyday life, such as allowing children to watch television when they want to or to play with their friends without adult supervision, are presented as part of a deliberate child-rearing philosophy grandly titled 'benign neglect'; while allowing a child to walk to school alone has become a fraught, self-conscious exercise in finding ways to inculcate independence, which can then fit with the identity work of being a 'good parent'. Above all, the 'backlash against overparenting' means that parents continue to behave in a fashion entirely consistent with intensive parenting culture, yet in the knowledge that there is something wrong – 'insane', or 'mad' (Gibbs, 2009; Warner, 2006) – about what they are doing.

Cotton wool kids

As Furedi (2008a) notes, there has been mounting concern, led primarily by developmental psychologists and those concerned with children's play, about the extent to which a risk-averse culture is creating a generation of 'cotton wool kids' whose development is stunted by their lack of freedom, and who lack the experiences to navigate dangers as they get older (Gill, 2007; Guldberg, 2009; Lindon, 1999; Skenazy, 2009). In recent years, there has been an increasing recognition in media and policy circles of the problem of raising a generation of children unwilling and unable to engage with the risks inherent in everyday life.

This often takes a highly instrumental form, to do with a concern about the capacity of young people to handle the challenges they will face as adult workers. For example, in 2007 Sir Digby Jones, former Director-General of the Confederation of British Industry (CBI), published a paper for the organization Heads, Teachers and Industry (HTI), titled *Cotton Wool Kids*. 'Overprotecting our children – swaddling them in cotton wool – is bad for society, the economy and young people's preparation for adulthood in a world full of uncertainties,' wrote HTI Chief Executive Anne Evans in the Foreword to the paper (Jones, 2007, p. 4).

Guldberg (2009) has made a deeper case for why children need to be able to grow up. In her introduction to *Reclaiming Childhood: Freedom and play in an age of fear*, Guldberg explains that the combination of research for a doctorate in developmental psychology and experience as a primary school teacher led her to the conviction that:

> Children need to be given space away from adults' watchful eyes – in order to play, experiment, take risks (within a sensible framework provided by adults), test boundaries, have arguments, fight, and learn how to resolve conflicts ... [W]atching the speed at which that free space is becoming eroded by a culture that prizes 'safety' above all else has weighed upon me as a grave concern. (Guldberg, 2009, p. 1)

For Guldberg, unsupervised play is crucial for children's personal development, in terms of enabling them to develop an understanding of the world, and to navigate risks and relationships. Allowing children the space to play requires acknowledging that parental determinism is a 'myth' – what makes us 'who we are' derives from a complex combination of experiences and relationships, and even the most controlling parent cannot guarantee their child's safety, or predict how the child will turn out. Allowing children the freedom to create their world – and, by the same token, allowing parents the freedom to let their children explore – is a vital part of childrearing (Guldberg, 2009, pp. 59–72, pp. 129–146).

Guldberg's emphasis on the freedom to play is echoed by the American writer Lenore Skenazy, who found herself labelled 'America's Worst Mom' after she allowed her nine-year-old son to ride the New York City subway alone, and then wrote about it in a newspaper column. The column 'ignited a global firestorm over what constitutes reasonable risk', reports Gibbs. 'Skenazy decided to fight back, arguing that we have lost our ability to assess risk. By worrying about the wrong things, we do actual damage to our children, raising them to be anxious and unadventurous or, as she puts it, "hothouse, mama-tied, danger-hallucinating joy extinguishers"' (Gibbs, 2009).

Skenazy's (2009) book, *Free-Range Kids: Giving our children the freedom we had without going nuts with worry*, speaks to the problem at the heart of the 'cotton wool kids' debate. Parents recognize that children need some freedom and independence and that these are good things to have; but this recognition takes place within a culture that emphasizes the need for safety and protection above all. Parents thus find themselves under contradictory pressures, not only to avoid stifling their children but also to keep them safe from possible harms to their physical safety or emotional well-being.

This contradiction is starkly revealed by Jenkins' (2006) study of the ways that families in the South Wales area of Britain constructed and articulated ideas about risk in relation to young people's outdoor play. Jenkins concluded that respondents were 'actively attempting to wrestle with competing sets of cultural orientations regarding the health and well being of their children', explaining this point as follows:

> Much of the anxiety parents reported experiencing stems from the development of an increasingly privatized approach to parenting. However, the interviews also revealed that the ways in which parents talked about risk contained sediment from a previous generation of parents, who perhaps tended to see the immediate outside world in far less hostile terms. Thus, although parents deeply feared the risk of their child being attacked by strangers, they also feared the damage excessive restriction would do to their offspring's social and physical development. (Jenkins, 2006, pp. 390–1)

Here, Jenkins relates the impact of risk-aversion to a wider experience of isolation, in which parents become both more susceptible to fears that other adults – 'strangers' – might harm their children, and less able to experience a situation in which unsupervised play between children can be entered into spontaneously. To put this another way: a child will not want to go and play outside on his or her own; so in a situation where most children are kept indoors, it requires a particular motivation on the part of the parent to push the child to be 'free range'. Jenkins' insights speak to the points discussed in Chapter 4, to do with how the wider breakdown of adult solidarity and the nervousness surrounding contact between the generations fuels the imperative of risk-aversion.

Jenkins also makes an important observation regarding the way that one's life experience and the experience absorbed 'from a previous generation of parents', provides a limit to the imperative of overprotection. The implication here is that the challenge to the excesses of parenting culture will come from the common sense of parents themselves. However, as Lee *et al.* note, in discussions about parenting and risk, it has become 'fashionable' to 'point the finger of blame at "helicopter parents" or to suggest that parents are damaging the next generation by raising cosseted "cotton-wool kids"' (Lee *et al.*, 2010, pp. 228–9). This is what we term the 'double bind' of parenting culture, in which parents, as the popular English saying would have it, 'can't do right for doing wrong'.

Helicopter parents

At the other end of childhood, the term 'helicopter parents' has become a commonly recognized phrase to denote the forms taken by parental over-protectiveness: where parents accompany teenage children to university interviews and involve themselves in discussions with tutors about grades or progress, or where parents become heavily involved with their child's job applications and workplace relations, to the point where, according to Howe and Strauss (2008), 'over one quarter of employers have had parents promote their children for a position, and 15% have had parents call to complain if the company does not hire their son or daughter' (Howe and Strauss, 2008, p. 5).

Somers' (2010) 'research towards a typology' of the helicopter parent offers the following definition:

> A helicopter parent (helopat for short) is a mother, father, or even a grandparent who 'hovers' over a student of any age by being involved – sometimes overly so – in student/school, student/employer, or student/social relationships. (Somers, 2010)

The term 'helicopter parent' is attributed to Charles Fay and Foster Cline, authors of the *Love and Logic* parenting series, and was popularized by Ned Zemen, writing in *Newsweek* in 1991. Zeman described the 'helicopter parent' as 'a nosy grown-up who's always hovering around. Quick to offer a teacher unwanted help' (Somers, 2010).

Neil Howe, a US consultant well known for his writing on generations, including a book on the 'Millennials' (born 'in or after 1982' (Howe and Strauss, 2000, p. 4)), has noted that the development and popularization of the term 'helicopter parent' coincides with the orientation of parenting culture around the priority of safety. An article reproduced on the website of LifeCourse Associates, of which Howe is President, summarizes his argument thus:

> Parents of millennials have been obsessive about ensuring the safety of their children … When the first wave was born in the early 1980s, "Baby on Board" signs began popping up on minivans. Children were buckled into child-safety seats, fitted with bicycle helmets, carpooled to numerous after-school activities and hovered over by what Howe describes as "helicopter parents." (LifeCourse Associates, 2003)

For Howe and Strauss (2000), the 'helicopter parent' is the result of an era in which children are 'wanted', 'protected', and 'worthy'. 'From conception to graduation, this 1982 cohort has marked a watershed in adult attitudes toward, treatment of, and expectations for children', they write:

> Over that eighteen-year span, whatever age bracket those 1982-born children have inhabited has been the target of intense hope, worry, and wonder from parents, pollsters, pundits, and politicians. Not since the Progressive Era, near the dawn of the twentieth century, has America greeted the arrival of a new generation with such a dramatic rise in adult attention to the needs of children. (Howe and Strauss, 2000, p. 32)

While the term 'helicopter parent' appears pejorative, and the phenomenon has attracted some critical commentary, implicit in all definitions of the 'helicopter parent' is that he or she is motivated by love and concern for the child. Thus, because the parent is following the central 'feeling rule' (Hochschild, 1979) of intensive parenting culture – where desire to do the best for one's child trumps all other considerations – criticism of the 'helicoptering' phenomenon is inconsistent.

The writer Katie Roiphe picks up on this inconsistency, contending that the orthodoxy of overprotection is so ingrained that it is often hard for parents even to know whether they are 'helicoptering' or not. 'In the recent clamor on the subject of whether this generation of parents is hovering too much and oversteering, overmanaging, and otherwise spoiling their children, I've heard parents say, "But we don't know any actual helicopter parents"', writes Roiphe (2012). 'They say this because they don't know anyone who fits the obvious caricatures – that is anyone who schedules Mandarin classes for their 5-year-old and dutifully shuttles them off every Saturday morning for theater-to-express-yourself classes. But the overabundance of extracurriculars is only one small part of [a] larger, disturbing phenomenon':

> The belief that we can control our children on a very high level and somehow program or train or condition them for a successful life however we define it is extremely prevalent and takes many forms. Do you not allow your children to watch television? Do you allow them any time on the Internet unsupervised? Are you keeping very close track of what they eat? Do you get a little too involved in homework? Do you barely ever hire baby sitters at night? I know parents who think of themselves as very unhelicoptery but who are just helicoptering in different ways. (Roiphe, 2012)

Critical commentary tends to focus less on a distinction between 'helicopter parenting' and 'non-helicopter parenting' than on a distinction between 'good helicoptering' and 'bad helicoptering'. Somers contends that '[h]elicopter behaviour can have a positive or a negative effect':

> Positive results accrue when the 'hovering' is age appropriate; when parents and students engage in a dialogue; when the student is empowered to act; and when parents intercede only if the student needs additional help. We label this behaviour positive parental engagement. Negative helicopter parents can be found in many settings, including educational, and are inappropriately (and at times surreptitiously) enmeshed in their children's lives and relationships. (Somers, 2010)

By attempting to distinguish between 'positive' and 'negative' helicopter parents, Somers highlights the fine line that the twenty-first century parent treads between showing that they are properly (and 'positively') engaged in, and concerned about, their children's lives, and being 'inappropriately' overprotective. From her research, she draws a typology of five helicopter parent 'types': *consumer advocates*, 'these parents view college not as an educational journey but as consumer transaction'; *equity or fairness advocates*, who 'demand fairness for their children'; *vicarious college students*, who 'missed out on many college experiences themselves and want to recreate those golden four (or five) years spent as undergraduates'; *toxic parents*, who 'have been written about extensively in self-help literature' – they have 'numerous psychological issues and are controlling, negative, and try at once to live their children's lives even as they "one-up" their children in the process'; and *safety patrol parents*. For Somers, only the 'toxic parent' is deeply problematic; for the other types, her article suggests ways in which they can best be 'handled' by college managers.

The attempt to differentiate between 'good' and 'bad' forms of helicopter parenting lies at the heart of the study by Fingerman *et al.* on 'Helicopter parents and landing pad kids'. The authors begin by noting that '[p]opular media describe adverse effects of helicopter parents who provide intense support to grown children'; however, but 'it remains unclear whether intense parental involvement is viewed as normative today and whether frequent support is detrimental or beneficial to the parents and grown children involved' (Fingerman *et al.*, 2012, pp. 880–1). This study found that parents and grown children alike found helicoptering 'non-normative', when it took the form of 'too much support'. However, 'grown children who received intense support reported better psychological adjustment and life satisfaction than grown children who did not receive intense support' (Fingerman *et al.*, 2012, p. 880). Thus, even though '[p]arents who perceived their grown children as needing too much support reported poorer life satisfaction', there is an implicit sentiment that some helicoptering might be beneficial for young people, and should therefore not be totally discouraged.

The notion that colleges and employers should see the role of the 'helicopter parent' as a potential advantage that simply needs to be managed appropriately is elaborated by Howe and Strauss (2008). 'While most employers see young workers' close relationships with parents as a problem, it is in fact an enormous opportunity', they assert, continuing:

> Handled properly, helicopter parents can be an enormous asset to employers' goals of recruitment, productivity, and retention. Instead of shutting out parents, employers can develop a strategic response to enroll parents as allies and harness these potential strengths. (Howe and Strauss, 2008, p. 2)

By the same token, argue these authors, even the reluctance of Millennials to move out of the family home and attempt an independent life should not be viewed as a 'failure to launch', but rather as 'a natural, even desirable step in their close relationship with parents and extended families' (Howe and Strauss, 2008, p. 2). The closeness of relationship between Baby Boomer parents and their adult children should, they contend, ultimately be viewed as a positive development to which society needs to adjust, rather than a negative trend towards infantilization.

From the discussion reviewed above, we can see that the ambivalence with which 'helicopter parenting' is perceived speaks to the contradictions within both the culture of intensive parenting and the backlash to it. What lies beneath this ambivalence is a wider anxiety, about the extent to which adults are seen to be capable of protecting children from the perceived 'toxicity' of the adult world.

Resistance to intensive parenting: navigating the contradictions

As discussed in Chapter 1, intensive parenting works as a cultural script to which responses are far from stable. The imperative of risk-aversion has had a powerful effect, but has not become a total orthodoxy: for the simple reason that it is practically impossible to raise children without encountering some kind of hazard on an everyday level. By a similar token, the imperative of 'concerted cultivation' (Lareau, 2003) raises as many problems for the concerned parent as it does solutions, first in deciding which of the myriad cultivation projects are the most important, and second in raising anxieties about whether a child's social or emotional development might suffer from too demanding a programme.

This conundrum was illustrated by the furore that greeted Amy Chua's book *Battle Hymn of the Tiger Mother*, published in 2011, in which she gave a personal account of practicing 'Chinese-style' parenting, with a heavy focus on academic achievement and musical accomplishment. The reaction to Chua both in the US and Britain can best be described as startled, as commentators simultaneously recoiled against the intensity of pressure that Chua seemed to be recommending should be put onto children, and recognized that many of the excesses of the 'Tiger Mother' were merely extreme versions of what passes as 'normal' parenting in middle-class western culture.

One interesting response came from the US commentator David Brooks, who criticized Chua not for the hardness of her approach but for its one-sidedness. 'She's protecting them from the most intellectually demanding activities because she doesn't understand what's cognitively difficult and what isn't,' Brooks argued, in response to Chua's admission that she refused to let her children attend sleepovers with their friends. 'Practicing a piece of music for four hours requires focused attention, but it is nowhere near as cognitively demanding as a sleepover with 14-year-old girls. Managing status rivalries, negotiating group dynamics, understanding social norms, navigating the distinction between self and group – these and other social tests impose cognitive demands that blow away any intense tutoring session or a class at Yale' (Brooks, 2011).

Brooks' criticism of Chua is thus that the imposition of a particular narrow set of adult goals and ambitions upon children fails to prepare them for the real world that they will have to navigate. This reveals how, within the culture of intensive parenting, it is possible to resist 'tiger mothering' without at all resisting the logic of intensive parenting, which is to attempt to ensure that everything possible is done to equip one's child for a life of happiness and success.

A similar tension is apparent in Cucchiara's (2013) study of American urban middle-class parents 'choosing an urban public school in an era of parental anxiety'.[1] In choosing to send their children to a particular public school, rather than following the path taken by other middle-class parents and sending their children to a private school, the parents interviewed by Cucchiara were self-consciously attempting to reject 'what is seen as intensive, hyper protective parenting' (Cucchiara, 2013, p. 90). However, acting on this desire to reject the orthodoxy took a significant amount of work. '[E]ven those who bemoaned contemporary "over-parenting" devoted significant time and energy to choosing a school and managing their children's experiences'; and the process of rejecting the 'focus on admissions to elite colleges as the ultimate indicator of "success"' required that parents engage in a dialogue about what other 'choices could count as "legitimate"' (Cucchiara, 2013, p. 90).

The parents in Cucchiara's study have thus internalized an anxiety about 'the negative consequences of "invasive parenting"', which operates against the anxiety that they will damage their children's life chances by *not* trying to ensure their children's academic success through choosing the best schools. In this way, we can see that the logic of risk-aversion that informs the orthodoxy of intensive parenting also informs the resistance to its excesses. Hence the headline of Cucchiara's study reads: '"Are we doing damage?"'

The diseasing of childhood

Some of those who have critiqued the phenomenon of 'cotton wool kids', such as Guldberg and Skenazy, are motivated by a concern about the impact of overprotection both on children and on their parents. Furedi's *Paranoid Parenting* stresses that the rearing of robust children relies on adults being confident in their own abilities; conversely, 'if parents stifle their children with their obsessions and restrict their scope to explore, then the young generation will become socialized to believe that vulnerability is the natural state of affairs' (Furedi, 2008a, p. 195). As discussed in Chapter 1, resistance to the orthodoxy of risk-averse parenting is, in these works, articulated as part of a call for a more open, expansive approach to adults and children interacting with each other, and with the world.

Others who critique the problem of 'cotton wool kids' or 'helicopter parents' take a different approach, in that their main concern appears to be a desire to free children from what is perceived to be a damaging, 'toxic' adult culture. In Britain, this view has been clearly articulated by Sue Palmer's (2006) book *Toxic Childhood: How modern life is damaging our children… and what we can do about it* and its sequel *Detoxing Childhood* (2007). Palmer summarizes the extent of 'toxicity' to surrounding the modern child as follows:

- 'Physical toxicity' (unhealthy food and a 'couch-potato screen-based lifestyle');
- 'Emotional toxicity' – parents being too busy with work to provide enough 'family time' and set clear routines and boundaries, family breakdown, and exposing children to 'emotionally destabilising' 'screen-based violence';
- 'Social toxicity' – the lack of unsupervised play outside the home, leading to an inability to form friendships and an unprecedented openness to 'marketeers, unsuitable role models and celebrity culture';
- 'Cognitive toxicity' – too little time with 'real-life adults' and too much time with the television leading to poor language development, while education in schools suffers from a preoccupation with targets and the threat of litigation. (Palmer, 2007, p. 5)

The positioning, here, of myriad features of everyday modern life as toxic influences upon the child speaks to a highly idealized (and inaccurate) notion of childhood as a period untainted by adulthood. This idea is a powerful strand in the arguments put forward by advocates for children's free play, and often leads to the argument that more should be done to free children from over-intervention by their parents. Here again, the contradictions of intensive parenting culture are starkly revealed.

While Guldberg, Skenazy, and Furedi view the problem with this culture as the extent to which it prevents children from growing into the adult world, Palmer's perspective views the problem as one where adult preoccupations and interventions despoil the innocence of childhood. Furthermore, campaigners and policymakers are highly selective about the kind of 'freedoms' they think children should be able to access. So for example, while unsupervised, outdoor play is increasingly lauded as important for children's development (and parents blamed for restricting children's access to it), parents are being increasingly pressured to engage in their children's activities on the Internet, providing more supervision rather than less.

Thus Claire Perry, the British Conservative MP who in 2012 chaired a parliamentary inquiry into 'online child protection' (Independent Parliamentary Inquiry into Online Child Protection, 2013), proclaimed in an interview with the *Daily Telegraph* newspaper: 'We need to take control' (Moreton, 2013). She continued:

> Parents say they want to be involved, but the children have overtaken them ... That's awful. We must be like the first generation whose children learnt to read and write, and we're all blundering about like illiterate ignoramuses. (Moreton, 2013)

The idea that today's parents lack both the skill and the will to protect their children from the myriad risks posed by the online world is a recurrent theme in policy debates about parenting. The presentation of parents here as incompetents – 'illiterate ignoramuses' – goes hand-in-hand with the presumption, described in Chapters 1 and 2 of this book, that parents can and should direct every influence that comes to their children via the online world.

The fraught character of discussions about outdoor play, or young people's use of the internet, reveal a set of wider anxieties about childhood, adulthood, and the modern world. Furedi describes this as the 'diseasing of childhood', where the metaphor of toxic childhood, 'which conveys the idea of the moral pollution of childhood, readily resonates with a cultural imagination that interprets every childhood experience as destructive and dangerous' (Furedi, 2008a, pp. 12–13). He continues:

> Proponents of this idea claim that everything is getting worse for children. Technological change, new digital applications, rampant consumerism, incompetent parenting, pressures of school exams, peer pressure and family breakdown are some of the forces considered to be fuelling toxic childhood ... Such pessimistic interpretations of childhood have little to do with the real life experience of children. They are fuelled by adult anxieties about the ability of mothers and fathers to parent and of children to deal with the challenges they face. (Furedi, 2008a, p. 13)

The imposition of adult anxieties onto the experience of children is starkly indicated by the American psychologist Madeline Levine, whose (2012) book *Teach Your Children Well: Parenting for authentic success* makes use of the metaphor of toxicity. In her favourable review, Judith Warner (2012) describes this book as 'a *cri de coeur* from a clinician on the front lines of the battle between our better natures – parents' deep and true love and concern for their kids – and our culture's worst competitive and materialistic influences'. 'When apples were sprayed with a chemical at my local supermarket, middle-aged moms turned out, picket signs and all, to protest the possible risk to their children's health,' says Levine. 'Yet I've seen no similar demonstrations about an educational system that has far more research documenting its own toxicity' (Warner, 2012).

The parents whom Levine is concerned about are those who 'run themselves ragged with work and hyper-parenting, presenting an "eviscerated vision of the successful life" that their children are then programmed to imitate', writes Warner:

> They're parents who are physically hyper-present but somehow psychologically M.I.A.: so caught up in the script that runs through their heads about how to 'do right' by their children that they can't see when the excesses of keeping up, bulking up, getting a leg up and generally running scared send the whole enterprise of ostensible care and nurturing right off the rails.

Judith Warner's own (2006) book was a high-profile critique of the 'Perfect Madness' of parenting culture, and many of its insights into the impact of society's one-sided approach to safety, achievement, and success illuminate well some of the tensions experienced by parents as they balance the imperative to be a good parent according to the accepted cultural script against their intuitive discomfort with some of the excesses of hyper-parenting. However, as the case of the helicopter parent and the cotton wool kid illustrates, the message that 'essentially, everything today's parents think they're doing right is actually wrong' (Warner, 2012) tends to dominate well-placed criticisms and concerns.

Conclusion: the double bind of parenting culture

Through the diseasing of childhood, parents are positioned as conduits for a 'toxic' adult culture. This reverses the traditional dynamic of adult–child relations, in which parents are expected to bring their children gently into the adult world and entrusted with the task of doing that. Rather, their role is positioned as keeping children apart from those aspects of adult culture that are perceived as negative, and continually checking their own behaviour to avoid imposing their own problematic expectations upon their children.

The main outcome of this process is not a balanced understanding of the problems of 'hyper-parenting', but a further development in the 'normalisation of parent-bashing' (Furedi, 2008a, p. 8). Parents are castigated for their failure to anticipate and manage bewildering range of risks to their child, and simultaneously criticized for their failure to 'let go', which would enable their children both to experience the joys and freedoms of childhood and to develop their own resources for dealing with risk.

This contradiction is, presently, particularly stark in relation to discussions about young people and the Internet, and this is an area of parenting culture that would benefit from further critical research. The fact that children may be using the relative freedom of the Internet to counteract the isolation of not being able to engage in unsupervised play in the 'real' world tends to be presented, less as a solution to a problem, than as yet another new and worrisome risk. Livingstone and Haddon's report *EU Kids Online* (2009) expresses this particular 'double bind' as follows:

> Balancing empowerment and protection is crucial, since increasing online access and use tends to increase online risks. Conversely, strategies to decrease risks can restrict children's online opportunities, possibly undermining children's rights or restricting their learning to cope with a degree of risk. (Livingstone and Haddon, 2009, p. 1)

It is, of course, important to acknowledge that 'overparenting' carries negative consequences for children's development. In this regard, it really is not 'better to be safe than sorry'. But when the whole of childhood experience (positive and negative) is framed in the language of competing risks, this presents little scope for the discussion that campaigners, policymakers, and scholars need to be having: about the kind of world we envisage for ourselves and our children, and how we might shape it.

Note

1. In the US, 'public school' means a school funded by public money – known in Britain as a 'state school'. In Britain, 'public school' refers to a fee-paying (private) school.

Further reading

Guldberg, H. (2009) *Reclaiming Childhood: Freedom and play in an age of fear* (London and New York: Routledge).
   Guldberg combines insights from child development theory with a cultural critique to show the various ways in which children's lives have become

constrained by overblown fears about the hazards of everyday life, from accidents to bullying to the risks posed by the Internet. *Reclaiming Childhood* has become an influential text for those studying the history, sociology, and psychology of childhood, and is equally important reading for students of parenting culture.

Skenazy, L. (2009) *Free-Range Kids: Giving our children the freedom we had without going nuts with worry* (San Francisco: Jossey-Bass).
This is a humorous riposte to the culture of fear surrounding children, packed with statistics revealing the extent to which children are, in many ways, safer than ever before. As well as in the book, Skenazy has pioneered an active movement promoting 'free range kids', which she has continued on her lively blog: http://www.freerangekids.com/.

Warner, J. (2006) *Perfect Madness: Motherhood in the age of anxiety* (London: Vermilion).
Providing a useful cross-cultural approach by drawing on her experiences of parenting in France, and comparing them with her native US, Warner examines why mothers who appear to 'have everything' are feeling exhausted, dissatisfied, and powerless. Exploring how the current generation of mothers in the US became a generation of 'desperate control freaks', she coins the term 'perfect madness' to show that women use mothering strategies as a way of patching over wider social insecurities.

Conclusion

Ellie Lee

As we were completing this book, British newspapers reported on the findings of a newly published study that had apparently discovered '[h]ow the breastfeeding effect altered the British class system' (Bingham, 2013). It has been 'revealed', we were told, that '[b]reastfeeding babies improves their chance of climbing the social ladder' (Cooper, 2013). Journalists in other parts of world repeated the same 'news', reporting that '[b]reast fed babies achieve higher social status' (Sifferlin, 2013), and even: 'Breast fed babies are more socially connected, less anxious, as adults, study finds' (NY Daily News, 2013).

It would be hard to think of a clearer example to testify to the pervasiveness of parental determinism. If we were to accept at face what we were being told, we would have to believe that, *quite literally*, how well a person does in life (defined as how far they 'climb the social ladder') is determined by how their mother fed them as babies, and that this is because breastfeeding breeds people who are 'more socially connected' and 'less anxious'. Indeed, just in case anyone were under any illusion about just how important breastfeeding is for the very structuring of society, it seems the British class system itself should be understood, in the light of this research, to be affected by feeding babies at the breast.

It was notable that in the news reports of this research, which was conducted by Sacker *et al.* (2013), no counter-opinion or voice of caution was apparently sought and then reported.[1] The journalists concerned did not seem to consider it necessary to ask even the obvious questions about the study: which could have been about methodology, the authors' definition and understanding of 'social mobility', the claim that 'neurological and stress mechanisms' provide a plausible causal explanation for the increased social mobility of persons who are breastfed, and how this might tally with marked levels of social inequality in societies where most babies *are* breastfed.

Given this sort of example of the way the everyday practices of parents are researched, and then discussed in public domains, it has been the first objective of this book to explain what we mean by parental determinism and document its rise. The fact that something as complex and socially significant as the class system can now be discussed as being affected by changes in rates of breastfeeding suggests, as this book has sought to argue, that parental determinism has become a very powerful worldview. Indeed, we have aimed in the preceding text to draw attention to the idea that this outlook is now at least as strong and influential as other sorts of better-recognized and widely discussed forms of deterministic thinking, such as economic or genetic determinism.

We have sought, secondly, to make the case for the interdisciplinary project of *Parenting Culture Studies*, in order to understand better, and to critique, parental determinism. Perhaps the key tension or sociopolitical contradiction that has emerged from our work so far is the widening gulf that has come to exist between the imperatives and assumptions of parental determinism, and the everyday, lived experience of parents.

This gulf is most obvious in field of policymaking. As discussed in Chapter 3, in 2011 the British government announced that it would be 'offering free parenting classes to over 50,000 mothers and fathers'. Under the Department of Education's (DfE) new scheme ('CANparent') parents would get vouchers to use to purchase parenting classes which, in line with the precepts of 'positive parenting' (Reece, 2013) would educate parents about the following:

- How to promote positive behaviour with better communication and listening skills;
- Managing conflict;
- The importance of mothers and fathers working as a team;
- The appropriate play for age/development;
- Understanding the importance of boundaries and routines to children;
- Firm, fair and consistent approaches to discipline; and
- Strengthening positive relationships in the family. (DfE, 2011)

In an undiluted invocation of the determinism discussed through this book, the then Children's Minister, Sarah Teather, promoted the scheme by commenting that:

The overwhelming evidence, from all the experts, is that a child's development in the first five years of their life is the single biggest factor influencing their future life chances, health and educational attainment. (DfE, 2011)

Teather's comments indicated just how far the politicization of parenting has gone. 'Armed with all this evidence, it is the Government's moral and social duty to make sure we support all parents at this critical time,' claimed Teather, contending further that no parent should go without government-funded parenting education: 'Parenting classes aren't just for struggling families with complex problems' (DfE, 2011). In this example of parental determinism in action, what happened in the subsequent months was especially notable.

When the CANparent scheme was announced, the government was at pains to suggest that its interpretation of matters was entirely in line with that of the nation's parents: 'Around three-quarters of parents say they want information and support to help their parenting' (DfE, 2011). Yet by March 2013, when the first evaluation of the scheme was published (Cullen *et al.*, 2013) it emerged that only two per cent of eligible parents had used the vouchers to go to classes (Boffey, 2013). The way that the official evaluation discussed this remarkable gap between policymakers' presumptions and parents' obvious lack of interest in the scheme spoke volumes of present attitudes towards parents.

The fact that 98 per cent of parents did not take up the offer of parenting classes would seem to be the most important matter. Yet this fact was only disclosed 52 pages into the evaluation report, and then buried in the form of one short bullet point, couched in evasive language:

> Only 6% of households had so far received a voucher. Amongst households which had received a voucher, about four in ten (43%) said they intended to use it (or had already done so). Fathers were less likely than mothers to have received vouchers. (Cullen *et al.*, 2013, p. 52)

In other words, of the small proportion of parents who showed an interest in the scheme and sent off for the voucher to which they were entitled (six per cent), almost two-thirds didn't even plan to use it. In particular fathers were uninterested; elsewhere in the report we are told that 94 per cent of those who did attend classes were female.

The way that the CANparent evaluation discusses this gulf between official enthusiasm for training parents and the desire of parents themselves (fathers especially) to be trained is also telling. The first key finding offered by the evaluators was: 'The trial has succeeded'. This is the case, apparently, because parents have been offered 'a wide choice of types of parenting programme and modes of delivery' (Cullen *et al.*, p. 10). Thus, success comes to turn in the first place on whether *parent trainers* think they made a good offer.

How was parents' lack of appreciation of the value of the classes then accounted for? Reading between the lines, it emerged from the evaluation that parents have other things to do than go to the classes, and ultimately do not consider they really have much to gain from them. The evaluators, however, have another way of describing this reality. Their key findings state: '*Lack of knowledge of positive outcomes* from parenting programmes and *time constraints* were the main inhibitors to participation' (Cullen *et al.*, p. 10, our emphasis). Given that parents' experience was interpreted in this way, the evaluators' conclusion was unsurprising: that more must be done to make sure parents 'know' about the 'positive outcomes' it assumed will accrue if they go to the classes. Hence, the evaluators' first recommendation was for policymakers '[t]o increase demand (desire for parenting support)' (Cullen *et al.*, p. 17). Along similar lines, in the face of especially marked 'lack of desire' among fathers, they recommend that policymakers 'should ... review current practice to explore how best to ensure large numbers of fathers ... are receiving vouchers, as well as mothers' (Cullen *et al.*, p. 18).

Overall, this episode highlights what needs to be a central concern for the study of parenting culture: the way that that parental determinism acts to disregard any possibility that learning by experience, and the tacit knowledge that accumulates this way, is a perfectly good and acceptable way to go about raising children. The belief that raising children is just too important and difficult to be left to mere parents, their families, and their communities has become a dogma, which allows no room for alternative evidence or viewpoints. Those who hold an *a priori* belief in the need for parenting education simply cannot accept that parents may neither need nor want expert advice: the only conclusion that they can draw is that more must be done to find ways to train parents and to increase 'demand' – that is, parents' willingness to be trained.

The CANparent example also indicates that policymakers and influential claimsmakers have constructed a parallel world to that of actual parents. In that world, those who think of 'parenting' as the determining cause of social problems inevitably and inexorably rub the experience of real parents out of the picture. Exploration of this gulf and its implications needs to be a point of departure for the future study of parenting culture. A better tomorrow can begin with making sense of genuine experiences, rather than with those which are the product of the prejudices and imaginations of those committed unquestioningly to the importance of 'training parents'. From this starting point we can encourage a dialogue and conversation where parents (and other adults) take seriously making sense of real world as they find it.

To this end, there are four connected areas that we think those interested in the study of parenting culture might put time and energy into researching:

1. **The social history of parental determinism.** As we have indicated throughout this book, deterministic thinking about children has historically formed an important component part of ways of thinking about the future, for example in Social Darwinism (see Chapter 2). The more recent preoccupation with children's brains (discussed in Jan Macvarish's essay in Part II) can be understood as a version of this biological determinism. We should seek to understand better the historical development of this way of thinking, to understand more fully the process we can, for now, call 'scientization': that is, the way informal relations between parents and children have become thoroughly saturated with the language and vocabulary of science, and described as unquestionable 'evidence'. The nature of the language that is now used to speak about this area of life needs more exploration, in terms of its origins, mechanisms for diffusion into hitherto informal relations, and international similarities and differences.

2. **Differences and similarities in the development of parenting culture in different parts of the world.** An important contribution was published recently, through the collection of essays by Faircloth *et al.* (2013) looking at the intensification of parenting comparatively and cross-culturally. Further exploration along these lines is needed, to bring to light how the scientization of childrearing is internalized by parents and other adults, and the differential effects of this aspect of the 'intensification' of parenting across and within cultures. The workings of the contemporary State with regard to parenting culture is an important area for this sort of work; for example in industrialized countries, the differential movement from the welfare state to the 'therapeutic' or 'interventionist' state is a key focus to consider further in a comparative sense.

3. **The problem of generations.** This is a third area raised in this book that would benefit from further exploration, in particular the ways that our current parenting culture calls into question the place of adults other than parents in the care of children, and how parents and families perceive and understand this aspect of the professionalization of parenting. The study of parenting culture should devote

energy to understanding the relation between this development and the wider reposing of social problems as ones of generational conflict. For example, the redefinition of what is wrong with society through the increasingly pronounced claims that the 'Baby Boomer' generation constitutes an unhealthy and unreliable influence over society (Beckett, 2010; Howker and Malik, 2010; Willetts, 2010) is an important process to understand and expose.

4. **Greater clarity to concepts and ideas.** There is a need for more dialogue about, and clarification of, key concepts that arise as the study of parenting culture develops. For example, the differences between privacy and informality on one hand, and individuation and privatization on the other, are important to understand in more depth. Similarly, this book points to an important distinction between morality and moralization, and contributing to the developing of ideas through engagement with the problems of parenting culture is an important task for this genuinely interdisciplinary project.

Through the network that has grown up around the Centre for Parenting Culture Studies, we have developed a space for ongoing research, collaboration, and engagement. We conclude this book with the aspiration that its readers will feel motivated to take forward research in this exciting field.

Notes

1. *The following comment about this study was posted on the Facebook page of the Centre for Parenting Culture Studies (CPCS), and we hope the observations made here will be developed in subsequent commentaries about the research and the reporting of it:*

    The claim that breastfeeding boosts 'social mobility' is all over the world's media this week. The article generating the claim is posted below. Here are responses from two CPCS Associates to the paper. Further comments and discussion are very welcome.

    Stuart Derbyshire: 'In this article the authors are implying causation (neurological effects of breastfeeding causes social mobility) from correlation. To an extent, they accept this. But they argue that the stratification allows them to make causal inferences. In essence, if you rule out all relevant sources of variance then it is reasonable to imply causation. We might legitimately argue about whether the authors have ruled out all relevant sources of variance, enabling them to isolate breastfeeding as causal. But, for the sake of argument, let's say they have and the study is sound. What are we left with?

    The first thing to note is that the odds ratios are small (odds ratios, incidentally are not the same as risk ratios, odds ratios are bigger. So an odds ratio of 1.24 does not mean that the breastfed infant is 1.24 times more likely to climb socially, the likelihood is much lower, around 1.06 times more likely). We are talking about a very small influence, and small influences are always tricky.

The second thing to note is that the mechanism remains uncertain. Maybe the enhanced nutrition improves brain development and cognition (though that link is tricky in itself). Maybe it is greater physical contact that increases calm and quiescence (I am deliberately avoiding the term 'stress' which I think is meaningless), which might improve learning. Even then, the step from improved cognition or better educational attainment or both to social mobility is highly uncertain.

The third thing to note is the dogmatism of the advice. Breast fed babies have better social mobility – so increase breast feeding. The authors fail to understand that if every baby were breast fed then any influence of breast feeding would be annihilated ... Ignoring that irritating fact, they fail to entertain the possibility that we mimic the effects of breast feeding through other, less intrusive and irritating, interventions such as improved formula nutrition, contact mimicking formula delivery or, possibly, educational programs for formula fed kids.'

Joan Wolf: 'This study, like the last one Iovacu and Kelly were involved in, did a good job of trying to control for obvious confounding variables. Like the last one, this study demonstrates that the more you control for other possible explanations of the putative benefits of breastfeeding, the smaller these benefits get. And, the smaller the benefits in an observational study, the more problematic the causal claim, particularly when your evidence for a causal link is wobbly (at best). In this case, as in so many others, it is entirely plausible that parents who breastfeed also engage in a range of behaviors that could slightly nudge their kids' social mobility.

There are myriad methodological problems here with cohort, operationalization of social class and other variables, and representation of past research on breastfeeding. And, of course, there are questions CPCS asks about motherhood, risk, and parenting. In short, I do not think this study moves us any closer to understanding the relative benefits of breast and bottlefeeding.'

Bibliography

4Children (2013) 'About', 'Foundation Years: From pregnancy to children Age 5', http://www.foundationyears.org.uk/about/, accessed 3 June 2013.

Ainsworth, M. Blehar, M., Waters, W. and Wall, S. (1978) *Patterns of Attachment: A psychological study of the strange situation* (Hillsdale, NJ: Lawrence Erlbaum Associates, Inc.).

Allen, G. (2011a) *Early Intervention: The next steps* (London: Cabinet Office).

Allen, G. (2011b) *Early Intervention: Smart investment, massive savings* (London: Cabinet Office).

Allen, G. and Duncan Smith, I. (2008) *Early Intervention: Good parents, great kids, better citizens* (London: Centre for Social Justice and the Smith Institute).

Allen, G. and Duncan Smith, I. (2009) *Early Intervention: Good parents, great kids, better citizens*, 2nd edn (London: Centre for Social Justice and the Smith Institute).

Apple, R. D. (1995) 'Constructing mothers: scientific motherhood in the nineteenth and twentieth centuries', *Social History of Medicine*, 8(2), 161–178.

Apple, R. (2006) *Perfect Motherhood: Science and childrearing in America* (New Brunswick, New Jersey and London: Rutgers University Press).

API (Attachment Parenting International) (2009) '8 Principles of AP', http://www.attachmentparenting.org/principles/principles.php, accessed 23 March 2013.

API (Attachment Parenting International) (2012) *Annual Report, 2012*, http://www.attachmentparenting.org/pdfs/API2012AnnualReport.pdf, accessed 26 February 2013.

Arai, L. (2009) *Teenage Pregnancy: The making and unmaking of a problem* (Bristol: The Policy Press).

Arendell, T. (2000) 'Conceiving and investigating motherhood: the decade's scholarship', *Journal of Marriage and the Family*, 62 (November), 1192–1207.

Ariès, P. (1968 [1962]) *Centuries of Childhood: A social history of family life* (New York: Vintage Books).

Armstrong, C. (2013) 'Why moderate drinking is hurting your baby', *HuffPost Lifestyle*, 21 June, http://www.huffingtonpost.co.uk/carrie-armstrong/drinking-is-hurting-your-baby_b_3465140.html, accessed 15 July 2013.

Armstrong, E. M. (2003) *Conceiving Risk, Bearing Responsibility: Fetal Alcohol Syndrome and the diagnosis of moral disorder* (Baltimore: The John Hopkins University Press).

Armstrong, E. M. (1998) 'Diagnosing moral disorder: the discovery and evolution of Fetal Alcohol Syndrome', *Social Science and Medicine*, 47(12), 2025–2042.

Armstrong, E. M. and Abel, E. L. (2000) 'Fetal Alcohol Syndrome: the origins of a moral panic', *Alcohol and Alcoholism*, 35(3), 276–282.

Arnup, K. (1994) *Education for Motherhood: Advice for mothers in twentieth-century Canada* (Toronto: University of Toronto Press).

Asher, R. (2011) *Shattered: Modern motherhood and the illusion of equality* (London: Harvill Secker).

Atkins, S. (n.d) http://sueatkinsparentingcoach.com/, accessed 15 February 2013.

Avishai, O. (2007) 'Managing the lactating body: the breast-feeding project and privileged motherhood', *Qualitative Sociology*, 30, 135–152.

Avishai, O. (2011) 'Managing the lactating body: The breastfeeding project in the Age of Anxiety', in P. Liamputtong (ed.) *Infant Feeding Practices: A Cross-Cultural Perspective* (New York: Springer).

Badinter, E. (1981 [1980]) *The Myth of Motherhood: A historical view of the maternal instinct* (trans. Roger De Garis) (London: Souvenir Press).

Ball, H. (2005) 'Infant social sleep: instinct and environment', Presentation at La Leche League Enrichment Day, Nottingham, 20 September.

Ball, H. (2007) 'Bed-sharing practices of initially breastfed infants in the first 6 months of life', *Infant and Child Development*, 16(4), 387–401.

BBC News Online (2007) 'Gang crime "due to absent dads"', 21 August, http://news.bbc.co.uk/1/hi/uk_politics/6956303.stm, accessed 1 April 2011.

BBC News Online (2010) 'Q&A: "Sarah's Law" explained', 28 September, http://www.bbc.co.uk/news/uk-england-11427787, accessed 1 July 2013.

BBC News Online (2011) 'England riots: Broken society is top priority – Cameron', 15 August, http://www.bbc.co.uk/news/uk-politics-14524834, accessed 15 August 2011.

BBC News Online (2012) 'Scottish charities call for smacking ban', 17 July, http://www.bbc.co.uk/news/uk-scotland-scotland-politics-18860950, accessed 28 May 2013.

Beck, U. (1992) *Risk Society: Towards a new modernity* (London: Sage).

Beck, U. and Beck-Gernsheim, E. (1995) *The Normal Chaos of Love* (Oxford: Polity Press).Bell, S. (2004) 'Intensive performances of mothering: a sociological perspective', *Qualitative Research*, 4(1), 45–75.

Belsky, J., Barnes, J. and Melhuish, E. (2007) *The National Evaluation of Sure Start: Does area-based early intervention work?* (Bristol: Policy Press).

Best, J. (1993a) *Threatened Children: Rhetoric and concern about child-victims* (Chicago: The University of Chicago Press).

Best, J. (1993b) 'But seriously folks: The limitations of the strict constructionist interpretation of social problems', in J.A. Holstein and G. Miller (eds) *Reconsidering Social Constructionism: Debates in Social Problems Theory* (New York: Aldine de Gruyter).

Best, J. (1995) 'Typification and social problem construction', in J. Best (ed.) *Images of Issues* (New York: Aldine de Gruyter).

Best, J. (ed.) (2001) *How Claims Spread: Cross-national diffusion of social problems* (New York: Aldine de Gruyter).

Best, J. (2011) 'Locating moral panics within the sociology of social problems', in S.P. Hier (ed.) *Moral Panics and the Politics of Anxiety* (London and New York: Routledge).

Bingham, J. (2012) 'Failure to treat tens of thousands of mothers creating riots generation', *Daily Telegraph*, 18 May, http://www.telegraph.co.uk/health/healthnews/9272927/Failure-to-treat-tens-of-thousands-of-mothers-creating-riots-generation.html, accessed 3 June 2013.

Bingham, J. (2013) 'How the "breastfeeding effect" altered the British class system', *Daily Telegraph*, 25 June, http://www.telegraph.co.uk/health/health-news/10139181/How-the-breastfeeding-effect-altered-the-British-class-system.html, accessed 3 July 2013.

Blair, T. (1999) 'Beveridge lecture, 18 March 1999', in R. Walker (ed.) *Ending Child Poverty: Popular Welfare for the 21st Century?* (Bristol: Policy Press).

Blair, T. (2005) 'Speech on improving parenting', http://www.britishpolitical-speech.org/speech-archive.htm?speech=291, accessed 1 July 2013.

Blaffer Hrdy, S. (2000) *Mother Nature: Maternal instincts and the shaping of the species* (London: Vintage).

Blum, L. (1999) *At the Breast: Ideologies of breastfeeding and motherhood in the contemporary United States* (Boston: Beacon Press).

Bobel, C. (2002) *The Paradox of Natural Mothering* (Philadelphia: Temple University Press).

Boffey, D. (2013) 'Free parenting classes scheme in meltdown', *Guardian*, 24 March, http://www.guardian.co.uk/money/2013/mar/24/free-parenting-classes-scheme?INTCMP=SRCH, accessed 8 July 2013.

Borland, S. (2012) 'Playground children having more accidents because parents are too busy playing on their smartphones', *Daily Mail Online*, 23 November, http://www.dailymail.co.uk/health/article-2237034/Unsupervised-children-having-accidents-parents-busy-playing-smartphones.html, accessed 1 July 2013.

Bogenschneider, K. (2000) 'Has family policy come of age? A decade review of the state of U.S. family policy in the 1990s', *Journal of Marriage and the Family*, 62, 1136–1159.

Bowlby, J. (1969) *Attachment* (London: Pelican).

Bowlby, J. (1995 [1952]) *Maternal Care and Mental Health* (Lanham: Jason Aronson Inc.).

Bowlby, J. (2005) [1988] *A Secure Base: Clinical applications of attachment theory* (London: Routledge).

Bristow, J. (2009) *Standing up to Supernanny* (Exeter: Imprint Academic).

Bristow, J. (2013) 'Reporting the riots: Parenting culture and the problem of authority in media analysis of August 2011', *Sociological Research Online*, 18(4), 11, http://www.socresonline.org.uk/18/4/11.html.

Broadhurst, K., Hall, C., Wastell, D., White, S. and Pithouse, A. (2010) 'Risk, instrumentalism and the humane project in social work: identifying the informal logics of risk management in children's statutory services', *British Journal of Social Work*, 40, 1046–1064.

Brooks, D. (2011) 'Amy Chua is a wimp', *New York Times*, 17 January, http://www.nytimes.com/2011/01/18/opinion/18brooks.html?_r=0, accessed 17 July 2013.

Brown, M. (1982) 'Corticotropin-releasing factor: actions on the sympathetic nervous system and metabolism', *Endocrinology*, 111, 928–931.

Bruer, John T. (1997) 'Education and the brain: a bridge too far', *Educational Researcher*, 26, 4–16.

Bruer, John T. (1998a) 'Brain science, brain fiction', *Educational Leadership*, 56(3), 14–18.

Bruer, John T. (1998b) 'Time for critical thinking', *Public Health Reports*, 113(5), 389–397.

Bruer, J. (1999) *The Myth of the First Three Years: A new understanding of early brain development and lifelong learning* (New York: The Free Press).

Burman, E. (2008) *Deconstructing Developmental Psychology* (London and New York: Routledge).

Buskens, P. (2001) 'The impossibility of "natural parenting" for modern mothers: on social structure and the formation of habit', *Association for Research on Mothering Journal*, Spring/Summer, 3.1, 75–86.

Cabinet Office (2006) *Reaching Out: An action plan on social exclusion* (London: Cabinet Office).

Cameron, C. (2001) 'Promise or problem? A review of the literature on men working in early childcare services', *Gender, Work and Organization*, 8(3), October.

Cameron, D. (2008) 'Speech introducing The Childhood Review' http://conservativehome.blogs.com/torydiary/files/cameron_speech_on_childhood.pdf, accessed 24 July 2013.

Carabine, J. (2007) 'New Labour's teenage pregnancy policy: constituting knowing responsible citizens?' *Cultural Studies*, 21(6), 952–973.

Carnegie Corporation (1994) *Starting Points: Meeting the needs of our youngest children*, abridged version (New York: Carnegie Corporation).

Casper, M. (1998) *The Making of the Unborn Patient: A social anatomy of fetal surgery* (New Brunswick, New Jersey and London: Rutgers University Press).

Chaffin, M. (2004) 'Is it time to rethink Healthy Start/Healthy Families?' *Child Abuse and Neglect*, 28, 589–595.

Chua, A. (2011) *Battle Hymn of the Tiger Mother* (London: Penguin).

Churchill, H. and Clarke, K. (2009) 'Investing in parenting education: a critical review of policy and provision in England', *Social Policy and Society*, 9(1), 39–53.

Clarke, K. (2006) 'Childhood, parenting and early intervention: a critical examination of the Sure Start national programme', *Critical Social Policy*, 26(4), 699–721.

Clarke, A. (2007) 'Consuming children and making mothers: birthday parties, gifts and the pursuits of sameness', *Hoizontes Antropoliogicos*, 13(28), 263–287.

Clayton, F., Sealy, J. and Pfeiffer, S. (2006) 'Weaning age among foragers at Matjes river rock shelter, South Africa, from stable nitrogen and carbon isotope Analyses', *American Journal of Physical Anthropology*, 129(2), 311–317.

Collier R. (2008) 'Engaging Fathers? Responsibility, Law and the "Problem of Fatherhood"', in J. Bridgeman, C. Lind and H. Keating (eds), *Responsibility, Law and the Family* (Aldershot: Ashgate Publishing), pp. 169–190.

Collier, R. and Sheldon, S. (2008) *Fragmenting Fatherhood: A socio-legal study* (Oxford: Hart).

Connell, R. (1995) *Masculinities* (Cambridge: Polity Press).

Cooper, C. (2013) 'Revealed: breastfeeding babies improves their chance of climbing the social ladder', *Independent*, 25 June, http://www.independent.co.uk/life-style/health-and-families/health-news/revealed-breastfeeding-babies-improves-their-chance-of-climbing-social-ladder-8672173.html, accessed 3 July 2013.

Copelton, D. (2008) 'Neutralization and emotion work in women's accounts of light drinking in pregnancy', in J. Nathanson and L. C. Tuley (eds), *Mother Knows Best: Talking back to the 'experts'* (Toronto: Demeter Press).

Council of Europe (2007) *Parenting in Europe: A positive approach* (Strasbourg: Council of Europe Publishing), http://www.coe.int/t/dg3/children/publications/ParentingContempory_en.asp, accessed 1 July 2013.

Cucchiara, M. (2013) '"Are we doing damage?" Choosing an urban public school in an era of parental anxiety', *Anthropology and Education Quarterly*, 44, 75–93.

Cullen, M. A., Cullen, S., Strand, S., Bakopoulou, I., Lindsay, G., Brind, R., Pickering, E., Bryson, C. and Purdon, S. (2013) *CANparent Trial Evaluation: First Interim Report* (London: Department for Education), http://www2.warwick.ac.uk/fac/soc/cedar/dfe-rr2801.pdf, accessed 8 July 2013.

Cunningham, H. (1995) *Children & Childhood in Western Society since 1500* (London: Longman).

Cunningham, H. (2006) *The Invention of Childhood* (London: BBC Books).

Daily Mail (2012) 'Smacking or shouting at your children "raises their risk of cancer, heart disease and asthma later in life"', 12 November, http://www.dailymail.co.uk/health/article-2231739/Smacking-shouting-children-raises-risk-cancer-heart-disease-asthma-later-life.html, accessed 1 July 2013.

Daily Telegraph (2009) 'Parent drivers "shouldn't over-react to vetting moves"', 14 September, http://www.telegraph.co.uk/news/uknews/6184668/Parent-drivers-shouldnt-over-react-to-vetting-moves.html, accessed 1 July 2013.

Daly, M. (2010) 'Shifts in family policy in the UK under New Labour', *Journal of European Social Policy*, 20(5), 433–443.

Daly, M. (2013) 'Parenting support policies in Europe', *Families, Relationships and Societies*, 2(2), 159–174.

Damasio, A. (2006) [1994] *Descartes' Error: Emotion, reason and the human brain* (London: Vintage Books).

Davis, R. A. (2010) 'Government intervention in child rearing: Governing infancy', *Educational Theory*, 60(3), 285–298.

Denney, D. (2005) *Risk and Society* (London: Sage Publications).

Department for Children, Schools and Families (DCSF) (2010) 'Vetting and Barring Facts', 8 February.

Department for Children, Schools and Families, Home Office, Department of Health (DCSF, HO, DH) (2007) *SVG Act 2006: ISA Scheme Consultation Document* (London: DCSF, HO, DH).

Department for Education (DfE) (2010) 'Parenting Experts and Practitioners' (Think Family Toolkit publication, February) (London: DfE).

Department for Education (DfE) (2011) 'Free parenting classes to be offered to over 50,000 mothers and fathers', 16 October, http://www.education.gov.uk/inthenews/inthenews/a00199302/free-parenting-classes-to-be-offered-to-over-50000-mothers-and-fathers, accessed 8 July 2013.

Department for Education (DfE) (2012) *Supporting Families in the Foundation Years*, http://www.education.gov.uk/childrenandyoungpeople/earlylearnin-gandchildcare/early/a00192398/supporting-families-in-the-foundation-years, accessed 2 May 2013.

Department for Education (DfE) (2013) *CANparent Trial Evaluation: First Interim Report*, https://www.gov.uk/government/uploads/system/uploads/attachment_data/file/190980/DFE-RR280.pdf, accessed 2 May 2013.

Department for Education and Employment (DfEE) (1998) *Meeting the Childcare Challenge* (Suffolk: DfEE).

Department for Education and Skills (2003) *Every Child Matters: A green paper*, September (London: The Stationery Office).

Department for Education and Skills (DfES) (2004) *Every Child Matters: Change for Children* (Nottingham: DfES).

Department for Education and Skills (DfES) (2006) *Parenting support: Guidance for local authorities in England* (London: DfES).

Department for Education and Skills (DfES) (2007) *Every Parent Matters* (Nottingham: DfES).

Department for Education, Department of Health, Home Office (DfE, DH, HO) (2011) *Vetting and Barring Scheme Remodelling Review – Report and Recommendations*, https://www.gov.uk/government/uploads/system/uploads/attachment_data/file/97748/vbs-report.pdf, accessed 10 July 2013.

Department of Health (DH) (2008) *The Child Health Promotion Programme: Pregnancy and the first five years of life*, April (London: DH).

Department of Health and Department for Education and Skills (DH and DfES) (2004) *National Service Framework for Children, Young People and Maternity Services* (London: HMSO).

Dermott, E. (2001) 'New Fatherhood in practice? – Parental leave in the UK', *International Journal of Sociology and Social Policy*, 21(4/5/6), 145–164.

Dermott, E. (2008) *Intimate Fatherhood: A sociological analysis* (London: Routledge).

Dettwyler, K. (1995) 'A Time to Wean: A hominid blueprint for the natural age of weaning', in P. Stuart-Macadam and K. Dettwyler (eds) *Breastfeeding: Bio-cultural Perspectives* (New York: Aldine de Gruyter), pp. 167–217.

Dodds, A. (2009) 'Families "at risk" and the Family Nurse Partnership: the intrusion of risk into social exclusion policy', *Journal of Social Policy*, 38(3), 499–514.

Dolev, R. and Zeedyk, M. S. (2006) 'How to be a good parent in bad times: constructing parenting advice about terrorism', *Child: Care, Health and Development*, 32(4), 467–476.

Donnelly, L. (2011) 'Working mothers spend 81 minutes per day looking after their children', *Sunday Telegraph*, 27 March, http://www.telegraph.co.uk/news/uknews/8408503/Working-mothers-spend-81-minutes-a-day-looking-after-their-children.html, accessed 3 December 2012.

Donzelot, J. (1980) *The Policing of Families: Welfare versus the state* (London: Hutchinson & Co.).

Doucet, A. (2006) *Do Men Mother? Fathering, care and domestic responsibility* (Toronto: University of Toronto Press).

Douglas, S. and Michaels, M. (2004) *The Mommy Myth: The idealization of motherhood and how it has undermined all women* (New York: Free Press).

Druckerman, P. (2012) *Bringing up Bébé: One American mother discovers the wisdom of French parenting* (London and New York: Penguin Books).

Duncan, S. (2007) 'What's the problem with teenage parents? And what's the problem with policy?' *Critical Social Policy*, 27(3), 307–334.

Duncan, S., Edwards, R. and Alexander, C. (eds) (2010) *Teenage Parenthood: What's the problem?* (London: the Tufnell Press).

Duncan, S., Edwards, R., Reynolds, T. and Alldred, P. (2003) 'Mothering, paid work and partnering: values and theories', *Work, Employment and Society*, 17(2), 309–330.

Economist (2009) 'Female power', 30 December, http://www.economist.com/node/15174418, accessed 27 November 2013.

Edwards, R. and Gillies, V. (2011) 'Clients or consumers, commonplace or pioneers? Navigating the contemporary class politics of family, parenting skills and education', *Ethics and Education*, 6(2), 141–154.

Edwards, R. and Gillies, V. (2013) '"Where are the parents?" Changing parenting responsibilities between the 1960s and the 2010s', in C. Faircloth *et al.* (eds) *Parenting in Global Perspective: Negotiating ideologies of kinship, self and politics* (London and New York: Routledge), pp. 21–36.

Egerton, J. (n/d) 'Fetal Alcohol Spectrum Disorder: Information Sheets', Worcestershire County Council, http://www.worcestershire.gov.uk/cms/PDF/FASD%20Information%20sheets%202009-02.pdf, accessed 3 June 2013.

Ehrenreich, B. and English, D. (1979) *For Her Own Good: 150 years of the experts' advice to women* (London: Pluto Press).

Elias, N. (1998) 'The Civilizing of Parents', in J. Goudsblom and S. Mennell (eds) *The Norbert Elias Reader* (Blackwell: Oxford), pp. 189–211.

Engels, F. (1972) [1884] *The Origin of the Family, Private Property and the State* (New York: Pathfinder).

Eyer, D. (1992) *Mother-Infant Bonding: A scientific fiction* (New Haven and London: Yale University Press).

Faircloth, C. (2013) *Militant Lactivism? Infant feeding and maternal accountability in the UK and France* (Oxford and New York: Berghahn Books).

Faircloth, C. (2010) '"If they want to risk the health and well-being of their child, that's up to them": long-term breastfeeding, risk and maternal identity', *Heath, Risk and Society*, 12(4), 357–367.

Faircloth, C. and Lee, E. (2010) 'Changing parenting culture', *Sociological Research Online*, 15(4), 1, http://www.socresonline.org.uk/15/4/1.html.

Faircloth, C., Hoffman, D. and Layne, L. (eds) (2013) *Parenting in Global Perspective: Negotiating ideologies of kinship, self and politics* (London and New York: Routledge).

Faircloth, C., Hoffman, D. and Layne, L. L. (2013) 'Introduction', in C. Faircloth et al. (eds) *Parenting in Global Perspective: Negotiating Ideologies of Kinship, Self and Politics* (London and New York: Routledge), pp. 1–19.

The Fatherhood Institute. (2009) *Think Fathers*, http://www.fatherhoodinstitute.org/2009/about-thethink-fathers-campaign/.

Fatherhood Institute (FI) (2010) *Guide for New Dads*, http://www.fatherhoodinstitute.org/wp-content/uploads/2010/02/Guide-for-New-Dads.pdf, accessed 2 May 2013.

Fatherhood Institute (FI) (2011) *FI Research Summary: Fathers, mothers, work and family*, http://www.fatherhoodinstitute.org/2011/fi-research-summary-fathers-mothers-work-and-family/, accessed 2 May 2013.

Featherstone, B. (2009) *Contemporary fathering: theory, policy and practice*. Bristol: Policy Press.

Featherstone, B., Morris, K. and White, S. (2013) 'A marriage made in hell: early intervention meets child protection', *British Journal of Social Work*, March, 1–15.

Field, F. (2010) *The Foundation Years: Preventing poor children becoming poor adults* (London: Cabinet Office).

Figert, A. E. (1996) *Women and the Ownership of PMS: The structuring of a psychiatric disorder* (New York: Aldine de Gruyter).

Figge, M. (1932) 'Studies in maternal overprotection and rejection: some factors in the etiology of maternal rejection', *Smith College Studies in Social Work*, 2, 237–260.

Fildes, V. (1986) *Breasts, Bottles, and Babies: A history of infant feeding* (Edinburgh: Edinburgh University Press).

Filler, D. M. (2001) 'Making the case for Megan's Law: a study in legislative rhetoric', *Indiana Law Journal*, 76(2), Article 2, 314–365.

Fingerman, K. L., Cheng, Y.-P., Wesselmann, E. D., Zarit, S., Furstenberg, F. and Birditt, K. S. (2012) 'Helicopter parents and landing pad kids: intense parental support of grown children', *Journal of Marriage and Family*, 74, 880–896.

Fisher, K., McCulloch, A. and Gershuny, J. (1999) *British Fathers and Children: A report for Channel 4 'Dispatches'*, Technical Report, Institute for Social and Economic Research, Colchester, UK.

Firestone, S. (1970) *The Dialectic of Sex: The case for feminist revolution* (New York: Bantam).

Foetal Alcohol Syndrome (FAS) Aware UK (2010) 'Baby Scan Video', 15 March http://www.youtube.com/watch?v=kk3i3kl_4yQ&feature=player_embedded, accessed 15 July 2013.

Fox, N. (1999) 'Postmodern reflections on "risk", "hazards" and life choices', in D. Lupton (ed.) *Risk and Sociocultural Theory: New Directions and Perspectives* (Cambridge: Cambridge University Press).

Fox, R., Heffernan, K. and Nicolson, P. (2009) '"I don't think it was such an issue back then": changing experiences of pregnancy across two generations of women in south-east England', *Gender, Place and Culture: A Journal of Feminist Geography*, 16(5), 553–568.

Fox Harding, L. M. (2000) 'Supporting Families/Controlling Families? – Towards a characterisation of New Labour's "family policy"', Working Paper No. 21 (Leeds: Centre for Research on Family, Kinship and Childhood).

Franklin, L. and Cromby, J. (2009) 'Everyday Fear: Parenting and Childhood in a Culture of Fear', in L. Franklin and R. Richardson (eds) *The Many Forms of Fear and Terror* (Oxford: Interdisciplinary Press), pp. 161–174.

Francis, B. (2010) *What Did the Baby Boomers Ever Do for Us? Why the children of the sixties lived the dream and failed the future* (London: Biteback).

Freely, M. (2000) *The Parent Trap: Children, families and the new morality* (London: Virago).

Furedi, F. (1997) *Culture of Fear: Risk-taking and the morality of low expectation* (London: Cassell).

Furedi, F. (2001) *Paranoid Parenting: Abandon your anxieties and be a good parent* (London: Allen Lane).

Furedi, F. (2002) *Paranoid Parenting: Why ignoring the experts may be best for your child* (Chicago: Chicago Review Press).

Furedi, F. (2004) *Therapy Culture: Cultivating vulnerability in an uncertain age* (London: Routledge).

Furedi, F. (2005) *Politics of Fear: Beyond left and right* (London and New York: Continuum).

Furedi, F. (2007) *Invitation to Terror: The expanding empire of the unknown* (London and New York: Continuum).

Furedi, F. (2008a) *Paranoid Parenting: Why ignoring the experts may be best for your child*, 2nd edn (London and New York: Continuum).

Furedi, F. (2008b) 'Politicising Science', *spiked*, 15 January 2008, http://www.spiked-online.com/index.php?/site/article/4275/, accessed 6 April 2008.

Furedi, F. (2009a) *Wasted: Why education isn't educating* (London: Continuum).

Furedi, F. (2009b) 'Precautionary culture and the rise of possibilistic risk assessment', *Erasmus Law Review*, 2(2), 197–220.

Furedi, F. (2011) 'The objectification of fear and the grammar of morality', in S.P. Hier (ed.) *Moral Panics and the Politics of Anxiety* (London and New York: Routledge).

Furedi, F. (2013a) 'The 20th Anniversary of James Bulger's death: a tragic episode and its shameful legacy', *The Independent*, 12 February, http://www.independent.co.uk/voices/comment/the-20th-anniversary-of-james-bulgers-death-a-tragic-episode-and-its-shameful-legacy-8490205.html, accessed 8 July 2013.

Furedi, F. (2013b) *Moral Crusades in an Age of Mistrust: The Jimmy Savile Scandal*, (Basingstoke: Palgrave).

Furedi, F. and Bristow, J. (2010) *Licensed to Hug: How child protection policies are poisoning the relationship between the generations and damaging the voluntary sector*, 2nd edn (London: Civitas).

Furstenburg, F. F. Jr (1991) 'As the pendulum swings: teenage childbearing and social concern', *Family Relations*, 40(2), 27–138.

Gabb, J. (2013) 'Embodying risk: managing father–child intimacy and the display of nudity in families', *Sociology*, August 2013, 47(4), 639–654.

Gabb, J. (2012) 'Embodying risk: managing father–child intimacy and display of nudity in families', *Sociology*, 0(0), 1–16.

Gardner, R. (1997) 'The embedment-in-the-brain-circuitry phenomenon: implications', *Journal of the American Academy of Psychoanalysis*, 25, 151–176.

Gatrell, C. (2005) *Hard Labour: The sociology of parenthood* (Maidenhead: Open University Press).

Gatrell, C. (2011) 'Policy and the pregnant body at work: strategies of secrecy, silence and supra-performance', *Gender, Work and Organization*, 18(2), 158–181.

Gatrell, C. (2013) 'Maternal body work: how women managers and professionals negotiate pregnancy and new motherhood at work', *Human Relations*, 66(5): 621–644.

Gauthier, A. *et al.* (2004) 'Are parents investing less time in children? Trends in selected industrialized countries', *Population and Development Review*, 30(4), 647–671.

Gavaghan, C. (2009) '"You can't handle the truth"; medical paternalism and prenatal alcohol use', *Journal of Medical Ethics*, 35, 300–303.

Godderis, R. (2010) 'Precarious beginnings: gendered risk discourses in psychiatric research literature about postpartum depression', *Health*, 14(5), 451–466.

Gerhardt, S. (2004) *Why Love Matters: How affection shapes a baby's brain* (London: Routledge).

Geronimus, A. T. (1997) 'Teenage childbearing and personal responsibility: an alternative view', *Political Science Quarterly*, 112(3), 405–430.

Gibbs, N. (2009) 'The Growing Backlash Against Overparenting', 30 November, http://www.time.com/time/magazine/article/0,9171,1940697,00.html#ixzz2Rx2e76ld, accessed 17 July 2013.

Giddens, A. (1991) *Modernity and Self-Identity: Self and society in the late modern age* (Cambridge: Polity).

Giddens, A. (1994) *Beyond Left and Right: The future of radical politics* (Palo Alto: Stanford University Press).

Giddens, A. (1999) *The Third Way: The renewal of social democracy* (Cambridge: Polity Press).

Gill, T. (2007) *No Fear: Growing up in a risk averse society* (London: Calouste Gulbenkian Foundation).

Gillies, V. (2005) 'Raising the meritocracy: parenting and the individualization of social class', *Sociology*, 39(5), 835–853.

Gillies, V. (2006) *Marginalised Mothers: Exploring working class parenting* (London and New York: Routledge).

Gillies, V. (2008) 'Perspectives on parenting responsibility: contextualising values and practices', *Journal of Law and Society*, 35(1), 95–112.

Gillies, V. (2009) 'Understandings and experiences of involved fathering in the United Kingdom: exploring classed dimensions', *The Annals of the American Academy of Political and Social Science*, 624, 49–60.

Gillies, V. (2011) 'From function to competence: engaging with the new politics of family', *Sociological Research Online*, 16(4), 11, http://www.socresonline.org.uk/16/4/11.html, accessed 15 July 2013.

Gillies, V. (2012) 'Family policy and the politics of parenting: from function to competence', in M. Richter and S. Andresen (eds) *The Politicization of Parenthood: Shifting Private and Public Responsibilities in Education and Child Rearing* (London and New York: Springer).

Gillies, V. (2013) 'From baby brain to conduct disorder: the new determinism in the classroom', paper given at the Gender and Education Association Conference, 25th April 2013, London: Weeks Centre for Social and Policy Research, London South Bank University, http://www.academia.edu/3549456/From_Baby_Brain_to_Conduct_Disorder_The_New_Determinism_in_the_Classroom, accessed 24 July 2013.

Gillis, J. (1995) 'Bringing up father: British paternal identities, 1700-present', *Masculinities*, 3(3), 1–27.

Gittins, D. (1993 [1985]) *The Family in Question: Changing households and family ideologies* (Basingstoke: Macmillan).

Godderis, R. (2010) 'Precarious beginnings: gendered risk discourses in psychiatric research literature about postpartum depression', *Health*, 14(5), 451–466.

Golden, J. (1999) '"An argument that goes back to the womb": the demedicalization of Fetal Alcohol Syndrome, 1973–1992', *Journal of Social History*, Winter, 269–298.

Golden, J. (2005) *Message in a Bottle: The making of Fetal Alcohol Syndrome* (Cambridge, MA and London: Harvard University Press).

Goldson, B. and Jamieson, J. (2002) 'Youth crime, the "parenting deficit" and state intervention: a contextual critique', *Youth Justice*, 2(2), 82–99.

Great Ormond Street Hospital (GOSH) (2011) 'The Role of Fathers', http://www.gosh.nhs.uk/parents-and-visitors/general-health-advice/parenting-advice/the-role-of-fathers/, accessed 1 May 2013.

Gross-Loh, C. (2007) *The Diaper-free Baby: The natural toilet training alternative for a happier, healthier baby or toddler* (New York: Harper Collins).

Guldberg, H. (2009) *Reclaiming Childhood: Freedom and play in an age of fear* (London and New York: Routledge).

HM Government (2011) *Consultation on Modern Workplaces*, https://www.gov.uk/government/uploads/system/uploads/attachment_data/file/31549/11-699-consultation-modern-workplaces.pdf, accessed 1 May 2013.

HM Treasury and Department for Education and Skills (DfES) (2007) *Aiming High for Children: Supporting families* (London: The Stationery Office).

Hardyment, C. (1995) *Perfect Parents: Baby-care advice past and present* (Oxford: Oxford University Press).

Hardyment, C. (2007) *Dream Babies: Childcare advice from John Locke to Gina Ford* (London: Francis Lincoln).

Hausman, B. (2003) *Mother's Milk: Breastfeeding controversies in American culture* (London: Routledge).

Hays, S. (1996) *The Cultural Contradictions of Motherhood* (New Haven and London: Yale University Press).

Heffernan, K., Nicolson, P. and Fox, R. (2011) 'The next generation of pregnant women: more freedom in the public sphere or just and illusion?' *Journal of Gender Studies*, 20(4), 321–332.

Hendrick, H. (1997) *Children, Childhood and English Society 1880–1990* (Cambridge: Cambridge University Press).

Henricson, C. (2008) 'Governing parenting: is there a case for a policy review and statement of parenting rights and responsibilities?' *Journal of Law and Society*, 35(1), 150–165.

Hess, E. (1966) 'Imprinting', in R. King (ed.) *Readings for an Introduction to Psychology* (New York: McGraw-Hill), pp. 39–46.

Hinton, D., Laverty, L. and Robinson, J. (2013) 'Negotiating (un)healthy lifestyles in an era of "intensive" parenting: ethnographic case studies from North West England, UK', in C. Faircloth *et al.* (eds) *Parenting in Global Perspective: Negotiating Ideologies of Kinship, Self and Politics* (London and New York: Routledge), pp. 71–86.

Hobson, B. (2002) *Making Men into Fathers: Men, masculinities and the social politics of fatherhood* (Cambridge: Cambridge University Press).

Hobson, B. and Morgan, D. (2002) 'Introduction', in B. Hobson (ed.) *Making Men into Fathers: Men, Masculinities and the Social Politics of Fatherhood* (Cambridge: Cambridge University Press), pp. 1–2.

Hochschild, A. R. (1979) 'Emotion work, feeling rules, and social structure', *The American Journal of Sociology*, 85(3), 551–575.

Hochschild, A. (2003) *The Second Shift* (London and New York: Penguin Books).

Hoffmann, D. (2010) 'Risky investments: parenting and the production of the "resilient child"', *Health, Risk and Society*, 12(4), 385–394.

Holt, L. Emmett. (1913) 'Infant Mortality, Ancient and Modern, An Historical Sketch', Presidential address before the American Association for the Study and Prevention of Infant Mortality, at the Fourth Annual Meeting, held at Washington, DC, November 14–17, 1913, published in *Archives of Pediatrics*, 30, 885–915, 1913, reproduced on Neonatology on the Web, http://www.neonatology.org/classics/holt.html, accessed 19 July 2013.

Home Office (1998) *Supporting Families: A consultation document* (London: Home Office).

Howe, N. and Strauss, W. (2000) *Millennials Rising: The next great generation* (New York: Vintage Books).

Howe, N. and William, S. (2008) *Helicopter Parents in the Workplace*, nGenera insight, http://www.wikinomics.com/blog/uploads/helicopter-parents-in-the-workplace.pdf, accessed 17 July 2013.

Howker, E. and Malik, S. (2010) *Jilted Generation: How Britain has bankrupted its youth* (London: Icon).

Hulbert, A. (2004) *Raising America: Experts, parents, and a century of advice about children* (New York: Vintage).

Humphriss, R., Hall, A., May, M., Zuccolo, L. and Mcleod, J. (2013) 'Prenatal alcohol exposure and childhood balance ability: findings from a UK birth cohort study', *BMJ Open* 3:e002718.doi: 10.1136/bmjopen-2013-002718.

Hunt, A. (2003) 'Risk and moralization in everyday life', in R.V. Erickson and A. Doyle (eds) *Risk and Morality* (Toronto: University of Toronto Press).

Hunt, A. (2011) 'Fractious rivals? Moral panics and moral regulation', in S.P. Hier (ed.) *Moral Panics and the Politics of Anxiety* (London and New York: Routledge).

Illouz, E. (2007) *Cold Intimacies: The making of emotional capitalism* (Cambridge: Polity Press).

Independent Parliamentary Inquiry into Online Child Protection (2013) *Findings and Recommendations*, April, http://www.claireperry.org.uk/down loads/independent-parliamentary-inquiry-into-online-child-protection.pdf, accessed 17 July 2013.

Ives, J. (2013) 'The Moral Habitus of Fatherhood: A study of how men negotiate the moral demands of becoming a father', University of Birmingham, http://www.birmingham.ac.uk/Documents/collegemds/haps/projects/MESH/habitus-fatherhood-report.pdf, accessed 1 May 2013.

Jackson, D. (2003) [1989] *Three in a Bed: The benefits of sleeping with your baby* (London: Bloomsbury).

Jackson, S. and Scott, S. (1999) 'Risk, anxiety and the social construction of children', in D. Lupton (ed.) *Risk and Socio-Cultural Theory: New Directions and Perspectives* (Cambridge: Cambridge University Press).

James, A., Jenks, C. and Prout, A. (1998) *Theorizing Childhood* (Cambridge: Polity Press).

Jamieson, L. (1998) *Intimacy: Personal Relationships in Modern Societies* (Cambridge: Polity Press).

Jaysane-Darr, A. (2013) 'Nurturing Sudanese, producing Americans: Refugee parents and personhood', in C. Faircloth *et al.* (eds) *Parenting in Global Perspective: Negotiating Ideologies of Kinship, Self and Politics* (London and New York: Routledge), pp. 101–117.

Jenkins, N. (2006) '"You can't wrap the up in cotton wool!" Constructing risk in young people's access to outdoor play', *Health, Risk and Society*, 8(4), 379–393.

Jenkins, P. (1998) *Moral Panic: Changing concepts of the child molester in modern America* (New Haven and London: Yale University Press).

Jensen, T. (2010) 'Warmth and wealth: re-imagining social class in taxonomies of good parenting', *Studies in the Maternal*, 2(1), http://www.mamsie.bbk.ac.uk/back_issues/issue_three/jensen.html.

Johnson, A. (2007) 'Cover letter to the launch of the report *Every Child Matters*' (London: Department for Education and Schools).

Johnston, D. and Swanson, D. (2006) 'Constructing the "Good Mother": the experience of mothering ideologies by work status', *Sex Roles*, 54, 509–519.

Jones, A. (2004) 'Risk anxiety, policy, and the spectre of sexual abuse in early childhood education', *Discourse: Studies in the Cultural Politics of Education*, 25(3), 321–334.

Jones, D. (2007) *Cotton Wool Kids: Releasing the potential for children to take risks and innovate*, Issues Paper 7 (London and Coventry: HTI), http://www.hti.org.uk/pdfs/pu/IssuesPaper7.pdf, accessed 17 July 2013.

Jones, G. (2007) 'Cameron Blames Fathers for "Broken' Society"', *Daily Telegraph*, 17 February, http://www.telegraph.co.uk/news/uknews/1542914/Cameron-blames-absent-fathers.html, accessed 4 July 2013.

Kagan, J. (1998) *Three Seductive Ideas* (Cambridge and London: Harvard University Press).

Kamerman, S. B. and Kahn, A. J. (2001) 'Child and family policies in the United States at the opening of the twenty-first century', *Social Policy and Administration*, 35(1), 69–84.

Kanieski, M. A. (2009) 'Best Be the Ties that Bind: The medicalization of mother love', paper presented at CPCS conference 'From child-rearing to "parenting": what's new about contemporary parenting culture?' January 2009, University of Kent, http://blogs.kent.ac.uk/parentingculturestudies/files/2010/12/Sem-1-kanieski-paper.pdf, accessed 12 June 2013.

Kanieski, M. A. (2010) 'Securing attachment: the shifting medicalization of attachment and attachment disorders', *Health, Risk and Society*, 12(4), 335–344.

Kanter, R. (1972) *Commitment and Community Communes and Utopias in Sociological Perspective* (Cambridge, MA: Harvard University Press).

Karpin, I. (2010) 'Taking care of the "health" of preconcevived human embryos or constaructing legal harms', in J. Nisker, F. Baylis, I. Karpin, C. McLeod and R. Mykituik (eds) *The 'Healthy' Embryo: Social, Biomedical, Legal and Philosophical Perspectives* (Cambridge: Cambridge University Press), pp. 136–149.

Kate Cairns Associates (2012) *Five to Thrive: The things you do every day that help your child's growing brain, a guide for parents and carers*, www.fivetothrive.org.uk, accessed 25 July 2013.

Keating, H. (2007) 'The "responsibility" of children in the criminal law', *Child and Family Law Quarterly*, 19(2), 183–203.

Kehily, M. J. (2010) 'Childhood in crisis? Tracing the contours of "crisis" and its impact upon contemporary parenting practices', *Media, Culture and Society*, 32(2), 171–185.

Kessen, W. (1979) 'The American child and other cultural inventions', *American Psychologist*, 34(10), 815–820.

King, J. R. (1998) *Uncommon Caring: Learning from men who teach young children* (New York: Teachers College Press).

Klaus, M. and Kennell, J. (1976) *Maternal-Infant Bonding: The impact of early separation or loss on family development* (St Louis: Mosby).

Klaus, M., Kennell, J. and Klaus, P. (1995) *Bonding: Building the foundations of secure attachment and independence* (Reading, MA: Addison-Wesley Publishing Company).

Klett-Davis M. (ed.) (2010) *Is Parenting a Class Issue?* (London: Family and Parenting Institute).

Kline, W. (2005) *Building a Better Race: Gender, sexuality and eugenics from the turn of the century to the baby boom* (Berkeley: University of California Press).

Knaak, S. (2005) 'Breast-feeding, bottle-feeding and Dr Spock: the shifting context of choice', *Canadian Review of Sociology and Anthropology*, 42(2), 197–216.

Knaak, S. (2006) 'The problem with breastfeeding discourse', *The Canadian Journal of Public Health*, 97(5), 412–414.

Knaak, S. (2010) 'Contextualising risk, constructing choice: breastfeeding and good mothering in risk society', *Heath, Risk and Society*, 12(4), 345–356.

Kukla, R. (2005) *Mass Hysteria: Medicine, culture and mothers' bodies* (New York: Rowman and Littlefield Publishers).

Kukla, R. (2006) 'Ethics and Ideology in Breastfeeding Advocacy Campaigns', *Hypatia*, 21(1), 157–180.

Kukla, R. (2008) 'Measuring motherhood', *The International Journal of Feminist Approaches to Bioethics*, 1(1), 67–90.

Kukla, R. (2010) 'The ethics and cultural politics of reproductive risk warnings: A case study of California's Proposition 65', *Health, Risk and Society*, 12(4), 323–334.

Landsman, G. (1998) 'Reconstructing motherhood in the age of "perfect" babies: mothers of infants and toddlers with disabilities', *Signs*, 24(1), 69–99.

Lareau, A. (2003) *Unequal Childhoods: Class, race, and family life* (Berkeley: University of California Press).

Lasch, C. (1977) *Haven in a Heartless World: The family besieged* (New York and London: Basic Books).

Lasch, C. (1979) *The Culture of Narcissism: American life in an age of diminishing expectations* (New York: Norton).

Layard, R. and Dunn, J. (2009) *A Good Childhood: Searching for values in a competitive age* (London: Penguin Books).

Layne, L. (2013) 'Intensive parenting alone: Negotiating the cultural contradictions of motherhood as a single mother by choice', in C. Faircloth *et al.* (eds) *Parenting in Global Perspective: Negotiating Ideologies of Kinship, Self and Politics* (London and New York: Routledge), pp. 213–229.

Lee, E. (2004) *Abortion, Motherhood and Mental Health: The medicalization of reproduction in the U.S. and Britain* (New York: Transaction Publishers).

Lee, E. (2007a) 'Health, morality, and infant feeding: British mothers' experiences of formula milk use in the early weeks', *Sociology of Health and Illness*, 29(7), 1075–1090.

Lee, E. (2007b) 'Infant feeding in risk society', *Health, Risk and Society*, 9(3), 295–309.

Lee, E. (2008) 'Living with risk in the age of "intensive motherhood": maternal identity and infant feeding', *Health, Risk and Society*, 10(5), 467–447.

Lee, E. (2010) 'Pathologising fatherhood: The case of male post natal depression in Britain', in S. Robertson and B. Gough (eds) *Men, Masculinities and Health: Critical Perspectives* (Basingstoke: Palgrave), pp. 161–177.

Lee, E. (2011) 'Breast-feeding advocacy, risk society and health moralism: a decade's scholarship', *Sociology Compass*, 5(12), 1058–1069.

Lee, E. and Bristow, J. (2009) 'Rules for feeding babies', in S. Day-Sclater, F. Ebtehaj, E. Jackson and M. Richards (eds) *Regulating Autonomy, Sex, Reproduction and the Family* (Oxford and Portland, Oregon: Hart Publishing), pp. 73–91.

Lee, E., Macvarish, J. and Bristow, J. (2010) 'Editorial: risk, health and parenting culture', *Health Risk and Society*, 12(4), 293–300.

Legrenzi, P. and Umilta, C. (2011) *Neuromania: On the limits of brain science* (Oxford: Oxford University Press).

Leppo, A. (2012) 'The emergence of the fetus: discourses on Fetal Alcohol Syndrome prevention and compulsory treatment in Finland', *Critical Public Health*, 22(2), 179–191.

Levine, M. (2012) *Teach Your Children Well: Parenting for authentic success* (New York: Harper/HarperCollins Publishers).

Levitas, R. (1998) *The Inclusive Society: Social exclusion and new labour* (Hampshire: Macmillan).

Levy, D. (1943) *Maternal Overprotection* (New York: Columbia University Press).

Lewis, J. (1980) *The Politics of Motherhood: Child and maternal welfare in England, 1900–1939* (London: Croom Helm).

Lewis, J. (2011) 'Parenting programmes in England: policy development and implementation issues, 2005–2010', *Journal of Social Welfare and Family Law*, 33(2), 107–21.

Liberman, E. (1999) 'Megan's Law's unintended result: Hysteria', *Providence Journal-Bulletin* (Rhode Island), 17 October.

Liedloff, J. (1985) *The Continuum Concept: In search of happiness lost* (Reading, MA: Addison-Wesley).

LifeCourse Associates (2003) Article reproduced in 'Media' section, 8 November, http://www.lifecourse.com/media/articles/lib/2003/081103-tajc.html, accessed 29 November 2013.

Lindon, J. (1999) *Too Safe for Their Own Good? Helping children learn about risk and lifeskills* (London: The National Early Years Network).

Livingstone, S. and Haddon, L. (2009) *EU Kids Online: Final report* (EC Safer Internet Plus Programme Deliverable D6.5) (London: LSE, EU Kids Online).

Lorenz, K. (1937) 'The nature of instinct', in C. Schiller (ed.) *Instinctive Behavior: The Development of a Modern Concept* (London: Methuen), pp. 129–175.

Lorenz, K. (1950) 'The comparative method of studying innate behavior patterns', *Symposia for the Society of Experimental Biology*, 4, 221–268.

Loseke, D. R. (1999) *Thinking about Social Problems: An introduction to constructionist perspectives* (New York: Aldine de Gruyter).

Lowe, P. and Lee, E. (2010a) 'Advocating alcohol abstinence to pregnant women: some observations about British policy', *Health, Risk and Society*, 12(4), 301–312.

Lowe, P. and Lee, E. (2010b) 'Under the influence? The construction of Fetal Alcohol Syndrome in UK Newspapers', *Sociological Research On line*, 15(4): 2 http://www.socresonline.org.uk/15/4/2.html.

Lucas, P. J. (2011) 'Some reflections on the rhetoric of parenting programmes: evidence, theory, and social policy', *Journal of Family Therapy*, 33, 181–198.

Luker, K. (1996) *Dubious Conceptions: The politics of teenage pregnancy* (Cambridge MA and London: Harvard University Press).

Lupton, D. (1999a) 'Risk and the ontology of pregnant embodiment', in D. Lupton (ed.) *Risk and Sociocultural Theory: New directions and perspectives* (Cambridge: Cambridge University Press).

Lupton, D. (1999b) 'Introduction', in D. Lupton (ed.) *Risk and Sociocultural Theory, New Directions and Perspectives* (Cambridge: Cambridge University Press).

Lupton, D. (2011) '"The best thing for the baby": Mothers' concepts and experiences related to promoting their infants' health and development', *Health, Risk & Society*, 13(7–8), 637–651.

Lupton, D. (2012a) 'Configuring Maternal, Preborn and Infant Embodiment', Sydney Health & Society Working Group Paper No. 2. (Sydney: Sydney Health & Society Group).

Lupton, D. (2012b) '"Precious cargo": fetal subjects, risk and reproductive citizenship', *Critical Public Health*, 22(3), 329–340.

Lupton, D. (2012c) '"I'm always on the look out for what could be going wrong": Mothers' concepts of health and illness in their young children', Sydney Health and Society Group Working Paper No. 1 (Sydney: Sydney Health & Society Group).

Lupton, D. (2013a). 'Infant embodiment and interembodiment: a review of sociocultural perspectives', *Childhood*, 20(1), 37–50.

Lupton, D. (2013b) *The Social Worlds of the Unborn* (Basingstoke: Palgrave Macmillan).

Lupton, D. and Barclay, L. (1997) *Constructing Fatherhood: Discourses and experiences* (London: Sage Publications).

Lupton, D. and Tulloch, J. (2002) Life would be pretty dull without risk: Voluntary risk-taking and its pleasures. *Health, Risk and Society* 4(2), 113–124.

Macvarish, J. (2009) Comments made at 'Changing Parenting Culture ESRC seminar series, Gender and Parenting Culture: Intensive fatherhood?' University of Cambridge, April http://blogs.kent.ac.uk/parentingculturestudies/files/2010/12/seminar-2-summary.pdf, accessed 1 May 2013.

Macvarish, J. (2010a) 'Understanding the significance of the teenage mother in contemporary culture', *Sociological Research Online*, 15(4), 3, http://www.socresonline.org.uk/15/4/3.html.

Macvarish, J. (2010b) 'The effect of "risk-thinking" on the contemporary construction of teenage motherhood', *Health, Risk and Society*, 12(4), 313–322.

Macvarish, J. and Billings, J. (2010) 'Challenging the irrational, amoral and antisocial construction of the "teenage mother"', in S. Duncan, R. Edwards and C. Alexander (eds) *Teenage Parenting – What's the problem?* (London: Tufnell Press).

Maher, V. (1992) *The Anthropology of Breastfeeding: Natural Law or Social Construct?* (Oxford: Berg).

Maher, J. and Saugeres, L. (2007) 'To be or not to be a mother? Women negotiating cultural representations of mothering', *Journal of Sociology*, 43(1), 5–21.

Mainstream Parenting Resources (2008) 'When proof is not proof', http://mainstreamparenting.wordpress.com/2008/01/23/when-proof-is-not-proof-apnp-research/, accessed 27 April 2009.

Manifesto Club (2006) *The Case against Vetting: How the child protection industry is poisoning adult-child relations*, http://www.manifestoclub.com/files/THE%20CASE%20AGAINST%20VETTING.pdf, accessed 10 July 2013.

Marano, H. (2008) *A Nation of Wimps: The high cost of invasive parenting* (New York: Broadway Books).

Marks, L. (2001) *Sexual Chemistry: A history of the contraceptive pill* (New Haven and London: Yale University Press).

Marsiglio, W., Amato, P., Day, R. and Lamb, M. (2000) 'Scholarship on fatherhood in the 1990s and beyond', *Journal of Marriage and the Family*, 62, 1173–1191.

Marshall, H. and Wollett, A. (2000) 'Fit to reproduce? The regulative role of pregnancy texts', *Feminism and Psychology*, 10(3), 351–366.

Maxwell, B. and Racine, E. (2012) 'Does the neuroscience research on early stress justify responsive childcare? Examining interwoven epistemological and ethical challenges', *Neuroethics*, 5, 159–172.

McAlinden, A. (2010) 'Vetting sexual offenders: state over-extension, the punishment deficit and the failure to manage risk', *Social Legal Studies*, 19(1), 25–48.

McEwen, B. (2000) 'The neurobiology of stress: from serendipity to clinical relevance', *Brain Research*, 886, 172–189.

McNamara, D. (2006) 'Parental control, overprotection associated with anxiety in children', *Clinical Psychiatry News*, 34(1), 44.

Milkie, M., Mattingly, M., Nomaguchi, K., Bianchi, S. and Robinson, J. (2004) 'The time squeeze: parental statuses and feelings about time with children', *Journal of Marriage and Family*, 66(3), 739–761.

Miller, T. (2011a) *Making Sense of Fatherhood* (Cambridge: Cambridge University Press).

Miller, T. 2011(b) 'Falling back into gender? Men's narratives and practices around first-time fatherhood', *Sociology*, 45(6), 1094–1109.

Moreton, C. (2013) 'Claire Perry MP: "Parents, take back control"', *Daily Telegraph*, 8 June, http://www.telegraph.co.uk/journalists/cole-moreton/10107771/Claire-Perry-MP-Parents-take-back-control.html, accessed 17 July 2013.

Moscucci, O. (2003) 'Holistic obstetrics: the origins of 'natural childbirth' in Britain', *Postgraduate Medical Journal*, 79, 168–173.

Moss, P. (ed.) (2011) *International Review of Leave Policies and Related Research 2011* (London: Institute of Education, University of London).

Murphy, C. (2010) 'Giving new life to the role of the father' *BBC News Online*, 20 January 2010, http://news.bbc.co.uk/1/hi/health/8468729.stm, accessed 2 May 2013.

Murphy, E. (1999) '"Breast is best": infant feeding decisions and maternal deviance', *Sociology of Health and Illness*, 21(2), 187–208.

Murphy, E. (2000) 'Risk, responsibility and rhetoric in infant feeding', *Journal of Contemporary Ethnography*, 3, 291–325.

Murphy, E. (2003) 'Expertise and forms of knowledge in the government of families', *The Sociological Review*, 51(4), 433–462.

Murphy, E. (2004) 'Risk, maternal ideologies and infant feeding', in J. Germov and L. Williams (eds) *A Sociology of Food and Nutrition* (Oxford: Oxford University Press).

Murray, S. B. (1996) '"We all love Charles": Men in child care and the social construction of gender', *Gender and Society*, 10(4), 368–385.

Murray, S. B. (2001) 'When a scratch becomes "a scary story": the social construction of micro panics in center-based child care', *The Sociological Review*, 49(4), 512–529.

Nadesan, M. H. (2002) 'Engineering the entrepreneurial infant: brain science, infant development toys, and governmentality', *Cultural Studies*, 16, 401–432.

Nathanson, J. and Tuley, L. C. (2008) *Mother Knows Best: Talking back to the 'experts'* (Toronto: Demeter Press).

National Fatherhood Initiative (2013) 'How to be a Dad: Reading to your child', http://www.fatherhood.org/fathers/how-to-be-a-dad/reading-to-your-children, accessed 1 May 2013.

National Health Service (NHS) (2012) 'Start for Life – Mums, Alcohol' (London: Department of Health), http://www.nhs.uk/start4life/Pages/alcohol-pregnant.aspx, accessed 17 June 2013.

National Health Service (NHS) (2013) 'Breastfeeding Help and Support', http://www.nhs.uk/conditions/pregnancy-and-baby/pages/breastfeeding-help-support.aspx#close, accessed 1 June 2013.

Nelson, M. (2008) 'Watching children: describing the use of baby monitors on Epinions.com', *Journal of Family Issues*, 29, 516–539.

Nelson, M. (2010) *Parenting Out of Control: Anxious parents in uncertain times* (New York and London: New York University Press).

Nicolson, P., Fox, R. and Heffernan, K. (2010) 'Constructions of pregnant and postnatal embodiment across three generations: mothers', daughters' and others' experiences of the transition to motherhood', *Journal of Health Psychology*, 15(4), 575–585.

NoFAS (n/d) 'About FASD', http://www.nofas.org/about-fasd/, accessed 17 June 2013.

Nolan, J. (1998) *The Therapeutic State: Justifying government at century's end* (New York: New York University Press).

NY Daily News (2013) 'Breast-fed babies are more socially connected, less anxious, as adults, study finds', *NY Daily News*, 25 June, http://www.nydailynews.com/life-style/health/breast-fed-babies-adult-social-climbers-study-article-1.1381933?localLinksEnabled=false, accessed 3 July 2013.

O'Connor, C. and Joffe, H. (2012) 'Media representations of early human development: Protecting, Feeding and Loving the Developing Brain', *Social Science and Medicine*, in press, published online http://dx.doi.org/10.1016/j.socscimed.2012.09.048, accessed 15 July 2013.

O'Connor, C. and Joffe, H. (2013) 'Media representations of early human development: Protecting, Feeding and Loving the Developing Brain', *Social Science and Medicine*, 97: 297–306.

O'Connor, C., Rees, G. and Joffe, H. (2012) Neuroscience in the public sphere. *Neuron*, 74(2), 220–226.

Oakley, A. (1974) *Housewife* (London: Allen Lane).

Oakley. A. (1986) *The Captured Womb: A history of the medical care of pregnant women* (Oxford: Basil Blackwell Ltd).

Palmer, G. (1993) [1988] *The Politics of Breastfeeding* 2nd edn (London: Pandora Press).

Palmer, S. (2006) *Toxic Childhood: How modern life is damaging our children ... and what we can do about it* (London: Orion).

Palmer, S. (2007) *Detoxing Childhood: What parents need to know to raise happy, successful children* (London: Orion).

Parents' Action for Children (2013) 'About us', http://www.parentsaction.org/pages/About-Us.html, accessed 23 April 2013.

Park, A. (2007) 'Baby Einsteins: Not So Smart After All', 6 August. http://www.time.com/time/health/article/0,8599,1650352,00.html, accessed 24 July 2013.

Parsons Leigh, J., Pacholok, S., Snape, T. and Gauthier, A. (2012) 'Trying to do more with less? Negotiating intensive mothering and financial strain in Canada', *Families, Relationships and Societies*, 1(3), 361–377.

Parton, N. (2006) *Safeguarding Childhood: Early intervention and surveillance in a late modern society* (Basingstoke: Palgrave Macmillan).

Parton, N. (2012) 'Reflections on "governing the family": the close relationship between child protection and social work in advanced Western societies – the example of England', *Families, Relationships and Societies*, 1(1), 87–101.

Perry, B. (1997) 'Incubated in terror: Neurodevelopmental factors in the "cycle of violence"', in J. Osofky (ed.) *Children in a Violent Society* (New York: Guilford Publications).

Perry, B., Pollard, R., Blakeley, T., Baker, W. and Vigilante, D. (1995) 'Childhood trauma, the neurobiology of adaptation and "use-dependent" development of the brain: how "states" become "traits"', *Infant Mental Health Journal*, 16, 271–291.

Phoenix, A. Wollett, A. and Lloyd, E. (eds) (1991) *Motherhood: Meanings, practices and ideologies* (London: Sage).

Piper, H. and Stronach, I. (2008) *Don't Touch! The educational story of a panic* (London and New York: Routledge).

Piper, H., Powell, J. and Smith, H. (2006) 'Parents, professionals, and paranoia: the touching of children in a culture of fear', *Journal of Social Work*, 6(2), 151–167.

Pitts-Taylor, V. (2010) 'The plastic brain: neoliberalism and the neuronal self', *Health*, 14, 635–652.

Pleck, J. (1993) 'Are "family-supportive" employer policies relevant to men?', in J. Hood (ed.) *Men, Work and Family* (Newbury Park, CA: Sage), pp. 217–237.

Porter, L. (2003) 'The Science of Attachment: The Biological Roots of Love', *Mothering Magazine* Issue 119, July/August 2003, Retrieved 8 March 2008 from http://www .mothering.com/community/a/the-science-of-attachment-the-biological-roots-of-love.

Postman, N. (1994) *The Disappearance of Childhood* (New York: Vintage Books).

Press Association (2013) 'Moderate drinking during pregnancy "does not harm baby's development"', *Guardian*, 18 June, http://www.guardian.co.uk/lifeandstyle/2013/jun/18/drinking-moderation-pregnancy-baby-development, accessed 21 June 2013.

Prout, A. (2000) 'Children's participation: control and self-realisation in British late modernity', *Children and Society*, 14, 304–315.

Prout, A. and James, A. (1990) 'A new paradigm for the sociology of childhood? Provenance, promise and problems', in A. James and A. Prout (eds) *Constructing and Reconstructing Childhood: Contemporary issues in the sociological study of childhood* (London and Washington, Falmer Press).

Prokos, A. (2002) 'Changing Fatherhood in the 21st Century: Incentives and Disincentives for Involved Parenting', Working Paper No. 45, May.

Pugh, A. (2005) 'Selling compromise: toys, motherhood, and the cultural deal', *Gender and Society*, 19, 729–749.

Ramaekers, S. and Suissa, J. (2011) 'Parents as "educators": languages of education, pedagogy and "parenting"', *Ethics and Education*, 6(2), 197–212.

Ramaekers, S. and Suissa, J. (2012) *The Claims of Parenting: Reasons, responsibility and society* (London and New York: Springer).

Reece, H. (2013) 'The Pitfalls of Positive Parenting', *Ethics and Education*, 8(1), 42–54.

Ribbens McCarthy, J. and Edwards, R. (2011) *Key Concepts in Family Studies* (London: Sage).

Rich Harris, J. (2009) *The Nurture Assumption: Why children turn out the way they do* (New York: Simon & Schuster).

Richardson, D. (1993) *Women, Mothering and Childrearing* (Basingstoke: Macmillan).

Richardson, H. (2012a) 'Warning Over Middle-Class Parents' Alcohol Habits', *BBC News Online*, 8 October, http://www.bbc.co.uk/news/education-19870190, accessed 1 July 2013.

Richardson, H. (2012b) 'Limit Children's Screen Time, Expert Urges', *BBC News Online*, 9 October, http://www.bbc.co.uk/news/education-19870199, accessed 1 July 2013.

Richter, M. and Andresen, S. (eds) (2012) *The Politicization of Parenthood: Shifting private and public responsibilities in education and child rearing (children's well-being: indicators and research)* (Dordrecht, Heidelberg, London, New York: Springer).

Riggs, J. (2005) 'Impressions of mothers and fathers on the periphery of child care', *Psychology of Women Quarterly*, 29, 58–62.

Riley, D. (1983) *War in the Nursery: Theories of the child and mother* (London: Virago).

Roach, C. (2013) 'Neuroscientist talk aims to give parents insight', *The Sudbury Star*, 10 April, http://www.thesudburystar.com/2013/04/10/neuroscientist-talk-aims-to-give-parents-insight, accessed 17 July 2013.

Roiphe, K. (2012) 'The Seven Myths of Helicopter Parenting', *Slate*, 31 July, http://www.slate.com/articles/double_x/roiphe/2012/07/madeline_levine_s_teach_your_children_well_we_are_all_helicopter_parents.html, accessed 17 July 2013.

Roisin, H. (2013) *The End of Men: And the rise of women* (London: Penguin).

Romagnoli, A. and Wall, G. (2012) '"I know I'm a good mom": young, low-income mothers' experiences with risk perception, intensive parenting ideology and parenting education programmes', *Health, Risk and Society*, 14(3), 273–289.

Rose, N. (1999) *Governing the soul: The shaping of the private self* (London: Free Association Books).

Rose, N. (2010) '"Screen and intervene": governing risky brains', *History of the Human Sciences*, 23(1), 79–105.

Rose, N. and Abi-Rached, J. M. (2013) *Neuro: The new brain sciences and the management of the mind* (Princeton and Oxford: Princeton University Press).

Ross, E. (1993) *Love and Toil: Motherhood in outcast London, 1870–1918* (Oxford: Oxford University Press).

Royal College of Midwives/The Fatherhood Institute (RCM/FI) (2013) 'Reaching Out: Involving Fathers in Maternity Care', www.rcm.org.uk/EasySiteWeb/ GatewayLink.aspx?alId=184428, accessed 1 May 2013.

Ruhl, L. (1999) 'Liberal governance and prenatal care: risk and regulation in pregnancy', *Economy and Society*, 28(1), 95–117.

Rumbelow, H. (2008) 'There's no jail like home', *The Times*, 11 April.

Rustin, S. (2012) 'Andrea Leadsom: Lobbying for more support for parents and children', *Guardian*, 27 November, http://www.guardian.co.uk/society/2012/ nov/27/andrea-leadsom-lobbying-parents-children, accessed 17 July 2013.

Rutter, M. (2011) Interviewed on BBC Radio 4 Analysis, 'Unsure about Sure Start', transcript of a recorded documentary, 11 July, p. 6, http://news.bbc. co.uk/nol/shared/spl/hi/programmes/analysis/transcripts/analysis_11_07_11. pdf, accessed 24 July 2013.

Sacker, A., Kelly, Y., Iacovou, M., Cable, N. and Bartley, M. (2013) 'Breast feeding and intergenerational social mobility: what are the mechanisms?' *Archives of Disease in Childhood Online First*: doi: 10.1136/archdischild-1012-303199.

Sayer, L. (2004) Are Parents Investing Less in Children? Trends in Mothers' and Fathers' Time with Children AJS Volume 110 Number 1 (July 2004), 1–43.

Sayer, L. C., Bianchi, S. M. and Robinson, J. P. (2004) 'Are parents investing less in children? Trends in mothers' and fathers' time with children', *American Journal of Sociology*, 1(July), 1–43.

Schneider, D. (1969) 'Kinship, nationality and religion in American culture: Towards a definition of kinship', in R. Spencer (ed.) *Forms of Symbolic Action: Proceedings of the 1969 Annual Spring Meeting of the American Ethnological Society* (Seattle: University of Washington Press), pp. 116–125.

Schore, A. (2001) 'The effects of early relational trauma on right brain development, affect regulation and infant mental health', *Infant Mental Health Journal*, 22(1–2): 201–269.

Scourfield, J. and Drakeford, M. (2002) 'New Labour and the "problem of men"', *Critical Social Policy*, 22(4), 619–640.Sears, W. and Sears, M. (1993) [1982] *The Baby Book: Everything you need to know about your baby* (Boston: Little Brown).

Sears, W. and Sears, M. (2001) *The Attachment Parenting Book: A commonsense guide to understanding and nurturing your baby* (London: Little, Brown and Company).

SEU (Social Exclusion Unit) (1999) *Teenage Pregnancy: Report by the Social Exclusion Unit* (London: Stationery Office).

Shaw, S. (2008) 'Family leisure and changing ideologies of parenthood', *Sociology Compass*, 2, 688–703.

Shilling, J. (2013) 'Parenting Wars', *The New Statesman*, 31 January, pp. 26–31.

Shirani, F., Henwood, K. and Coltart, C. (2012) 'Meeting the challenges of intensive parenting culture: gender, risk management and the moral parent', *Sociology*, 46(1), 25–40.

Shklar, J. N. (1987) *Men and Citizens: A study of Rousseau's social theory* (Cambridge: Cambridge University Press).

Sifferlin, A. (2013) 'Breast-fed babies achieve higher social status', *Time*, 25 June, http://healthland.time.com/2013/06/25/breastfed-babies-achieve-higher-social-status/, accessed 3 July 2013.

Skenazy, L. (2009) *Free-Range Kids: Giving our children the freedom we had without going nuts with worry* (San Francisco: Jossey-Bass).

Small, M. (1998) *Our Babies, Ourselves: How biology and culture shape the way we parent* (New York: Random House).

Smart, C. (2007) *Personal Life: New directions in sociological thinking* (Cambridge, Polity).

Smeyers, P. (2008) 'Child-rearing: on government intervention and the discourse of experts', *Educational Philosophy and Theory*, 40(6), 719–738.

Smeyers, P. (2010) 'State intervention and the technologization and regulation of parenting', *Educational Theory*, 60(3), 265–270.

Smeaton, D. and Marsh, A. (2006) 'Maternity and paternity rights and benefits: survey of parents 2005', *Employment Relations Research Series*, No. 50 (Department of Trade and Industry).

Smith, R. (2010) 'Total Parenting', *Educational Theory*, 60(3), 357–369.

Smyth, C. (2012) 'Warning tiny amount of alcohol during pregnancy can harm child's IQ', *The Times*, 15 November, http://www.thetimes.co.uk/tto/health/news/article3600232.ece, accessed 1 July 2013.

Somers, P. (2010) 'The Helicopter Parent: Research toward a typology (Part I)', *College and University*, 86(1), 18–24.

Spangler, G., Schieche, M., Ilg, U., Maier, U. and Ackerman, C. (1994) 'Maternal sensitivity as an organizer for biobehavioral regulation in infancy', *Developmental Psychobiology*, 27, 425–437.

Spurr, P. (2012) 'Parents must fight the "sound-bite" urge', *Sunday Telegraph*, 4 November, http://www.telegraph.co.uk/health/children_shealth/9654567/Parents-must-fight-the-sound-bite-urge.html, accessed 1 July 2013.

Start for Life (S4L) (2013) 'Tips and ideas for dads-to-be to help their partners have a healthy pregnancy', http://www.nhs.uk/start4life/Pages/health-advice-dads.aspx, accessed 1 May 2013.

Stearns, P. (2003) *Anxious Parents: A history of modern childrearing in America* (New York and London: New York University Press).

Stearns, P. N. (2009) 'Analyzing the role of culture in shaping American childhood: a twentieth-century case', *European Journal of Developmental Psychology*, 6(1), 34–52.

Straw, J. and Anderson, J. (1996) *Parenting: A discussion paper* (London: The Labour Party).

Sumsion, J. (2000) 'Negotiating "otherness": a male early childhood educator's gender positioning', *International Journal of Early Years Education*, 8(2), 129–140.

Sunderland, J. (2006) '"Parenting" or "mothering"? The case of modern childcare magazines', *Discourse and Society*, 17(4), 503–527.

Sunderland, M. (2006) *The Science of Parenting: Practical guidance on sleep, crying, play and building emotional wellbeing for life* (London: Dorling Kindersley).

Tallis, R. (2011) *Aping Mankind: Neuromanin, Darwinitis and the misrepresentation of humanity* (Durham: Acumen).

Thompson, R. A. and Nelson, C. A. (2001) 'Developmental science and the media: early brain development', *American Psychologist*, 56(1), 5–15.

Thornton, D. J. (2011) 'Neuroscience, affect, and the entrepreneurialization of motherhood', *Communication and Critical/Cultural Studies*, 8, 399–424.

Tronick, E. and Weinberg, M. (1997) 'Depressed mothers and infants: Failure to form dyadic states of consciousness', in L. Murray and P. Cooper (eds), *Postpartum Depression in Child Development* (New York: Guilford Press), pp. 54–84.

Tronto, J. C. (2002) 'The "Nanny" question in feminism', *Hypatia*, 17, 34–51.

Umansky, L. (1996) *Motherhood Reconceived: Feminism and the legacies of the Sixties* (New York: New York University Press).

UNICEF (2013) 'Baby Friendly Hospital Initiative: Skin to skin contact', http://www.unicef.org.uk/BabyFriendly/Resources/Guidance-for-Health-Professionals/Learning-about-breastfeeding/Skin-to-skin-contact/, accessed 26 February 2013.

Urwin, C. and Sharland, E. (1992) 'From bodies to minds in childcare literature: Advice to parents in inter-war Britain', in R. Cooter (ed.) *In the Name of the Child: Health and Welfare 1880–1940* (London and New York: Routledge).

Valentine, G. (1997) '"Oh yes I can." "Oh no you can't": children and parents' understandings of kids' competence to negotiate public space safely', *Antipode*, 29(1), 1–100.

van Ijzendoorn, M. and Kroonberg, P. (1988) 'Cross-cultural patterns of attachment: a meta-analysis of the strange situation', *Child Development*, 59, 147–156.

Vansieleghem, N. (2010) 'The residual parent to come: on the need for parental expertise and advice, *Educational Theory*, 6(3), 341–355.

Villalobos, A. (2009) *Motherload: How mothers bear the weight of societal insecurity*, PhD thesis, University of California, Berkley, 2009.

Vincent, C. and Ball, S. (2006) *Childcare, Choice and Class Practices* (London: Routledge).

Vinovskis, M. A. (1988) *An 'Epidemic' of Adolescent Pregnancy? Some historical and policy considerations* (Oxford: Oxford University Press).

Waiton, S. and Knight, S. (2007) 'The roots of "paedophobia"', *Scottish Youth Issues Journal*, 9, 89–94.

Wall, G. (2001) 'Moral constructions of motherhood in breastfeeding discourse', *Gender and Society*, 15(4), 590–608.

Wall, G. (2004) 'Is your child's brain potential maximized? Mothering in an age of new brain research', *Atlantis*, 28(2), 41–50.

Wall, G. (2010) 'Mothers' experiences with intensive parenting and brain development discourse', *Women's Studies International Forum*, 33(3), 253–263.

Wall, G. and Arnold, S. (2007) 'How involved is involved fathering?' *Gender and Society*, 21(4), 508–527.

Warner, J. (2006) *Perfect Madness: Motherhood in the age of anxiety* (London: Vermilion).

Warner, J. (2012) 'How to Raise a Child', *New York Times*, 27 July, http://www.nytimes.com/2012/07/29/books/review/teach-your-children-well-by-madeline-levine.html?pagewanted=all, accessed 17 July 2013.

Wasoff, F. and Dey, I. (2000) *Family Policy* (Oxon: Routledge).

Wastell, D. and White, S. (2012) 'Blinded by neuroscience: social policy, the family and the infant brain', *Families, Relationships and Societies*, 1(3), 397–414.

Watson, J. (1928) *Psychological Care of Infant and Child* (New York: W. W. Norton and Company, Inc.).

Wave Trust (2013) 'Conception to Age 2 – the Age of Opportunity' (Croydon: The Wave Trust), http://www.wavetrust.org/sites/default/files/reports/conception_to_age_2_-_the_age_of_opportunity_addendum_to_the_governments_vision_for_the_foundation_years-_supporting_families_in_the_foundation_years.pdf, accessed 3 June 2013.

Wells J. (2006) 'The role of cultural factors in human breastfeeding: Adaptive behaviour or biopower?', in K. Bose (ed.) *Ecology, Culture, Nutrition, Health and Disease* (Delhi, India: Kamla-Raj Enterprises), pp. 14, 39–47.

Welshman, J. (2008) 'The cycle of deprivation: myths and misconceptions', *Children and Society*, 22, 75–85.

Welshman, J. (2010) 'From Head Start to Sure Start: reflections on policy transfer', *Children and Society*, 24, 89–99.

Willetts, D. (2010) *The Pinch: How the baby boomers took their children's future – and why they should give it back* (London: Atlantic Books).

Wilson, H. (2002) 'Brain science, early intervention and "at risk" families: implications for parents, professionals and social policy', *Social Policy and Society*, 1(3), 191–202.

Wolf, J. (2007) 'Is breast really best? Risk and total motherhood in the National Breastfeeding Awareness Campaign', *Journal of Health Politics, Policy and Law*, 32(4), 595–636.

Wolf, J. (2011) *Is Breast Best? Taking on the breastfeeding experts and the new high stakes of motherhood* (New York: New York University Press).

Wrennall, L. (2010) 'Surveillance and child protection: de-mystifying the Trojan Horse', *Surveillance and Society*, 7(3/4), 304–324.

Yaqub, S. (2002) '"Poor children grow into poor adults": harmful mechanisms or over-deterministic theory?' *Journal of International Development*, 14, 1081–1093.

Zedner, L. (2009) 'Fixing the future? The pre-emptive turn in criminal Justice', in B. McSherry, A. Norrie and S. Bronitt (eds) *Regulating Deviance: The Redirection of Criminalisation and the Futures of Criminal Law* (Oxford: Hart Publishing).

Zelizer, V. (1994) *Pricing the Priceless Child: The changing social value of children* (Princeton: Princeton University Press).

Index

Printed and bound in the United States of America